Selected Works of
Ida B. Wells-Barnett

THE SCHOMBURG LIBRARY OF
NINETEENTH-CENTURY BLACK WOMEN WRITERS

Henry Louis Gates, Jr.
General Editor

Titles are listed chronologically; collections that
include works published over a span of years are listed according to
the publication date of their initial work.

Phillis Wheatley, *The Collected Works of Phillis Wheatley*
Six Women's Slave Narratives: M. Prince; Old Elizabeth;
    M. J. Jackson; L. A. Delaney; K. Drumgoold; A. L. Burton
Spiritual Narratives: M. W. Stewart; J. Lee; J. A. J. Foote;
    V. W. Broughton
Ann Plato, *Essays*
Collected Black Women's Narratives: N. Prince; L. Picquet;
    B. Veney; S. K. Taylor
Sojourner Truth, *Narrative of Sojourner Truth; A Bondswoman
    of Olden Time, With a History of Her Labors and Correspondence
    Drawn from Her "Book of Life"*
Frances E. W. Harper, *Complete Poems of Frances E. W. Harper*
Charlotte Forten Grimké, *The Journals of Charlotte Forten Grimké*
Two Biographies by African-American Women: J. Brown; F. A. Rollin
Mary Seacole, *Wonderful Adventures of Mrs. Seacole in Many Lands*
Eliza Potter, *A Hairdresser's Experience in High Life*
Harriet Jacobs, *Incidents in the Life of a Slave Girl*
Collected Black Women's Poetry, Volumes 1–4: M. E. Tucker;
    A. I. Menken; M. W. Fordham; P. J. Thompson;
    C. A. Thompson; H. C. Ray; L. A. J. Moorer; J. D. Heard; E. Bibb;
    M. P. Johnson; Mrs. H. Linden
Elizabeth Keckley, *Behind the Scenes. Or, Thirty Years a Slave,
    and Four Years in the White House*
C. W. Larison, M.D., *Silvia Dubois, A Biografy of the Slav
    Who Whipt Her Mistres and Gand Her Fredom*

Katherine Davis Chapman Tillman, *The Works of Katherine Davis Chapman Tillman*

Mrs. A. E. Johnson, *Clarence and Corinne; or, God's Way*

Octavia V. Rogers Albert, *The House of Bondage: or Charlotte Brooks and Other Slaves*

Emma Dunham Kelley, *Megda*

Anna Julia Cooper, *A Voice From the South*

Frances E. W. Harper, *Iola Leroy, or Shadows Uplifted*

Ida B. Wells-Barnett, *Selected Works of Ida B. Wells-Barnett*

Amanda Smith, *An Autobiography: The Story of the Lord's Dealings with Mrs. Amanda Smith the Colored Evangelist*

Mrs. A. E. Johnson, *The Hazeley Family*

Mrs. N. F. Mossell, *The Work of the Afro-American Woman*

Alice Dunbar-Nelson, *The Works of Alice Dunbar-Nelson*, Volumes 1–3

Emma D. Kelley-Hawkins, *Four Girls at Cottage City*

Olivia Ward Bush-Banks, *The Collected Works of Olivia Ward Bush-Banks*

Angelina Weld Grimké, *Selected Works of Angelina Weld Grimké*

Pauline E. Hopkins, *Contending Forces: A Romance Illustrative of Negro Life North and South*

Short Fiction by Black Women, 1900–1920: P. E. Hopkins; A. W. Grimké; A. B. Scales; G. F. Stewart; G. Mossell; R. D. Todd; G. H. D. Browne; F. B. Williams; M. L. Burgess-Ware; K. D. Sweetser; L. Plummer; E. E. Bulkley; F. Nordstrom; G. E. Tompkins; M. K. Griffin; J. Fauset; L. B. Dixon; A. Dunbar-Nelson; M. Jones; A. McCrary; E. E. Butler; H. G. Ricks; A. F. Ries; L. A. Pendleton; E. M. Harrold; A. S. Coleman

Pauline Hopkins, *The Magazine Novels of Pauline Hopkins*

Effie Waller Smith, *The Collected Works of Effie Waller Smith*

Hallie Q. Brown, *Homespun Heroines and Other Women of Distinction*

Jean Fagan Yellin and Cynthia D. Bond (Comps.), *The Pen Is Ours: A Listing of Writings by and about African-American Women before 1910. With Secondary Bibliography to the Present*

IDA B. WELLS-BARNETT

Selected Works

of

Ida B. Wells-Barnett

Compiled with an Introduction by
TRUDIER HARRIS

New York   Oxford
OXFORD UNIVERSITY PRESS
1991

Oxford University Press

Oxford   New York   Toronto
Delhi   Bombay   Calcutta   Madras   Karachi
Petaling Jaya   Singapore   Hong Kong   Tokyo
Nairobi   Dar es Salaam   Cape Town
Melbourne   Auckland

and associated companies in
Berlin   Ibadan

Library of Congress Cataloging-in-Publication Data
Wells-Barnett, Ida B., 1862–1931.
[Works. 1991]
Selected works of Ida B. Wells-Barnett /
compiled with an introduction by Trudier Harris.
p.   cm.—(Schomburg library of nineteenth-century Black women writers)
ISBN 0-19-506202-7
1. Afro-Americans.   I. Harris, Trudier.   II. Title.   III. Series.
E185.97.W55A2   1991
973'.0496073—dc20   90-41973   CIP

2 4 6 8 10 9 7 5 3 1

Printed in the United States of America
on acid free paper

The
Schomburg Library
of
Nineteenth-Century
Black Women Writers
Is
Dedicated
in Memory
of
PAULINE AUGUSTA COLEMAN GATES

1916–1987

PUBLISHER'S NOTE

FOREWORD TO THE
SCHOMBURG SUPPLEMENT

Henry Louis Gates, Jr.

The enthusiastic reception by students, scholars, and the general public to the 1988 publication of the Schomburg Library of Nineteenth-Century Black Women Writers more than justified the efforts of twenty-five scholars and the staff of the Black Periodical Literature Project to piece together the fragments of knowledge about the writings of African-American women between 1773 and 1910. The Library's republication of those writings in thirty volumes—ranging from the poetry of Phillis Wheatley to the enormous body of work that emerged out of the "Black Woman's Era" at the turn of this century—was a *beginning* for the restoration of the written sensibilities of a group of writers who confronted the twin barriers of racism and sexism in America. Through their poetry, diaries, speeches, biographies, essays, fictional narratives, and autobiographies, these writers transcended the boundaries of racial prejudice and sexual discrimination by recording the thoughts and feelings of Americans who were, at once, black *and* female. Taken together, these works configure into a literary tradition because their authors read, critiqued, and revised each other's words, in textual groundings with their sisters.

Indeed, by publishing these texts together as a "library," and by presenting them as part of a larger discourse on race and gender, we hoped to enable readers to chart the formal specificities of this tradition and to trace its origins. As a whole, the works in the Schomburg Library demonstrate that the contemporary literary movement of African-American women writers is heir to a legacy that was born in 1773, when Phillis Wheatley's *Poems on Various Subjects, Religious and Moral* first unveiled the mind of a black woman to the world. The fact that the Wheatley volume has proven to be the most popular in the Schomburg set is a testament to her role as the "founder" of both the black American's and the black woman's literary tradition.

Even before the Library was published, however, I began to receive queries about producing a supplement that would incorporate works that had not been included initially. Often these exchanges were quite dramatic. For instance, shortly before a lecture I was about to deliver at the University of Cincinnati, Professor Sharon Dean asked me if the Library would be reprinting the 1859 autobiography of Eliza Potter, a black hairdresser who had lived and worked in Cincinnati. I had never heard of Potter, I replied. Did Dean have a copy of her book? No, but there *was* a copy at the Cincinnati Historical Society. As I delivered my lecture, I could not help thinking about this "lost" text and its great significance. In fact, after the lecture, Dean and I rushed from the building and drove to the Historical Society, arriving just a few moments before closing time. A patient librarian brought us the book, and as I leafed through it, I was once again confronted with the realization that so often accompanied the research behind the Library's first thirty volumes—the exciting, yet poignant awareness that there probably exist *dozens* of works like Potter's, buried in research libraries, waiting only to be uncovered through an accident of contiguity like that which placed Sharon Dean in Cincinnati, roaming the shelves of its Historical Society. Another scholar wrote to me about work being done on the poet Effie Waller Smith. Several other scholars also wrote to share their research on other authors and their works. A supplement to the Library clearly was necessary.

Thus we have now added ten volumes, among them Potter's autobiography and Smith's collected poetry, as well as a narrative by Sojourner Truth, several pamphlets by Ida B. Wells-Barnett, and two biographies by Josephine Brown and Frances Rollin. Also included are books consisting of various essays, stories, poems, and plays whose authors did not, or could not, collect their writings into a full-length volume. The works of Olivia Ward Bush-Banks, Angelina Weld Grimké, and Katherine Davis Chapman Tillman are in this category. A related volume is an anthology of short fiction published by black women in the *Colored American Magazine* and *Crisis* magazine—a collection that reveals the shaping influence which certain periodicals had upon the generation of specific genres within the black women's literary tradition. Both types of collected books are intended to kindle an interest in still another series of works that bring together for the first time either the complete *oeuvre* of one writer or that of one genre within the periodical press. Indeed, there are several authors whose collected works will establish them as major forces in the nineteenth- and early twentieth-century black women's intellectual community. Compiling, editing, and publishing these volumes will be as important a factor in constructing the black women's literary tradition as has been the republication of books long out of print.

Finally, the Library now includes a detailed bibliography of the writings of black women in the nineteenth and early twentieth centuries. Prepared by Jean Fagan Yellin and Cynthia Bond, this bibliography is the result of years of research and will serve as an indispensable resource in future investigations of black women writers, particularly those whose works appeared frequently throughout the nineteenth century in the principal conduit of writing for black women *or* men, the African-American periodical press.

The publication of this ten-volume supplement, we hope, will make a sound contribution toward reestablishing the importance of the creative works of African-American women and reevaluating the relation of these works not only to each other but also to African-American *and* American literature and history as a whole. These works are invaluable sources for readers intent upon understanding the complex interplay of ethnicity and gender, of racism and sexism—of how "race" becomes gendered and how gender becomes racialized—in American society.

FOREWORD
In Her Own Write

Henry Louis Gates, Jr.

One muffled strain in the Silent South, a jarring chord and a vague and uncomprehended cadenza has been and still is the Negro. And of that muffled chord, the one mute and voiceless note has been the sadly expectant Black Women, ...

The "other side" has not been represented by one who "lives there." And not many can more sensibly realize and more accurately tell the weight and the fret of the "long dull pain" than the open-eyed but hitherto voiceless Black Woman of America.

. . . as our Caucasian barristers are not to blame if they cannot *quite* put themselves in the dark man's place, neither should the dark man be wholly expected fully and adequately to reproduce the exact Voice of the Black Woman.

—ANNA JULIA COOPER
A Voice From the South (1892)

The birth of the African-American literary tradition occurred in 1773, when Phillis Wheatley published a book of poetry. Despite the fact that her book garnered for her a remarkable amount of attention, Wheatley's journey to the printer had been a most arduous one. Sometime in 1772, a young African girl walked demurely into a room in Boston to undergo an oral examination, the results of which would determine the direction of her life and work. Perhaps she was shocked

upon entering the appointed room. For there, perhaps gathered in a semicircle, sat eighteen of Boston's most notable
citizens. Among them were John Erving, a prominent Boston merchant; the Reverend Charles Chauncy, pastor of the
Tenth Congregational Church; and John Hancock, who would
later gain fame for his signature on the Declaration of Independence. At the center of this group was His Excellency,
Thomas Hutchinson, governor of Massachusetts, with Andrew Oliver, his lieutenant governor, close by his side.

Why had this august group been assembled? Why had it
seen fit to summon this young African girl, scarcely eighteen
years old, before it? This group of "the most respectable
Characters in *Boston*," as it would define itself, had assembled
to question closely the African adolescent on the slender sheaf
of poems that she claimed to have "written by herself." We
can only speculate on the nature of the questions posed to the
fledgling poet. Perhaps they asked her to identify and explain—for all to hear—exactly who were the Greek and Latin
gods and poets alluded to so frequently in her work. Perhaps
they asked her to conjugate a verb in Latin or even to trans-
late randomly selected passages from the Latin, which she
and her master, John Wheatley, claimed that she "had made
some Progress in." Or perhaps they asked her to recite from
memory key passages from the texts of John Milton and
Alexander Pope, the two poets by whom the African claimed
to be most directly influenced. We do not know.

We do know, however, that the African poet's responses
were more than sufficient to prompt the eighteen august
gentlemen to compose, sign, and publish a two-paragraph
"Attestation," an open letter "To the Publick" that prefaces
Phillis Wheatley's book and that reads in part:

> We whose Names are under-written, do assure the World,
> that the Poems specified in the following Page, were (as we

verily believe) written by Phillis, a young Negro Girl, who was but a few Years since, brought an uncultivated Barbarian from *Africa*, and has ever since been, and now is, under the Disadvantage of serving as a Slave in a Family in this Town. She has been examined by some of the best Judges, and is thought qualified to write them.

So important was this document in securing a publisher for Wheatley's poems that it forms the signal element in the prefatory matter preceding her *Poems on Various Subjects, Religious and Moral,* published in London in 1773.

Without the published "Attestation," Wheatley's publisher claimed, few would believe that an African could possibly have written poetry all by herself. As the eighteen put the matter clearly in their letter, "Numbers would be ready to suspect they were not really the Writings of Phillis." Wheatley and her master, John Wheatley, had attempted to publish a similar volume in 1772 in Boston, but Boston publishers had been incredulous. One year later, "Attestation" in hand, Phillis Wheatley and her master's son, Nathaniel Wheatley, sailed for England, where they completed arrangements for the publication of a volume of her poems with the aid of the Countess of Huntington and the Earl of Dartmouth.

This curious anecdote, surely one of the oddest oral examinations on record, is only a tiny part of a larger, and even more curious, episode in the Enlightenment. Since the beginning of the sixteenth century, Europeans had wondered aloud whether or not the African "species of men," as they were most commonly called, *could* ever create formal literature, could ever master "the arts and sciences." If they could, the argument ran, then the African variety of humanity was fundamentally related to the European variety. If not, then it seemed clear that the African was destined by nature to be a slave. This was the burden shouldered by Phillis Wheatley when she successfully defended herself and the authorship of her book against counterclaims and doubts.

Indeed, with her successful defense, Wheatley launched two traditions at once—the black American literary tradition *and* the black woman's literary tradition. If it is extraordinary that not just one but both of these traditions were founded simultaneously by a black woman—certainly an event unique in the history of literature—it is also ironic that this important fact of common, coterminous literary origins seems to have escaped most scholars.

That the progenitor of the black literary tradition was a woman means, in the most strictly literal sense, that all subsequent black writers have evolved in a matrilinear line of descent, and that each, consciously or unconsciously, has extended and revised a canon whose foundation was the poetry of a black woman. Early black writers seem to have been keenly aware of Wheatley's founding role, even if most of her white reviewers were more concerned with the implications of her race than her gender. Jupiter Hammon, for example, whose 1760 broadside "An Evening Thought. Salvation by Christ, With Penitential Cries" was the first individual poem published by a black American, acknowledged Wheatley's influence by selecting her as the subject of his second broadside, "An Address to Miss Phillis Wheatly [*sic*], Ethiopian Poetess, in Boston," which was published in Hartford in 1778. And George Moses Horton, the second African American to publish a book of poetry in English (1829), brought out in 1838 an edition of his *Poems By A Slave* bound together with Wheatley's work. Indeed, for fifty-six years, between 1773 and 1829, when Horton published *The Hope of Liberty*, Wheatley was the *only* black person to have published a book of imaginative literature in English. So central was this black woman's role in the shaping of the

African-American literary tradition that, as one historian has maintained, the history of the reception of Phillis Wheatley's poetry *is* the history of African-American literary criticism. Well into the nineteenth century, Wheatley and the black literary tradition were the same entity.

But Wheatley is not the only black woman writer who stands as a pioneering figure in African-American literature. Just as Wheatley gave birth to the genre of black poetry, Ann Plato was the first African American to publish a book of essays (1841) and Harriet E. Wilson was the first black person to publish a novel in the United States (1859).

Despite this pioneering role of black women in the tradition, however, many of their contributions before this century have been all but lost or unrecognized. As Hortense Spillers observed as recently as 1983,

> With the exception of a handful of autobiographical narratives from the nineteenth century, the black woman's realities are virtually suppressed until the period of the Harlem Renaissance and later. Essentially the black woman as artist, as intellectual spokesperson for her own cultural apprenticeship, has not existed before, for anyone. At the source of [their] own symbol-making task, [the community of black women writers] confronts, therefore, a tradition of work that is quite recent, its continuities, broken and sporadic.

Until now, it has been extraordinarily difficult to establish the formal connections between early black women's writing and that of the present, precisely because our knowledge of their work has been broken and sporadic. Phillis Wheatley, for example, while certainly the most reprinted and discussed poet in the tradition, is also one of the least understood. Ann Plato's seminal work, *Essays* (which includes biographies and poems), has not been reprinted since it was published a century and a half ago. And Harriet Wilson's *Our Nig*, her

compelling novel of a black woman's expanding consciousness in a racist Northern antebellum environment, never received even *one* review or comment at a time when virtually
all works written by black people were heralded by abolitionists as salient arguments against the existence of human slavery. Many of the books reprinted in this set experienced a
similar fate, the most dreadful fate for an author: that of
being ignored then relegated to the obscurity of the rare book
section of a university library. We can only wonder how
many other texts in the black woman's tradition have been
lost to this generation of readers or remain unclassified or
uncatalogued and, hence, unread.

This was not always so, however. Black women writers
dominated the final decade of the nineteenth century, perhaps
spurred to publish by an 1886 essay entitled "The Coming
American Novelist," which was published in *Lippincott's
Monthly Magazine* and written by "A Lady From Philadelphia." This pseudonymous essay argued that the "Great
American Novel" would be written by a black person. Her
argument is so curious that it deserves to be repeated:

> When we come to formulate our demands of the Coming
> American Novelist, we will agree that he must be native-
> born. His ancestors may come from where they will, but we
> must give him a birthplace and have the raising of him.
> Still, the longer his family has been here the better he will
> represent us. Suppose he should have no country but ours,
> no traditions but those he has learned here, no longings apart
> from us, no future except in our future—the orphan of the
> world, he finds with us his home. And with all this, suppose
> he refuses to be fused into that grand conglomerate we call
> the "American type." With us, he is not of us. He is origi-
> nal, he has humor, he is tender, he is passive and fiery, he
> has been taught what we call justice, and he has his own
> opinion about it. He has suffered everything a poet, a dra-

matist, a novelist need suffer before he comes to have his lips anointed. And with it all he is in one sense a spectator, a little out of the race. How would these conditions go towards forming an original development? In a word, suppose the coming novelist is of African origin? When one comes to consider the subject, there is no improbability in it. One thing is certain,—our great novel will not be written by the typical American.

An atypical American, indeed. Not only would the great American novel be written by an African American, it would be written by an African-American *woman:*

Yet farther: I have used the generic masculine pronoun because it is convenient; but Fate keeps revenge in store. It was a woman who, taking the wrongs of the African as her theme, wrote the novel that awakened the world to their reality, and why should not the coming novelist be a woman as well as an African? She—the woman of that race—has some claims on Fate which are not yet paid up.

It is these claims on fate that we seek to pay by publishing The Schomburg Library of Nineteenth-Century Black Women Writers.

This theme would be repeated by several black women authors, most notably by Anna Julia Cooper, a prototypical black feminist whose 1892 *A Voice From the South* can be considered to be one of the original texts of the black feminist movement. It was Cooper who first analyzed the fallacy of referring to "the Black man" when speaking of black people and who argued that just as white men cannot speak through the consciousness of black men, neither can black *men* "fully and adequately . . . reproduce the exact Voice of the Black Woman." Gender and race, she argues, cannot be conflated, except in the instance of a black woman's voice, and it is this voice which must be uttered and to which we must listen. As Cooper puts the matter so compellingly:

It is not the intelligent woman vs. the ignorant woman; nor the white woman vs. the black, the brown, and the red,—it is not even the cause of woman vs. man. Nay, 'tis woman's strongest vindication for speaking that *the world needs to hear her voice*. It would be subversive of every human interest that the cry of one-half the human family be stifled. Woman in stepping from the pedestal of statue-like inactivity in the domestic shrine, and daring to think and move and speak,—to undertake to help shape, mold, and direct the thought of her age, is merely completing the circle of the world's vision. Hers is every interest that has lacked an interpreter and a defender. Her cause is linked with that of every agony that has been dumb—every wrong that needs a voice.

It is no fault of man's that he has not been able to see truth from her standpoint. It does credit both to his head and heart that no greater mistakes have been committed or even wrongs perpetrated while she sat making tatting and snipping paper flowers. Man's own innate chivalry and the mutual interdependence of their interests have insured his treating her cause, in the main at least, as his own. And he is pardonably surprised and even a little chagrined, perhaps, to find his legislation not considered "perfectly lovely" in every respect. But in any case his work is only impoverished by her remaining dumb. The world has had to limp along with the wobbling gait and one-sided hesitancy of a man with one eye. Suddenly the bandage is removed from the other eye and the whole body is filled with light. It sees a circle where before it saw a segment. The darkened eye restored, every member rejoices with it.

The myopic sight of the darkened eye can only be restored when the full range of the black woman's voice, with its own special timbres and shadings, remains mute no longer.

Similarly, Victoria Earle Matthews, an author of short stories and essays, and a cofounder in 1896 of the National Association of Colored Women, wrote in her stunning essay,

"The Value of Race Literature" (1895), that "when the literature of our race is developed, it will of necessity be different in all essential points of greatness, true heroism and real Christianity from what we may at the present time, for convenience, call American literature." Matthews argued that this great tradition of African-American literature would be the textual outlet "for the unnaturally suppressed inner lives which our people have been compelled to lead." Once these "unnaturally suppressed inner lives" of black people are unveiled, no "grander diffusion of mental light" will shine more brightly, she concludes, than that of the articulate African-American woman:

> And now comes the question, What part shall we women play in the Race Literature of the future? . . . within the compass of one small journal ["Woman's Era"] we have struck out a new line of departure—a journal, a record of Race interests gathered from all parts of the United States, carefully selected, moistened, winnowed and garnered by the ablest intellects of educated colored women, shrinking at no lofty theme, shirking no serious duty, aiming at every possible excellence, and determined to do their part in the future uplifting of the race.
>
> If twenty women, by their concentrated efforts in one literary movement, can meet with such success as has engendered, planned out, and so successfully consummated this convention, what much more glorious results, what wider spread success, what grander diffusion of mental light will not come forth at the bidding of the enlarged hosts of women writers, already called into being by the stimulus of your efforts?
>
> And here let me speak one word for my journalistic sisters who have already entered the broad arena of journalism. Before the "Woman's Era" had come into existence, no one except themselves can appreciate the bitter experience and sore

> disappointments under which they have at all times been compelled to pursue their chosen vocations.
>
> If their brothers of the press have had their difficulties to contend with, I am here as a sister journalist to state, from the fullness of knowledge, that their task has been an easy one compared with that of the colored woman in journalism.
>
> Woman's part in Race Literature, as in Race building, is the most important part and has been so in all ages. . . . All through the most remote epochs she has done her share in literature. . . .

One of the most important aspects of this set is the republication of the salient texts from 1890 to 1910, which literary historians could well call the "Black Woman's Era." In addition to Mary Helen Washington's definitive edition of Cooper's *A Voice From the South,* we have reprinted two novels by Amelia Johnson, Frances Harper's *Iola Leroy,* two novels by Emma Dunham Kelley, Alice Dunbar-Nelson's two impressive collections of short stories, and Pauline Hopkins's three serialized novels as well as her monumental novel, *Contending Forces*—all published between 1890 and 1910. Indeed, black women published more works of fiction in these two decades than black men had published in the previous half century. Nevertheless, this great achievement has been ignored.

Moreover, the writings of nineteenth-century African-American women in general have remained buried in obscurity, accessible only in research libraries or in overpriced and poorly edited reprints. Many of these books have never been reprinted at all; in some instances only one or two copies are extant. In these works of fiction, poetry, autobiography, biography, essays, and journalism resides the mind of the nineteenth-century African-American woman. Until these works are made readily available to teachers and their students, a significant segment of the black tradition will remain silent.

Oxford University Press, in collaboration with the Schomburg Center for Research in Black Culture, is publishing thirty volumes of these compelling works, each of which contains an introduction by an expert in the field. The set includes such rare texts as Johnson's *The Hazeley Family* and *Clarence and Corinne*, Plato's *Essays*, the most complete edition of Phillis Wheatley's poems and letters, Emma Dunham Kelley's pioneering novel *Megda*, several previously unpublished stories and a novel by Alice Dunbar-Nelson, and the first collected volumes of Pauline Hopkins's three serialized novels and Frances Harper's poetry. We also present four volumes of poetry by such women as Henrietta Cordelia Ray, Adah Menken, Josephine Heard, and Maggie Johnson. Numerous slave and spiritual narratives, a newly discovered novel—*Four Girls at Cottage City*—by Emma Dunham Kelley (-Hawkins), and the first American edition of *Wonderful Adventures of Mrs. Seacole in Many Lands* are also among the texts included.

In addition to resurrecting the works of black women authors, it is our hope that this set will facilitate the resurrection of the African-American woman's literary tradition itself by unearthing its nineteenth-century roots. In the works of Nella Larsen and Jessie Fauset, Zora Neale Hurston and Ann Petry, Lorraine Hansberry and Gwendolyn Brooks, Paule Marshall and Toni Cade Bambara, Audre Lorde and Rita Dove, Toni Morrison and Alice Walker, Gloria Naylor and Jamaica Kincaid, these roots have branched luxuriantly. The eighteenth- and nineteenth-century authors whose works are presented in this set founded and nurtured the black women's literary tradition, which must be revived, explicated, analyzed, and debated before we can understand more completely the formal shaping of this tradition within a tradition, a coded literary universe through which, regrettably, we are only just beginning to navigate our way. As Anna Cooper said nearly one hundred years ago, we have been blinded by the loss of sight in one eye and have therefore been unable to detect the full *shape* of the African-American literary tradition.

Literary works configure into a tradition not because of some mystical collective unconscious determined by the biology of race or gender, but because writers read other writers and *ground* their representations of experience in models of language provided largely by other writers to whom they feel akin. It is through this mode of literary revision, amply evident in the *texts* themselves—in formal echoes, recast metaphors, even in parody—that a "tradition" emerges and defines itself.

This is formal bonding, and it is only through formal bonding that we can know a literary tradition. The collective publication of these works by black women now, for the first time, makes it possible for scholars and critics, male and female, black and white, to *demonstrate* that black women writers read, and revised, other black women writers. To demonstrate this set of formal literary relations is to demonstrate that sexuality, race, and gender are both the condition and the basis of *tradition*—but tradition as found in discrete acts of language use.

A word is in order about the history of this set. For the past decade, I have taught a course, first at Yale and then at Cornell, entitled "Black Woman and Their Fictions," a course that I inherited from Toni Morrison, who developed it in the mid-1970s for Yale's Program in Afro-American Studies. Although the course was inspired by the remarkable accomplishments of black women novelists since 1970, I gradually extended its beginning date to the late nineteenth century, studying Frances Harper's *Iola Leroy* and Anna Julia Cooper's *A Voice From the South*, both published in 1892. With the discovery of Harriet E. Wilson's seminal novel, *Our Nig* (1859), and Jean Yellin's authentication of Harriet Jacobs's brilliant slave narrative, *Incidents in the Life of a Slave Girl* (1861), a survey course spanning over a century and a quarter emerged.

But the discovery of *Our Nig*, as well as the interest in nineteenth-century black women's writing that this discovery generated, convinced me that even the most curious and diligent scholars knew very little of the extensive history of the creative writings of African-American women before 1900. Indeed, most scholars of African-American literature had never even read most of the books published by black women, simply because these books—of poetry, novels, short stories, essays, and autobiography—were mostly accessible only in rare book sections of university libraries. For reasons unclear to me even today, few of these marvelous renderings of the African-American woman's consciousness were reprinted in the late 1960s and early 1970s, when so many other texts of the African-American literary tradition were resurrected from the dark and silent graveyard of the out-of-print and were reissued in facsimile editions aimed at the hungry readership for canonical texts in the nascent field of black studies.

So, with the help of several superb research assistants—including David Curtis, Nicola Shilliam, Wendy Jones, Sam Otter, Janadas Devan, Suvir Kaul, Cynthia Bond, Elizabeth Alexander, and Adele Alexander—and with the expert advice of scholars such as William Robinson, William Andrews, Mary Helen Washington, Maryemma Graham, Jean Yellin, Houston A. Baker, Jr., Richard Yarborough, Hazel Carby, Joan R. Sherman, Frances Foster, and William French, dozens of bibliographies were used to compile a list of books written or narrated by black women mostly before 1910. Without the assistance provided through this shared experience of scholarship, the scholar's true legacy, this project would not have been conceived. As the list grew, I was struck by how very many of these titles that I, for example, had never even heard of, let alone read, such as Ann Plato's *Essays*, Louisa Picquet's slave narrative, or Amelia Johnson's two novels, *Clarence and Corinne* and *The Hazeley Family*. Through our research with the Black Periodical Fiction and Poetry Project (funded by NEH and the Ford Foundation), I also realized that several novels by black women, including three works of fiction by Pauline Hopkins, had been serialized in black periodicals, but had never been collected and published as books. Nor had the several books of poetry published by black women, such as the prolific Frances E. W. Harper, been collected and edited. When I discovered still another "lost" novel by an African-American woman (*Four Girls at Cottage City*, published in 1898 by Emma Dunham Kelley-Hawkins), I decided to attempt to edit a collection of reprints of these works and to publish them as a "library" of black women's writings, in part so that I could read them myself.

Convincing university and trade publishers to undertake this project proved to be a difficult task. Despite the commercial success of *Our Nig* and of the several reprint series of women's works (such as Virago, the Beacon Black Women Writers Series, and Rutgers' American Women Writers Series), several presses rejected the project as "too large," "too limited," or as "commercially unviable." Only two publishers recognized the viability and the import of the project and, of these, Oxford's commitment to publish the titles simultaneously as a set made the press's offer irresistible.

While attempting to locate original copies of these exceedingly rare books, I discovered that most of the texts were housed at the Schomburg Center for Research in Black Culture, a branch of The New York Public Library, under the

direction of Howard Dodson. Dodson's infectious enthusiasm for the project and his generous collaboration, as well as
that of his stellar staff (especially Diana Lachatanere, Sharon
Howard, Ellis Haizip, Richard Newman, and Betty Gub-
ert), led to a joint publishing initiative that produced this set
as part of the Schomburg's major fund-raising campaign.
Without Dodson's foresight and generosity of spirit, the set
would not have materialized. Without William P. Sisler's
masterful editorship at Oxford and his staff's careful attention to detail, the set would have remained just another grand
idea that tends to languish in a scholar's file cabinet.

I would also like to thank Dr. Michael Winston and Dr.
Thomas C. Battle, Vice-President of Academic Affairs and
the Director of the Moorland-Spingarn Research Center (respectively) at Howard University, for their unending encouragement, support, and collaboration in this project, and
Esme E. Bhan at Howard for her meticulous research and
bibliographical skills. In addition, I would like to acknowl-
edge the aid of the staff at the libraries of Duke University,
Cornell University (especially Tom Weissinger and Donald
Eddy), the Boston Public Library, the Western Reserve
Historical Society, the Library of Congress, and Yale University. Linda Robbins, Marion Osmun, Sarah Flanagan,
and Gerard Case, all members of the staff at Oxford, were
extraordinarily effective at coordinating, editing, and producing the various segments of each text in the set. Candy
Ruck, Nina de Tar, and Phillis Molock expertly typed reams
of correspondence and manuscripts connected to the project.

I would also like to express my gratitude to my colleagues
who edited and introduced the individual titles in the set.
Without their attention to detail, their willingness to meet
strict deadlines, and their sheer enthusiasm for this project,
the set could not have been published. But finally and ulti-

mately, I would hope that the publication of the set would help to generate even more scholarly interest in the black women authors whose work is presented here. Struggling against the seemingly insurmountable barriers of racism *and* sexism, while often raising families and fulfilling full-time professional obligations, these women managed nevertheless to record their thoughts and feelings and to *testify* to all who dare read them that the will to harness the power of collective endurance and survival is the will to write.

The Schomburg Library of Nineteenth-Century Black Women Writers is dedicated in memory of Pauline Augusta Coleman Gates, who died in the spring of 1987. It was she who inspired in me the love of learning and the love of literature. I have encountered in the books of this set no will more determined, no courage more noble, no mind more sublime, no self more celebratory of the achievements of all African-American women, and indeed of life itself, than her own.

A NOTE FROM
THE SCHOMBURG CENTER

Howard Dodson

The Schomburg Center for Research in Black Culture, The New York Public Library, is pleased to join with Dr. Henry Louis Gates and Oxford University Press in presenting The Schomburg Library of Nineteenth-Century Black Women Writers. This thirty-volume set includes the work of a generation of black women whose writing has only been available previously in rare book collections. The materials reprinted in twenty-four of the thirty volumes are drawn from the unique holdings of the Schomburg Center.

A research unit of The New York Public Library, the Schomburg Center has been in the forefront of those institutions dedicated to collecting, preserving, and providing access to the records of the black past. In the course of its two generations of acquisition and conservation activity, the Center has amassed collections totaling more than 5 million items. They include over 100,000 bound volumes, 85,000 reels and sets of microforms, 300 manuscript collections containing some 3.5 million items, 300,000 photographs and extensive holdings of prints, sound recordings, film and videotape, newspapers, artworks, artifacts, and other book and nonbook materials. Together they vividly document the history and cultural heritages of people of African descent worldwide.

Though established some sixty-two years ago, the Center's book collections date from the sixteenth century. Its oldest item, an Ethiopian Coptic Tunic, dates from the eighth or ninth century. Rare materials, however, are most available for the nineteenth-century African-American experience. It is from these holdings that the majority of the titles selected for inclusion in this set are drawn.

The nineteenth century was a formative period in African-American literary and cultural history. Prior to the Civil War, the majority of black Americans living in the United States were held in bondage. Law and practice forbade teaching them to read or write. Even after the war, many of the impediments to learning and literary productivity remained. Nevertheless, black men and women of the nineteenth century persevered in both areas. Moreover, more African Americans than we yet realize turned their observations, feelings, social viewpoints, and creative impulses into published works. In time, this nineteenth-century printed record included poetry, short stories, histories, novels, autobiographies, social criticism, and theology, as well as economic and philosophical treatises. Unfortunately, much of this body of literature remained, until very recently, relatively inaccessible to twentieth-century scholars, teachers, creative artists, and others interested in black life. Prior to the late 1960s, most Americans (black as well as white) had never heard of these nineteenth-century authors, much less read their works.

The civil rights and black power movements created unprecedented interest in the thought, behavior, and achievements of black people. Publishers responded by revising traditional texts, introducing the American public to a new generation of African-American writers, publishing a variety of thematic anthologies, and reprinting a plethora of "classic texts" in African-American history, literature, and art. The reprints usually appeared as individual titles or in a series of bound volumes or microform formats.

The Schomburg Center, which has a long history of supporting publishing that deals with the history and culture of Africans in diaspora, became an active participant in many of the reprint revivals of the 1960s. Since hard copies of original printed works are the preferred formats for producing facsimile reproductions, publishers frequently turned to the Schomburg Center for copies of these original titles. In addition to providing such material, Schomburg Center staff members offered advice and consultation, wrote introductions, and occasionally entered into formal copublishing arrangements in some projects.

Most of the nineteenth-century titles reprinted during the 1960s, however, were by and about black men. A few black women were included in the longer series, but works by lesser known black women were generally overlooked. The Schomburg Library of Nineteenth-Century Black Women Writers is both a corrective to these previous omissions and an important contribution to African-American literary history in its own right. Through this collection of volumes, the thoughts, perspectives, and creative abilities of nineteenth-century African-American women, as captured in books and pamphlets published in large part before 1910, are again being made available to the general public. The Schomburg Center is pleased to be a part of this historic endeavor.

I would like to thank Professor Gates for initiating this project. Thanks are due both to him and Mr. William P. Sisler of Oxford University Press for giving the Schomburg Center an opportunity to play such a prominent role in the set. Thanks are also due to my colleagues at The New York Public Library and the Schomburg Center, especially Dr. Vartan Gregorian, Richard De Gennaro, Paul Fasana, Betsy Pinover, Richard Newman, Diana Lachatanere, Glenderlyn Johnson, and Harold Anderson for their assistance and support. I can think of no better way of demonstrating than in this set the role the Schomburg Center plays in assuring that the black heritage will be available for future generations.

CONTENTS

Introduction by Trudier Harris   3

Southern Horrors: Lynch Law in All Its Phases (1892)   14

The Reason Why the Colored American Is Not in the World's Columbian Exposition (1893)   46

A Red Record: Tabulated Statistics and Alleged Causes of Lynchings in the United States, 1892–1893–1894 (1895)   138

Mob Rule in New Orleans: Robert Charles and His Fight to the Death (1900)   253

INTRODUCTION

Trudier Harris

From the perspective of the last few years of the twentieth century, it is easy to romanticize the work of a woman like Ida B. Wells-Barnett. We can admire the fortitude and courage it took for her to wage a crusade against lynching for almost four decades in this country, frequently without the assistance of law officers and other legal personnel, and often without the support of the very African-American communities that she sought to protect. To idealize her, to make her larger than life, however, is perhaps to minimize the persistence of effort and the human toll this woman paid for demanding that the United States be as democratic and as humane as it professed to be.

The history of the crusade against lynching in the United States (not just hanging captured individuals by the neck until dead, but any execution conducted by mobs with impunity) would be incomplete without Ida B. Wells-Barnett. Self-appointed to take stands against the atrocities being committed in the summary execution of black people in the 1880s and 1890s, Wells-Barnett set out to show that the causes of lynching were rooted in the economic and social repression of the race, not in the emotionally charged accusations of rape that usually led to the deaths of black men. In the volatile post-Reconstruction climate of Ku Klux Klan activity and increasing Jim Crow laws, Wells-Barnett made herself a target of threatened violence by refusing to be silent in the face of intensified lynchings and the attendant horrors with which these deaths were caused.

3

Born the eldest of eight children in Holly Springs, Mississippi, on 16 July 1862, Wells acquired from her slave parents a love of liberty and a self-sufficiency that characterized her throughout her life. Upon the death of her parents during a yellow fever epidemic in 1878, when the young Ida was visiting her grandmother in another town, she resisted warnings to stay away from the plague-infested area and returned to care for her younger siblings. When the youngest child also died, and Mr. Wells's Mason brothers determined that the surviving children should be divided among well-intentioned neighbors and friends, Ida refused the offers and assumed responsibility for the lot of them. Drawing upon the resources she had acquired by regularly attending Shaw University (later Rust College) in Holly Springs, Ida was able to make a good start at keeping her resolve. By teaching at a nearby school during the week and returning on weekends, she was able to keep the family together until sometime in 1883, when she moved to Memphis to secure more lucrative employment. Although the family was divided at this point to give her greater freedom to work, she nevertheless remained devoted to her siblings, including a sister handicapped by curvature of the spine.

Wells's determination to fight the odds and keep her family as a unit matched her determination in Memphis to challenge unfair laws in public accommodations. On a train ride to her teaching job just outside Memphis in May of 1884, she was asked to transfer to the smoking car. Her refusal prompted the conductor and a couple of white men to move her bodily while onlooking whites cheered. She got off at the next stop and initiated a suit against the railroad upon her return to Memphis. Although she was awarded damages of five hundred dollars in December of that year, a higher court reversed the lower court's decision. Nevertheless, disappointment with that result did not in any way minimize Wells's use of the legal system as a means of bringing about justice for black people.

As early as 1887, Wells found what would become her life's work. She submitted articles to a church newspaper, which led to her journalistic work and editorship of the Memphis *Free Speech and Headlight* (later *Free Speech*). She became one-third owner of the paper. When her articles critical of the "colored" schools in Memphis led to her dismissal as a teacher in 1891, she devoted her attention exclusively to newspaper work.

Wells-Barnett's fame and the good she did are ironically based on one of the ugliest chapters in American history, that of lynching. On 9 March 1892, while Wells was in Natchez, Mississippi, in connection with her newspaper work, three young black businessmen, deemed too prosperous by white competitors, were summarily lynched in Memphis: "They were loaded on a switch engine of the railroad which ran back of the jail, carried a mile north of the city limits, and horribly shot to death" (Duster, p. 50). One of the three, Thomas Moss, was reputed to have advised his fellow blacks to go West because there was no justice for them in Memphis. Wells, who knew Moss and his wife, was godmother to their child, and considered them her best friends in Memphis, took up the pen that would spew forth fire about the horrors of lynching for the next several decades. Three young black men were dead, and their families and community were understandably aggrieved, but the country reaped a champion for the safety of black lives. Wells initially used her paper to advise all who could to take Moss's advice and leave Memphis:

> The city of Memphis has demonstrated that neither char-
> acter nor standing avails the Negro if he dares to protect
> himself against the white man or become his rival. There is

nothing we can do about the lynching now, as we are out-
numbered and without arms. The white mob could help itself
to ammunition without pay, but the order was rigidly enforced
against the selling of guns to Negroes. There is therefore
only one thing left that we can do; save our money and leave
a town which will neither protect our lives and property, nor
give us a fair trial in the courts, but takes us out and murders
us in cold blood when accused by white persons. (Duster, p.
52)

For nearly three months, black people left Memphis "by
scores and hundreds," supported financially by Wells and
others who remained in town. This continued until the white
citizenry, feeling the loss of manual labor and business
income, appealed to Wells to halt the exodus. She refused.
Shortly, in response to other lynchings, she committed the
ultimate sin of impugning Southern white womanhood by
asserting that the notion of black men raping white women
was a "thread bare lie"; indeed, many white women became
involved with black men voluntarily. That editorial, appear-
ing in a May 1892 issue of *Free Speech*, led whites in
Memphis to destroy Wells's newspaper office and to run her
business manager out of town. Luckily for her, she was on
vacation in New York, but to ensure that she would remain
out of Memphis, her life was threatened.

These events simply served to change the locale of Wells's
assault. As she was already visiting T. Thomas Fortune, the
editor of the *New York Age*, he offered her a job on the
paper. Though their relations would be strained in later
years, he readily supported her during this crisis. Wells
initially published a seven-column article on the front page
of the *New York Age*, "giving names, dates, and places of
many lynchings for alleged rape" (Duster, p. 69). She had
earlier chosen the pen name "Iola," but her increased exposure

through her columns encouraged many groups to invite her to discuss the Memphis lynchings publicly. At a meeting in New York presided by Victoria Earle Matthews, Wells made her first public presentation. Later, in Philadelphia, she was the guest of abolitionist William Still, another of the famous personages with whom she would have constant contact for the remainder of her life.

The Memphis lynchings also inspired the first of Wells's publications beyond newspaper work. In 1892 she published *Southern Horrors: Lynch Law in All Its Phases* (an expansion of the seven-column article she had written for the *New York Age*), which was funded by a "testimonial gift" organized under Mrs. Matthews's leadership to support Wells's anti-lynching crusade (Thompson, p. 61). Historians studying lynching have pointed out that 1892 was a peak year for such brutalities; the number of lynchings had ranged around 150 per year in the 1880s and going into the 1890s. That number reached 235 in 1892. Other keepers of statistics maintain that between 1882 and 1927, an estimated 3,513 black persons were lynched in the United States, seventy-six of them women (White, p. 229); murder, rape, and "minor offenses" were listed as the major causes. Historian James E. Cutler, in *Lynch-Law*, states that of the 2,060 blacks lynched for "various causes" between 1882 and 1903, 783 were lynched for murder, 707 for rape ("either attempted, alleged, or actually committed"), and 208 for "minor offenses"; many were also burned or "roasted alive" (pp. 175–76).

Though the number of black men lynched for rape comprised only one-third of the total, that accusation became the most emotional incentive for gathering a crowd and executing a prisoner; it was therefore the target upon which Wells centered her attacks. She maintained that such accusations were designed to keep blacks suppressed, to prevent them from getting the education and acquiring the wealth that would place them on a more equal footing with whites. Her suspicions were borne out by Richard Wright, who related in his autobiography, *Black Boy*, the story of how his uncle was killed in Arkansas early in the twentieth century because his saloon had become more profitable than the whites thought it should be.

Perhaps Wells's most inflammatory publication was *A Red Record: Tabulated Statistics and Alleged Causes of Lynchings in the United States, 1892–1893–1894*, which appeared in 1895. It provided provocative information on lynchings and burnings believed to be the result of alleged attacks on white women by black men (Chapter 6). Her basic contention here, as earlier, was that white women willingly consorted with black men until someone in the white community discovered the liaisons; then, to save their reputations, the women either screamed rape of their own volition or were forced to do so by the avenging mobs.

In her effort to decentralize lynching from its position as "an almost integral part of our national folkways," as Walter White put it, Wells, upon the invitation of a British woman she had met through William Still, took her campaign against American lynching to the British Isles. Just as she was convinced that only white people of good will in the United States could bring about change in contemporary practices, she was equally convinced that England, held in high esteem by most Americans, could expedite the necessary alterations.

Wells encountered some initial reactions of disbelief, but her trip to England in 1893 and her more extended visit in 1894 alternately succeeded in garnering much support from British royalty, clergy, and laypersons for her cause. During her second visit, she was sponsored in part by the *Chicago Inter-Ocean*, which hired her as a correspondent for the six months of the trip. She wrote a series of letters about her reactions to the people she met and the places she visited, as well as about the foreign reaction to her and her antilynching presentations. Between the two foreign visits, she had moved from New York to Chicago, where she became involved with women's clubs and where the issue of the exclusion of black Americans from the Chicago World's Fair of 1893 provided another political arena. She urged Frederick Douglass and others to join her in the publication of *The Reason Why the Colored American Is Not in the World's Columbian Exposition*. While she and Douglass agreed on the need for this pamphlet, she felt somewhat betrayed when he later agreed to plan a "Negro Day" for the fair, though in time she was able to understand his decision.

After coming back to the United States in 1894, Wells worked briefly with Susan B. Anthony and for a year traveled around the country campaigning against lynching. Returning to Chicago in 1895, she married Ferdinand L. Barnett, a local lawyer, on 27 June. She also founded the Ida B. Wells Club of Chicago, a move that would increase her involvement in women's club work in subsequent years.

After 1895 Wells-Barnett's life took on all the typical problems of a working wife and mother. She did not stop her campaign against lynching, but instead resumed her travels, albeit with nursing babies and with promises that child care would be available to her from one train stop to another. Of her dual professions as activist and mother, she wrote: "I had already found that motherhood was a profession by itself, just like schoolteaching and lecturing, and that once one was launched on such a career, she owed it to herself to become as expert as possible in the practice of her profession" (Duster, pp. 250–51). Although she maintained that her "early entrance into public life" may have initially smothered

her mothering instinct, she asserted that the joy of motherhood
had revived those smothered tendencies. Indeed, motherhood
may have increased her inclinations to activism, for it was
after the birth of her first child that she worked to establish
a kindergarten in Chicago. She also continued her antilynching crusade by investigating lynchings in Missouri in 1900
and by publishing *Mob Rule in New Orleans* in that same
year.

Two stand-out antilynching cases in which she was involved
occurred in 1910 and 1915. In 1910 Steve Green, a tenant
farmer in Arkansas, was accused of killing the landowner
from whom he rented. Escaping to Chicago, he was arrested
and put on a train back to Arkansas before Wells-Barnett was
able to intervene; however, she succeeded in getting him
rearrested and returned to Chicago before his extradition
could be completed. He was still living in Chicago at the
time she began writing her autobiography in 1928. The other
case, focusing on Joseph Campbell, had to do with the
questionable circumstances of a prison fire in Joliet, Illinois,
in which the warden's wife had been killed. Although the
wife was scheduled to speak on Campbell's behalf at his parole
hearing the following day, he was nonetheless accused of
setting the fire that killed her; naturally, feeling ran high to
lynch him. Wells-Barnett went to the Joliet prison to interview Campbell; her husband then spent several weeks defending his case. Campbell was sentenced to be hanged, but
lawyer Barnett was able to get the sentence commuted to life
imprisonment, and the husband and wife team succeeded in
moving Campbell out of that prison and away from the
warden's revenge. While the life sentence may not have been
cause for celebration, especially when Wells-Barnett knew the
man was innocent, it nonetheless reflected the best she and
her husband could effect under an almost impossible system.

She also campaigned to have sheriffs held responsible for the abduction and lynching of their prisoners. In one famous case, that of Sheriff Frank Davis of Springfield, Illinois, who had allowed a mob to take and lynch a black prisoner of his, Wells-Barnett succeeded in getting the governor not to reappoint Davis. She gathered evidence, read the brief her husband had prepared, and even argued the case in court.

It would be erroneous to conclude that all of Wells-Barnett's undertakings were successful or that she was universally, warmly received. That is certainly not the case. Black people were frequently as much her enemies as were the lynching variety of whites. In a time when their own situation was precarious, some African-Americans objected to Wells-Barnett's activities for further upsetting whites who already could take black lives at whim. While she was certainly celebrated by blacks, some of them nevertheless painted her as egotistical, or as a crazy woman, a loner who did not represent the sentiments of the majority of forward-thinking black intellectuals. Where others were willing to compromise, she was not. Her stances not only caused T. Thomas Fortune to declare publicly that the majority of blacks did not agree with her, but they also caused her to lose elections for offices in some of the women's clubs. She got her knocks for opposing the accommodationist policies of Booker T. Washington as well. Even young W. E. B. Du Bois, who is usually heralded as the nemesis of conservatism, was skeptical of Wells-Barnett's leadership. Perhaps, in a society where the few blacks who were educated usually stood head and shoulders above those who were not, it was rather an enigma that Wells-Barnett, who did not have a college degree, had an international reputation.

Yet for all the resistance she faced, Ida B. Wells-Barnett still made a substantial mark on American history. In addition

to her antilynching crusade, she was influential in establishing
the black women's club movement in this country, served as
a probation officer for young black men in Chicago and
helped them find jobs when the white YMCA refused them
such help, provided a place for new arrivals to Chicago to
stay, established a theater in Chicago, assisted in the founding
of the NAACP, and was involved in many other race-related
endeavors. If she had done nothing but fight against lynching,
however, her place in American history would be ensured.

It is one of the most shameful facts of the American
democratic process that no federal legislation against lynching
in this country was ever passed. The Dyer Anti-Lynching
bill was presented many times, but it was never made into
law. Whatever the reasons for that embarrassment, it was
certainly not due to lack of effort on the part of Ida B. Wells-
Barnett.

WORKS CONSULTED

Cutler, James E. *Lynch-Law: An Investigation into the History of
    Lynching in the United States*. New York: Longmans, Green,
    and Co., 1905.

Duster, Alfreda M., ed. *Crusade for Justice: The Autobiography of
    Ida B. Wells*. Chicago and London: The University of
    Chicago Press, 1970.

Ginzburg, Ralph. *100 Years of Lynching*. New York: Lancer Books,
    1962.

Hall, Jacquelyn Dowd. *Revolt Against Chivalry: Jessie Daniel Ames
    and the Women's Campaign Against Lynching*. New York:
    Columbia University Press, 1979.

Harris, Trudier. *Exorcising Blackness: Historical and Literary Lynch-
    ing and Burning Rituals*. Bloomington: Indiana University
    Press, 1984.

Hernton, Calvin C. *Sex and Racism in America*. New York: Grove Press, 1965.

Jordan, Winthrop D. *White Over Black: American Attitudes Toward the Negro: 1550–1812*. New York: Penguin, 1969.

NAACP. *Thirty Years of Lynching in the United States, 1889–1918*. New York: Arno Press and the *New York Times*, 1969.

Raper, Arthur F. *The Tragedy of Lynching*. Chapel Hill: The University of North Carolina Press, 1933.

Thompson, Mildred. *Ida B. Wells-Barnett: An Exploratory Study of an American Black Woman, 1893–1930*. Ann Arbor: University Microfilms International, 1979.

Tucker, David M. "Miss Ida B. Wells and Memphis Lynching." *Phylon* 32 (Summer 1971): 112–22.

Wells, Ida B. "Lynch Law in All Its Phases.'" *Our Day* 9 (May 1893).

White, Walter F. *Rope and Faggot: A Biography of Judge Lynch*. New York: Knopf, 1929.

Wright, Richard. *Black Boy*. New York: Harper and Row, 1945.

Zangrando, Robert L. *The NAACP Crusade Against Lynching, 1909–1950*. Philadelphia: Temple University Press, 1980.

SOUTHERN HORRORS
Lynch Law in All Its Phases

PREFACE

The greater part of what is contained in these pages was published in the New York *Age* June 25, 1892, in explanation of the editorial which the Memphis whites considered sufficiently infamous to justify the destruction of my paper, *The Free Speech*.

Since the appearance of that statement, requests have come from all parts of the country that "Exiled," (the name under which it then appeared) be issued in pamphlet form. Some donations were made, but not enough for that purpose. The noble effort of the ladies of New York and Brooklyn Oct 5 have enabled me to comply with this request and give the world a true, unvarnished account of the causes of lynch law in the South.

This statement is not a shield for the despoiler of virtue, nor altogether a defense for the poor blind Afro-American Sampsons who suffer themselves to be betrayed by white Delilahs. It is a contribution to truth, an array of facts, the perusal of which it is hoped will stimulate this great American Republic to demand that justice be done though the heavens fall.

It is with no pleasure I have dipped my hands in the corruption here exposed. Somebody must show that the Afro-American race is more sinned against than sinning, and it

Originally published in 1892 by the New York *Age Print*, New York.

seems to have fallen upon me to do so. The awful death-roll that Judge Lynch is calling every week is appalling, not only because of the lives it takes, the rank cruelty and outrage to the victims, but because of the prejudice it fosters and the stain it places against the good name of a weak race.

The Afro-American is not a bestial race. If this work can contribute in any way toward proving this, and at the same time arouse the conscience of the American people to a demand for justice to every citizen, and punishment by law for the lawless, I shall feel I have done my race a service. Other considerations are of minor importance.

IDA B. WELLS.

New York City, Oct. 26, 1892.

To the Afro-American women of New York and Brooklyn, whose race love, earnest zeal and unselfish effort at Lyric Hall, in the City of New York, on the night of October 5th, 1892,—made possible its publication, this pamphlet is gratefully dedicated by the author.

HON. FRED. DOUGLASS'S LETTER

Dear Miss Wells:

Let me give you thanks for your faithful paper on the lynch abomination now generally practiced against colored people in the South. There has been no word equal to it in convincing power. I have spoken, but my word is feeble in comparison. You give us what you know and testify from actual knowledge. You have dealt with the facts with cool, painstaking fidelity and left those naked and uncontradicted facts to speak for themselves.

Brave woman! you have done your people and mine a service which can neither be weighed nor measured. If American conscience were only half alive, if the American church and clergy were only half christianized, if American moral sensibility were not hardened by persistent infliction of outrage and crime against colored people, a scream of horror, shame and indignation would rise to Heaven wherever your pamphlet shall be read.

But alas! even crime has power to reproduce itself and create conditions favorable to its own existence. It sometimes seems we are deserted by earth and Heaven—yet we must still think, speak and work, and trust in the power of a merciful God for final deliverance.

Very truly and gratefully yours,
FREDERICK DOUGLASS.
Cedar Hill, Anacostia, D.C., Oct. 25, 1892.

CHAPTER I
THE OFFENSE

Wednesday evening May 24th, 1892, the city of Memphis was filled with excitement. Editorials in the daily papers of that date caused a meeting to be held in the Cotton Exchange Building; a committee was sent for the editors of the "Free Speech" and Afro-American journal published in that city, and the only reason the open threats of lynching that were made were not carried out was because they could not be found. The cause of all this commotion was the following editorial published in the "Free Speech" May 21st, 1892, the Saturday previous.

"Eight negroes lynched since last issue of the 'Free Speech'

one at Little Rock, Ark., last Saturday morning where the
citizens broke (?) into the penitentiary and got their man;
three near Anniston, Ala., one near New Orleans; and three
at Clarksville, Ga., the last three for killing a white man,
and five on the same old racket—the new alarm about raping
white women. The same programme of hanging, then shooting bullets into the lifeless bodies was carried out to the letter.

["]Nobody in this section of the country believes the old
thread bare lie that Negro men rape white women. If Southern
white men are not careful, they will over-reach themselves
and public sentiment will have a reaction; a conclusion will
then be reached which will be very damaging to the moral
reputation of their women."

"The Daily Commercial" of Wednesday following, May
25th, contained the following leader:

"Those negroes who are attempting to make the lynching
of individuals of their race a means for arousing the worst
passions of their kind are playing with a dangerous sentiment.
The negroes may as well understand that there is no mercy
for the negro rapist and little patience with his defenders. A
negro organ printed in this city, in a recent issue publishes
the following atrocious paragraph: 'Nobody in this section of
the country believes the old thread-bare lie that negro men
rape white women. If Southern white men are not careful
they will over-reach themselves, and public sentiment will
have a reaction; and a conclusion will be reached which will
be very damaging to the moral reputation of their women.'

["]The fact that a black scoundrel is allowed to live and
utter such loathsome and repulsive calumnies is a volume of
evidence as to the wonderful patience of Southern whites. But
we have had enough of it.

["]There are some things that the Southern white man will

not tolerate, and the obscene intimations of the foregoing have brought the writer to the very outermost limit of public patience. We hope we have said enough."

The "Evening Scimitar" of same date, copied the "Commercial's" editorial with these words of comment: "Patience under such circumstances is not a virtue. If the negroes themselves do not apply the remedy without delay it will be the duty of those whom he has attacked to tie the wretch who utters these calumnies to a stake at the intersection of Main and Madison Sts., brand him in the forehead with a hot iron and perform upon him a surgical operation with a pair of tailor's shears."

Acting upon this advice, the leading citizens met in the Cotton Exchange Building the same evening, and threats of lynching were freely indulged, not by the lawless element upon which the deviltry of the South is usually saddled—but by the leading business men, in the leading business centre. Mr. Fleming, the business manager and owning a half interest the Free Speech, had to leave town to escape the mob, and was afterwards ordered not to return; letters and telegrams sent me in New York where I was spending my vacation advised me that bodily harm awaited my return. Creditors took possession of the office and sold the outfit, and the "Free Speech" was as if it had never been.

The editorial in question was prompted by the many inhuman and fiendish lynchings of Afro-Americans which have recently taken place and was meant as a warning. Eight lynched in one week and five of them charged with rape! The thinking public will not easily believe freedom and education more brutalizing than slavery, and the world knows that the crime of rape was unknown during four years of civil war, when the white women of the South were at the mercy of the race which is all at once charged with being a bestial one.

Since my business has been destroyed and I am an exile from home because of that editorial, the issue has been forced, and as the writer of it I feel that the race and the public generally should have a statement of the facts as they exist. They will serve at the same time as a defense for the Afro-Americans Sampsons who suffer themselves to be betrayed by white Delilahs.

The whites of Montgomery, Ala., knew J. C. Duke sounded the keynote of the situation—which they would gladly hide from the world, when he said in his paper, "The Herald," five years ago: "Why is it that white women attract negro men now more than in former days? There was a time when such a thing was unheard of. There is a secret to this thing, and we greatly suspect it is the growing appreciation of white Juliets for colored Romeos." Mr. Duke, like the "Free Speech" proprietors, was forced to leave the city for reflecting on the "honah" of white women and his paper suppressed; but the truth remains that Afro-American men do not always rape (?) white women without their consent.

Mr. Duke, before leaving Montgomery, signed a card disclaiming any intention of slandering Southern white women. The editor of the "Free Speech" has no disclaimer to enter, but asserts instead that there are many white women in the South who would marry colored men if such an act would not place them at once beyond the pale of society and within the clutches of the law. The miscegnation laws of the South only operate against the legitimate union of the races; they leave the white man free to seduce all the colored girls he can, but it is death to the colored man who yields to the force and advances of a similar attraction in white women. White men lynch the offending Afro-American, not because he is a despoiler of virtue, but because he succumbs to the smiles of white women.

CHAPTER II
THE BLACK AND WHITE OF IT

The "Cleveland Gazette" of January 16, 1892, publishes a case in point. Mrs. J. S. Underwood, the wife of a minister of Elyria, Ohio, accused an Afro-American of rape. She told her husband that during his absence in 1888, stumping the State for the Prohibition Party, the man came to the kitchen door, forced his way in the house and insulted her. She tried to drive him out with a heavy poker, but he overpowered and chloroformed her, and when she revived her clothing was torn and she was in a horrible condition. She did not know the man but could identify him. She pointed out William Offett, a married man, who was arrested and, being in Ohio, was granted a trial.

The prisoner vehemently denied the charge of rape, but confessed he went to Mrs. Underwood's residence at her invitation and was criminally intimate with her at her request. This availed him nothing against the sworn testimony of a minister's wife, a lady of the highest respectability. He was found guilty, and entered the penitentiary, December 14, 1888, for fifteen years. Some time afterwards the woman's remorse led her to confess to her husband that the man was innocent.

These are her words: "I met Offett at the Post Office. It was raining. He was polite to me, and as I had several bundles in my arms he offered to carry them home for me, which he did. He had a strange fascination for me, and I invited him to call on me. He called, bringing chestnuts and candy for the children. By this means we got them to leave us alone in the room. Then I sat on his lap. He made a proposal to me and I readily consented. Why I did so, I do not know, but that I did is true. He visited me several times after that and each time I was indiscreet. I did not care after the first time. In fact I could not have resisted, and had no desire to resist."

When asked by her husband why she told him she had been outraged, she said: "I had several reasons for telling you. One was the neighbors saw the fellow here, another was, I was afraid I had contracted a loathsome disease, and still another was that I feared I might give birth to a Negro baby. I hoped to save my reputation by telling you a deliberate lie." Her husband horrified by the confession had Offett, who had already served four years, released and secured a divorce.

There are thousands of such cases throughout the South, with the difference that the Southern white men in insatiate fury wreak their vengeance without intervention of law upon the Afro-Americans who consort with their women. A few instances to substantiate the assertion that some white women love the company of the Afro-American will not be out of place. Most of these cases were reported by the daily papers of the South.

In the winter of 1885–6 the wife of a practicing physician in Memphis, in good social standing whose name has escaped me, left home, husband and children, and ran away with her black coachman. She was with him a month before the husband found and brought her home. The coachman could not be found. The doctor moved his family away from Memphis, and is living in another city under an assumed name.

In the same city last year a white girl in the dusk of evening screamed at the approach of some parties that a Negro had assaulted her on the street. He was captured, tried by a white judge and jury, that acquitted him of the charge. It is needless to add if there had been a scrap of evidence on which to convict him of so grave a charge he would have been convicted.

Sarah Clark of Memphis loved a black man and lived openly with him. When she was indicted last spring for miscegenation, she swore in court that she was *not* a white woman. This she did to escape the penitentiary and continued her illicit relation undisturbed. That she is of the lower class of whites, does not disturb the fact that she is a white woman. "The leading citizens" of Memphis are defending the "honor" of *all* white women, *demi-monde* included.

Since the manager of the "Free Speech" has been run away from Memphis by the guardians of the honor of Southern white women, a young girl living on Poplar St., who was discovered in intimate relations with a handsome mulatto young colored man, Will Morgan by name, stole her father's money to send the young fellow away from that father's wrath. She has since joined him in Chicago.

The Memphis "Ledger" for June 8th has the following; "If Lillie Bailey, a rather pretty white girl seventeen years of age, who is now at the City Hospital, would be somewhat less reserved about her disgrace there would be some very nauseating details in the story of her life. She is the mother of a little coon. The truth might reveal fearful depravity or it might reveal the evidence of a rank outrage. She will not divulge the name of the man who has left such black evidence of her disgrace, and, in fact, says it is a matter in which there can be no interest to the outside world. She came to Memphis nearly three months ago and was taken in at the Women's Refuge in the southern part of the city. She remained there until a few weeks ago, when the child was born. The ladies in charge of the Refuge were horrified. The girl was at once sent to the City Hospital, where she has been since May

30th. She is a country girl. She came to Memphis from her father's farm, a short distance from Hernando, Miss. Just when she left there she would not say. In fact she says she came to Memphis from Arkansas, and says her home is in that State. She is rather good looking, has blue eyes, a low forehead and dark red hair. The ladies at the Woman's Refuge do not know anything about the girl further than what they learned when she was an inmate of the institution; and she would not tell much. When the child was born an attempt was made to get the girl to reveal the name of the Negro who had disgraced her, she obstinately refused and it was impossible to elicit any information from her on the subject."

Note the wording. "The truth might reveal fearful depravity or rank outrage." If it had been a white child or Lillie Bailey had told a pitiful story of Negro outrage, it would have been a case of woman's weakness or assault and she could have remained at the Woman's Refuge. But a Negro child and to withhold its father's name and thus prevent the killing of another Negro "rapist." A case of "fearful depravity."

The very week the "leading citizens" of Memphis were making a spectacle of themselves in defense of all white women of every kind, an Afro-American, M. Stricklin, was found in a white woman's room in that city. Although she made no outcry of rape, he was jailed and would have been lynched, but the woman stated she bought curtains of him (he was a furniture dealer) and his business in her room that night was to put them up. A white woman's word was taken as absolutely in this case as when the cry of rape is made, and he was freed.

What is true of Memphis is true of the entire South. The daily papers last year reported a farmer's wife in Alabama had given birth to a Negro child. When the Negro farm hand who was plowing in the field heard it he took the mule from the plow and fled. The dispatches also told of a woman in South Carolina who gave birth to a Negro child and charged three men with being its father, *every one of whom has since disappeared.* In Tuscumbia, Ala., the colored boy who was lynched there last year for assaulting a white girl told her before his accusers that he had met her there in the woods often before.

Frank Weems of Chattanooga who was not lynched in May only because the prominent citizens became his body guard until the doors of the penitentiary closed on him, had letters in his pocket from the white woman in the case, making the appointment with him. Edward Coy who was burned alive in Texarkana, January 1, 1892, died protesting his innocence. Investigation since as given by the Bystander in the Chicago Inter-Ocean, October 1, proves:

"1. The woman who was paraded as a victim of violence was of bad character; her husband was a drunkard and a gambler.

2. She was publicly reported and generally known to have been criminally intimate with Coy for more than a year previous.

3. She was compelled by threats, if not by violence, to make the charge against the victim.

4. When she came to apply the match Coy asked her if she would burn him after they had 'been sweethearting' so long.

5. A large majority of the 'superior' white men prominent in the affair are the reputed fathers of mulatto children.

These are not pleasant facts, but they are illustrative of the vital phase of the so-called 'race question,' which should properly be designated an earnest inquiry as to the best methods by which religion, science, law and political power may be employed to excuse injustice, barbarity and crime done to a people because of race and color. There can be no possible belief that these people were inspired by any consum-ming zeal to vindicate God's law against miscegnationists of the most practical sort. The woman was a willing partner in the victim's guilt, and being of the 'superior' race must naturally have been more guilty."

In Natchez, Miss., Mrs. Marshall, one of the *creme de la creme* of the city, created a tremendous sensation several years ago. She has a black coachman who was married, and had been in her employ several years. During this time she gave birth to a child whose color was remarked, but traced to some brunette ancestor, and one of the fashionable dames of the city was its godmother. Mrs. Marshall's social position was unquestioned, and wealth showered every dainty on this child which was idolized with its brothers and sisters by its white papa. In course of time another child appeared on the scene, but it was unmistakably dark. All were alarmed, and "rush of blood, strangulation" were the conjectures, but the doctor, when asked the cause, grimly told them it was a Negro child. There was a family conclave, the coachman heard of it and leaving his own family went West, and has never returned. As soon as Mrs. Marshall was able to travel she was sent away in deep disgrace. Her husband died within the year of a broken heart.

Ebenzer Fowler, the wealthiest colored man in Issaquena County, Miss., was shot down on the street in Mayersville, January 30, 1885, just before dark by an armed body of white men who filled his body with bullets. They charged him with writing a note to a white woman of the place, which they intercepted and which proved there was an intimacy existing between them.

Hundreds of such cases might be cited, but enough have

been given to prove the assertion that there are white women in the South who love the Afro-American's company even as there are white men notorious for their preference for Afro-American women.

There is hardly a town in the South which has not an instance of the kind which is well-known, and hence the assertion is reiterated that "nobody in the South believes the old thread bare lie that negro men rape white women." Hence there is a growing demand among Afro-Americans that the guilt or innocence of parties accused of rape be fully established. They know the men of the section of the country who refuse this are not so desirous of punishing rapists as they pretend. The utterances of the leading white men show that with them it is not the crime but the *class*. Bishop Fitzgerald has become apologist for lynchers of the rapists of *white* women only. Governor Tillman, of South Carolina, in the month of June, standing under the tree in Barnwell, S.C., on which eight Afro-Americans were hung last year, declared that he would ["]lead a mob to lynch a *negro* who raped a *white* woman." So say the pulpits, officials and newspapers of the South. But when the victim is a colored woman it is different.

Last winter in Baltimore, Md., three white ruffians assaulted a Miss Camphor, a young Afro-American girl, while out walking with a young man of her own race. They held her escort and outraged the girl. It was a deed dastardly enough to arouse Southern blood, which gives its horror of rape as excuse for lawlessness, but she was an Afro-American. The case went to the courts, an Afro-American lawyer defended the men and they were acquitted.

In Nashville, Tenn., there is a white man, Pat Hanifan, who outraged a little Afro-American girl, and, from the physical injuries received, she has been ruined for life. He was jailed for six months, discharged, and is now a detective in that city. In the same city, last May, a white man outraged an Afro-American girl in a drug store. He was arrested, and released on bail at the trial. It was rumored that five hundred Afro-Americans had organized to lynch him. Two hundred and fifty white citizens armed themselves with Winchesters and guarded him. A cannon was placed in front of his home, and the Buchanan Rifles (State Militia) ordered to the scene for his protection. The Afro-American mob did not materialize. Only two weeks before Eph. Grizzard, who had only been *charged* with rape upon a white woman, had been taken from the jail, with Governor Buchanan and the police and militia standing by, dragged through the streets in broad daylight, knives plunged into him at every step, and with every fiendish cruelty a frenzied mob could devise, he was at last swung out on the bridge with hands cut to pieces as he tried to climb up the stanchions. A naked, bloody example of the blood-thirstiness of the nineteenth century civilization of the Athens of the South! No cannon or military was called out in his defense. He dared to visit a white woman.

At the very moment these civilized whites were announcing their determination " to protect their wives and daughters," by murdering Grizzard, a white man was in the same jail for raping eight-year-old Maggie Reese, an Afro-American girl. He was not harmed. The "honor" of grown women who were glad enough to be supported by the Grizzard boys and Ed Coy, as long as the liaison was not known, needed protection; they were white. The outrage upon helpless childhood needed no avenging in this case; she was black.

A white man in Guthrie, Oklahoma Territory, two months ago inflicted such injuries upon another Afro-American child that she died. He was not punished, but an attempt was made in the same town in the month of June to lynch an Afro-American who visited a white woman.

In Memphis, Tenn., in the month of June, Ellerton L. Dorr, who is the husband of Russell Hancock's widow, was arrested for attempted rape on Mattie Cole, a neighbor's cook; he was only prevented from accomplishing his purpose, by the appearance of Mattie's employer. Dorr's friends say he was drunk and not responsible for his actions. The grand jury refused to indict him and he was discharged.

CHAPTER III
THE NEW CRY

The appeal of Southern whites to Northern sympathy and sanction, the adroit, insiduous plea made by Bishop Fitzgerald for suspension of judgment because those "who condemn lynching express no sympathy for the *white* woman in the case," falls to the ground in the light of the foregoing.

From this exposition of the race issue in lynch law, the whole matter is explained by the well-known opposition growing out of slavery to the progress of the race. This is crystalized in the oft-repeated slogan: "This is a white man's country and the white man must rule." The South resented giving the Afro-American his freedom, the ballot box and the Civil Rights Law. The raids of the Ku-Klux and White Liners to subvert reconstruction government, the Hamburg and Ellerton, S.C., the Copiah County Miss., and the Lay-fayette Parish, La., massacres were excused as the natural resentment of intelligence against government by ignorance.

Honest white men practically conceded the necessity of intelligence murdering ignorance to correct the mistake of

the general government, and the race was left to the tender
mercies of the solid South. Thoughtful Afro-Americans with
the strong arm of the government withdrawn and with the
hope to stop such wholesale massacres urged the race to
sacrifice its political rights for sake of peace. They honestly
believed the race should fit itself for government, and when
that should be done, the objection to race participation in
politics would be removed.

But the sacrifice did not remove the trouble, nor move the
South to justice. One by one the Southern States have legally
(?) disfranchised the Afro-American, and since the repeal of
the Civil Rights Bill nearly every Southern State has passed
separate car laws with a penalty against their infringement.
The race regardless of advancement is penned into filthy,
stifling partitions cut off from smoking cars. All this while,
although the political cause has been removed, the butcheries
of black men at Barnwell, S.C., Carrolton, Miss., Waycross,
Ga., and Memphis, Tenn., have gone on; also the flaying
alive of a man in Kentucky, the burning of one in Arkansas,
the hanging of a fifteen year girl in Louisiana, a woman in
Jackson, Tenn., and one in Hollendale, Miss., until the dark
and bloody record of the South shows 728 Afro-Americans
lynched during the past 8 years. Not 50 of these were for
political causes; the rest were for all manner of accusations
from that of rape of white woman, to the case of the boy
Will Lewis who was hanged at Tullahoma, Tenn., last year
for being drunk and "sassy" to white folks.

These statistics compiled by the Chicago "Tribune" were
given the first of this year (1892). Since then, not less than
one hundred and fifty have been known to have met violent
death at the hands of cruel bloodthirsty mobs during the past
nine months.

To palliate this record (which grows worse as the Afro-

American becomes intelligent) and excuse some of the most
heinous crimes that ever stained the history of a country, the
South is shielding itself behind the plausible screen of defending the honor of its women. This, too, in the face of the
fact that only *one-third* of the 728 victims to mobs have been
charged with rape, to say nothing of those of that one-third
who were innocent of the charge. A white correspondent of
the Baltimore Sun declares that the Afro-American who was
lynched in Chestertown, Md., in May for assault on a white
girl was innocent; that the deed was done by a white man
who had since disappeared. The girl herself maintained that
her assailant was a white man. When the poor Afro-American
was murdered, the whites excused their refusal of a trial on
the ground that they wished so spare the white girl the
mortification of having to testify in court.

This cry has had its effect. It has closed the heart, stifled
the conscience, warped the judgment and hushed the voice of
press and pulpit on the subject of lynch law throughout this
"land of liberty." Men who stand high in the esteem of the
public for christian character, for moral and physical courage,
for devotion to the principles of equal and exact justice to all,
and for great sagacity, stand as cowards who fear to open
their mouths before this great outrage. They do not see that
by their tacit encouragement, their silent acquiescence, the
black shadow of lawlessness in the form of lynch law is
spreading its wings over the whole country.

Men who, like Governor Tillman, start the ball of lynch
law rolling for a certain crime, are powerless to stop it when
drunken or criminal white toughs feel like hanging an Afro-
American on any pretext.

Even to the better class of Afro-Americans the crime of
rape is so revolting they have too often taken the white man's

word and given lynch law neither the investigation nor condemnation it deserved.

They forget that a concession of the right to lynch a man for a certain crime, not only concedes the right to lynch any person for any crime, but (so frequently is the cry of rape now raised) it is in a fair way to stamp us a race of rapists and desperadoes. They have gone on hoping and believing that general education and financial strength would solve the difficulty, and are devoting their energies to the accumulation of both.

The mob spirit has grown with the increasing intelligence of the Afro-American. It has left the out-of-the-way places where ignorance prevails, has thrown off the mask and with this new cry stalks in broad daylight in large cities, the centres of civilization, and is encouraged by the "leading citizens" and the press.

CHAPTER IV
THE MALICIOUS AND
UNTRUTHFUL WHITE PRESS

The "Daily Commercial" and "Evening Scimitar" of Memphis, Tenn., are owned by leading business men of that city, and yet, in spite of the fact that there had been no white woman in Memphis outraged by an Afro-American, and that Memphis possessed a thrifty law-abiding, property owning class of Afro-Americans the "Commercial" of May 17th, under the head of "More Rapes, More Lynchings" gave utterance to the following:

["]The lynching of three Negro scoundrels reported in our dispatches from Anniston, Ala., for a brutal outrage committed upon a white woman will be a text for much comment on "Southern barbarism" by Northern newspapers; but we fancy it will hardly prove effective for campaign purposes among intelligent people. The frequency of these lynchings calls attention to the frequency of the crimes which causes lynching. The "Southern barbarism" which deserves the serious attention of all people North and South, is the barbarism which preys upon weak and defenseless women. Nothing but the most prompt, speedy and extreme punishment can hold in check the horrible and beastial propensities of the Negro race. There is a strange similarity about the number of cases of this character which have lately occurred.

["]In each case the crime was deliberately planned and perpetrated by several Negroes. They watched for an opportunity when the women were left without a protector. It was not a sudden yielding to a fit of passion, but the consummation of a devilish purpose which has been seeking and waiting for the opportunity. This feature of the crime not only makes it the most fiendishly brutal, but it adds to the terror of the situation in the thinly settled country communities. No man can leave his family at night without the dread that some roving Negro ruffian is watching and waiting for this opportunity. The swift punishment which invariably follows these horrible crimes doubtless acts as a deterring effect upon the Negroes in that immediate neighborhood for a short time. But the lesson is not widely learned nor long remembered. Then such crimes, equally atrocious, have happened in quick succession, one in Tennessee, one in Arkansas, and one in Alabama. The facts of the crime appear to appeal more to the Negro's lustful imagination than the facts of the punishment do to his fears. He sets aside all fear of death in any form when opportunity is found for the gratification of his bestial desires.

["]There is small reason to hope for any change for the better. The commission of this crime grows more frequent every year. The generation of Negroes which have grown up since the war have lost in large measure the traditional and wholesome awe of the white race which kept the Negroes in subjection, even when their masters were in the army, and their families left unprotected except by the slaves themselves. There is no longer a restraint upon the brute passion of the Negro.

["]What is to be done? The crime of rape is always horrible, but the Southern man there is nothing which so fills the soul with horror, loathing and fury as the outraging of a white woman by a Negro. It is the race question in the ugliest, vilest, most dangerous aspect. The Negro as a political factor can be controlled. But neither laws nor lynchings can subdue his lusts. Sooner or later it will force a crisis. We do not know in what form it will come."

In its issue of June 4th, the Memphis "Evening Scimitar" gives the following excuse for lynch law:

"Aside from the violation of white women by Negroes, which is the outcropping of a bestial perversion of instinct, the chief cause of trouble between the races in the South is the Negro's lack of manners. In the state of slavery he learned politeness from association with white people, who took pains to teach him. Soon the emancipation came and the tie of mutual interest and regard between master and servant was broken, the Negro has drifted away into a state which is neither freedom nor bondage. Lacking the proper inspiration of the one and the restraining force of the other he has taken up the idea that boorish insolence is independence, and the exercise of a decent degree of breeding toward white people is identical with servile submission. In consequence of the prevalence of this notion there are many Negroes who use every opportunity to make themselves offensive, particularly when they think it can be done with impunity.

["]We have had too many instances right here in Memphis to doubt this, and our experience is not exceptional. *The white people won't stand this sort of thing, and whether they be insulted as individuals [or] as a race, the response will be prompt and effectual.* The bloody riot of 1866, in which so many Negroes perished, was brought on principally by the outrageous conduct of the blacks toward the whites on the streets. It is also a remarkable and discouraging fact that the majority of such scoundrels are Negroes who have received educational advantages at the hands of the white taxpayers. They have got just enough of learning to make them realize how hopelessly their race is behind the other in everything that makes a great people, and they attempt to "get even" by insolence, which is ever the resentment of inferiors. There are well-bred Negroes among us, and it is truly unfortunate that they should have to pay, even in part, the penalty of the offenses committed by the baser sort, but this is the way of the world. The innocent must suffer for the guilty. If the Negroes as a people possessed a hundredth part of the self-respect which is evidenced by the courteous bearing of some that the "Scimitar" could name, the friction between the races would be reduced to a minimum. It will not do to beg the question by pleading that many white men are also stirring up strife. The Caucasian blackguard simply obeys the promptings of a depraved disposition, and he is seldom deliberately rough or offensive toward strangers or unprotected women.

["]The Negro tough, on the contrary, is given to just that kind of offending, and he almost invariably singles out white people as his victims."

On March 9th, 1892, there were lynched in this same city

three of the best specimens of young since-the-war Afro-American manhood. They were peaceful, law-abiding citizens and energetic business men.

They believed the problem was to be solved by eschewing politics and putting money in the purse. They owned a flourishing grocery business in a thickly populated suburb of Memphis, and a white man named Barrett had one on the opposite corner. After a personal difficulty which Barrett sought by going into the "People's Grocery" drawing a pistol and was thrashed by Calvin McDowell, he (Barrett) threatened to "clean them out." These men were a mile beyond the city limits and police protection; hearing that Barrett's crowd was coming to attack them Saturday night, they mustered forces and prepared to defend themselves against the attack.

When Barrett came he led a *posse* of officers, twelve in number, who afterward claimed to be hunting a man for whom they had a warrant. That twelve men in citizen's clothes should think it necessary to go in the night to hunt one man who had never before been arrested, or made any record as a criminal has never been explained. When they entered the back door the young men thought the threatened attack was on, and fired into them. Three of the officers were wounded, and when the *defending* party found it was officers of the law upon whom they had fired, they ceased and got away.

Thirty-one men were arrested and thrown in jail as "conspirators," although they all declared more than once they did not know they were firing on officers. Excitement was at fever heat until the morning papers, two days after, announced that the wounded deputy sheriffs were out of danger. This hindered rather than helped the plans of the whites. There was no law on the statute books which would execute an Afro-American for wounding a white man, but the "un-written law" did. Three of these men, the president, the manager and clerk of the grocery—"the leaders of the con-spiracy"—were secretly taken from jail and lynched in a shockingly brutal manner. "The Negroes are getting too independent," they say, "we must teach them a lesson."

"What lesson?["] The lesson of subordination. "Kill the leaders and it will cow the Negro who dares to shoot a white man, even in self-defense."

Although the race was wild over the outrage, the mockery of law and justice which disarmed men and locked them up in jails where they could be easily and safely reached by the mob—the Afro-American ministers, newspapers and leaders counselled obedience to the law which did not protect them.

Their counsel was heeded and not a hand was uplifted to resent the outrage; following the advice of the "Free Speech," people left the city in great numbers.

The dailies and associated press reports heralded these men to the country as "toughs," and "Negro desperadoes who kept a low dive." This same press service printed that the Negro who was lynched at Indianola, Miss., in May, had outraged the sheriff's eight-year-old daughter. The girl was more than eighteen years old, and was found by her father in this man's room, who was a servant on the place.

Not content with misrepresenting the race, the mob-spirit was not to be satisfied until the paper which was doing all it could to counteract this impression was silenced. The colored people were resenting their bad treatment in a way to make itself felt, yet gave the mob no excuse for further murder, until the appearance of the editorial which is construed as a reflection on the "honor" of the Southern white women. It is not half so libelous as that of the "Commercial" which appeared four days before, and which has been given in these pages. They would have lynched the manager of the "Free Speech" for exercising the right of free speech if they had found him as quickly as they would have hung a rapist, and glad of the excuse to do so. The owners were ordered not to return, "The Free Speech" was suspended with as little compunction as the business of the "People's Grocery" broken up and the proprietors murdered.

CHAPTER V
THE SOUTH'S POSITION

Henry W. Grady in his well-mannered speeches in New England and New York pictured the Afro-American as incapable of self-government. Through him and other leading men the cry of the South to the country has been "Hands off! Leave us to solve our problem." To the Afro-American the South says, "the white man must and will rule." There is little difference between the Ante-bellum South and the New South.

Her white citizens are wedded to any method however revolting, any measure however extreme, for the subjugation of the young manhood of the race. They have cheated him out of his ballot, deprived him of civil rights or redress therefor in the civil courts, robbed him of the fruits of his labor, and are still murdering, burning and lynching him.

The result is a growing disregard of human life. Lynch law has spread its insiduous influence till men in New York State, Pennsylvania and on the free Western plains feel they can take the law in their own hands with impunity, especially where an Afro-American is concerned. The South is brutalized to a degree not realized by its own inhabitants, and the very foundation of government, law and order, are imperilled.

Public sentiment has had a slight "reaction" though not sufficient to stop the crusade of lawlessness and lynching. The spirit of christianity of the great M. E. Church was aroused to the frequent and revolting crimes against a weak people, enough to pass strong condemnatory resolutions at its General Conference in Omaha last May. The spirit of justice of the grand old party asserted itself sufficiently to secure a denunciation of the wrongs, and a feeble declaration of the belief in human rights in the Republican platform at Minneapolis, June 7th. Some of the great dailies and weeklies have swung into line declaring that lynch law must go. The President of the United States issued a proclamation that it be not tolerated in the territories over which he has jurisdiction. Governor Northern and Chief Justice Bleckley of Georgia have proclaimed against it. The citizens of Chattanooga, Tenn., have set a worthy example in that they not only condemn lynch law, but her public men demanded a trial for Weems, the accused rapist, and guarded him while the trial was in progress. The trial only lasted ten minutes, and Weems chose to plead guilty and accept twenty-one years sentence, than invite the certain death which awaited him outside that cordon of police if he had told the truth and shown the letters he had from the white woman in the case.

Col. A. S. Colyar, of Nashville, Tenn., is so overcome with the horrible state of affairs that he addressed the following earnest letter to the Nashville "American." "Nothing since I have been a reading man has so impressed me with the decay of manhood among the people of Tennessee as the dastardly submission to the mob reign. We have reached the unprecedented low level; the awful criminal depravity of substituting the mob for the court and jury, by giving up the jail keys to the mob whenever they are demanded. We do it in the largest cities and in the country towns; we do it in midday; we do it after full, not to say formal, notice, and so thoroughly and generally is it acquiesced in that the murderers have discarded the formula of masks. They go into the town where everybody knows them, sometimes under the gaze of the governor, in the presence of the courts, in the presence of the sheriff and his deputies, in the presence of the entire police force, take out the prisoner, take his life, often with fiendish glee, and often with acts of cruelty and barbarism which impress the reader with a degeneracy rapidly approaching savage life. That the State is disgraced but faintly expresses the humiliation which has settled upon the once proud people of Tennessee. The State, in its majesty, through its organized life, for which the people pay liberally, makes but one record, but one note, and that a criminal falsehood, 'was hung by persons to the jury unknown.' The murder at Shelbyville is only a verification of what every intelligent man knew would come, because with a mob a rumor is as good as a proof."

These efforts brought forth apologies and a short halt, but the lynching mania was raged again through the past three months with unabated fury.

The strong arm of the law must be brought to bear upon lynchers in severe punishment, but this cannot and will not be done unless a healthy public sentiment demands and sustains such action.

The men and women in the South who disapprove of lynching and remain silent on the perpetration of such outrages, are particeps criminis, accomplices, accessories before and after the fact, equally guilty with the actual law-breakers who would not persist if they did not know that neither the law nor militia would be employed against them.

CHAPTER VI
SELF HELP

In the creation of this healthier public sentiment, the Afro-American can do for himself what no one else can do for him. The world looks on with wonder that we have conceded so much and remain law-abiding under such great outrage and provocation.

To Northern capital and Afro-American labor the South owes its rehabilitation. If labor is withdrawn capital will not remain. The Afro-American is thus the backbone of the South. A thorough knowledge and judicious exercise of this power in lynching localities could many times effect a blood-less revolution. The white man's dollar is his god, and to stop this will be to stop outrages in many localities.

The Afro-Americans of Memphis denounced the lynching of three of their best citizens, and urged and waited for the authorities to act in the matter and bring the lynchers to justice. No attempt was made to do so, and the black men left the city by thousands, bringing about great stagnation in every branch of business. Those who remained so injured the business of the street car company by staying off the cars, that the superintendent, manager and treasurer called person-ally on the editor of the "Free Speech," asked them to urge our people to give them their patronage again. Other business men became alarmed over the situation and the "Free Speech" was run away that the colored people might be more easily controlled. A meeting of white citizens in June, three months after the lynching, passed resolutions for the first time, condemning it. *But they did not punish the lynchers.* Every one of them was known by name, because they had been elected to do the dirty work, by some of the very citizens who passed these resolutions. Memphis is fast losing her black population, who proclaim as they go that there is no protection for the life and property of any Afro-American citizen in Memphis who is not a slave.

The Afro-American citizens of Kentucky, whose intellectual and financial improvement has been phenomenal, have never had a separate car law until now. Delegations and petitions poured into the Legislature against it, yet the bill passed and the Jim Crow Car of Kentucky is a legalized institution. Will the great mass of Negroes continue to patronize the railroad? A special from Covington, Ky., says:

Covington, June 13th.—The railroads of the State are beginning to feel very markedly, the effects of the separate coach bill recently passed by the Legislature. No class of people in the State have so many and so largely attended excursions as the blacks. All these have been abandoned, and regular travel is reduced to a minimum. A competent authority says the loss to the various roads will reach $1,000,000 this year.

A call to a State Conference in Lexington, Ky., last June had delegates from every country in the State. Those delegates, the ministers, teachers, heads of secret and others orders, and the head of every every family should [pass] the word around for every member of the race in Kentucky to stay off railroads unless obliged to ride. If they did so, and their advice was followed persistently the convention would not need to petition the Legislature to repeal the law or raise money to file a suit. The railroad corporations would be so effected they would in self-defense lobby to have the separate car law repealed. On the other hand, as long as the railroads can get Afro-American excursions they will always have plenty of money to fight all the suits brought against them. They will be aided in so doing by the same partisan public sentiment which passed the law. White men passed the law, and white judges and juries would pass upon the suits against the law, and render judgment in line with their prejudices and in deference to the greater financial power.

The appeal to the white man's pocket has ever been more effectual than all the appeals ever made to his conscience. Nothing, absolutely nothing, is to be gained by a further sacrifice of manhood and self-respect. By the right exercise of his power as the industrial factor of the South, the Afro-American can demand and secure his rights, the punishment of lynchers, and a fair trial for accused rapists.

Of the many inhuman outrages of this present year, the only case where the proposed lynching did *not* occur, was where the men armed themselves in Jacksonville, Fla., and Paducah, Ky., and prevented it. The only times an Afro-American who was assaulted got away has been when he had a gun and used it in self-defense.

The lesson this teaches and which every Afro-American should ponder well, is that a Winchester rifle should have a place of honor in every black home, and it should be used for that protection which the law refuses to give. When the white man who is always the aggressor knows he runs as great risk of biting the dust every time his Afro-American victim does, he will have greater respect for Afro-American life. The more the Afro-American yields and cringes and begs, the more he has to do so, the more he is insulted, outraged and lynched.

The assertion has been substantiated throughout these pages that the press contains unreliable and doctored reports of lynchings, and one of the most necessary things for the race to do is to get these facts before the public. The people must know before they can act, and there is no educator to compare with the press.

The Afro-American papers are the only ones which will

print the truth, and they lack means to employ agents and detectives to get at the facts. The race must rally a mighty host to the support of their journals, and thus enable them to do much in the way of investigation.

A lynching occurred at Port Jarvis, N.Y., the first week in June. A white and colored man were implicated in the assault upon a white girl. It was charged that the white man paid the colored boy to make the assault, which he did on the public highway in broad day time, and was lynched. This, too, was done by "parties unknown." The white man in the case still lives. He was imprisoned and promises to fight the case on trial. At the preliminary examination, it developed that he had been a suitor of the girl's. She had repulsed and refused him, yet had given him money, and he had sent threatening letters demanding more.

The day before this examination she was so wrought up, she left home and wandered miles away. When found she said she did so because she was afraid of the man's testimony. Why should she be afraid of the prisoner? Why should she yield to his demands for money if not to prevent him exposing something he knew? It seems explainable only on the hypothesis that a *liaison* existed between the colored boy and the girl, and the white man knew of it. The press is singularly silent. Has it a motive? We owe it to ourselves to find out.

The story comes from Larned, Kansas, Oct. 1st, that a young white lady held at bay until daylight, without alarming any one in the house, "a burly Negro" who entered her room and bed. The 'burly Negro" was promptly lynched without investigation or examination of inconsistent stories.

A house was found burned down near Montgomery, Ala., in Monroe County, Oct. 13th, a few weeks ago; also the burned bodies of the owners and melted piles of gold and silver.

These discoveries led to the conclusion that the awful crime was not prompted by motives of robbery. The suggestion of the whites was that "brutal lust was the incentive, and as there are nearly 200 Negroes living within a radius of five miles of the place the conclusion was inevitable that some of them were the perpetrators."

Upon this "suggestion" probably made by the real criminal, the mob acted upon the "conclusion" and arrested ten Afro-Americans, four of whom, they tell the world, confessed to the deed of murdering Richard L. Johnson and outraging his daughter, Jeanette. These four men, Berrell Jones, Moses Johnson, Jim and John Packer, none of them 25 years of age, upon this conclusion, were taken from jail, hanged, shot, and burned while yet alive the night of Oct. 12th. The same report says Mr. Johnson was on the best of terms with his Negro tenants.

The race thus outraged must find out the facts of this awful hurling of men into eternity on supposition, and give them to the indifferent and apathetic country. We feel this to be a garbled report, but how can we prove it?

Near Vicksburg, Miss., a murder was committed by a gang of burglars. Of course it must have been done by Negroes, and Negroes were arrested for it. It is believed that 2 men, Smith Tooley and John Adams belonged to a gang controlled by white men and, fearing exposure, on the night of July 4th, they were hanged in the Court House yard by those interested in silencing them. Robberies since committed in the same vicinity have been known to be by white men who had their faces blackened. We strongly believe in the innocence of these murdered men, but we have no proof. No other news goes out to the world save that which stamps us as a race of cut-throats, robbers and lustful wild beasts. So great is Southern hate and prejudice, they legally (?) hung poor little thirteen year old Mildred Brown at Columbia,

S.C., Oct. 7th, on the circumstantial evidence that she poisoned a white infant. If her guilt had been proven unmistakably, had she been white, Mildred Brown would never have been hung.

The country would have been aroused and South Carolina disgraced forever for such a crime. The Afro-American himself did not know as he should have known as his journals should be in a position to have him know and act.

Nothing is more definitely settled than he must act for himself. I have shown how he may employ the boycott, emigration and the press, and I feel that by a combination of all these agencies can be effectually stamped out lynch law, that last relic of barbarism and slavery. "The gods help those who help themselves."

THE REASON WHY
The Colored American Is Not in the World's Columbian Exposition

The Afro-American's Contribution to Columbian Literature

PREFACE

À Tout Chercheur de Vérité:

L'Amérique a convié le monde civilisé à se jomdre à elle pour célébrer le quatre-centième anniversaire de la découverte de l'Amérique, et son invitation a été acceptée.

Certes, le parc Jackson fait largement connaitre ses ressources naturelles et ses progrès dans les arts et dans les sciences; mais on a oublié justement ce qui devait donner le plus d'éclat à son élévation morale.

En mettant en effet sous les yeux les progrès qu'a faits en 25 ans de liberté une race sortant d'un escalvage de 250 ans, on eût rendu à la grandeur et au développement des institutions américaines le tribut le plus beau que pourrait voir le monde. Les gens de couleur de cette grande République sont au nombre de huit millions, plus du dix-septième de la population totale des Etats-Unis. Ils ont été parmi les plus anciens colons de ce continent, arrivant à Jamestown, Virginie, en 1619 dams un canot d'esclave avant les Puritans qui débarquèrent à Plymouth en 1620. Ils ont contribué dans une large mesure à la prospérité et à la civilisation de l'Amérique. Ce sont eux qui ont accompli et accomplissent encore la moitié du travail de ce pays; c'est le produit, le

Compiled and published by Ida B. Wells in 1893 in Chicago. Parts of Wells's own chapter (4) in this pamphlet were later reprinted in *A Red Record*.

46

résultat de leur travail qui a été la base du premier crédit que son commerce a obtenu de l'étranger. Si la race blanche a pu prendre son temps pour les grands progrès auxquels elle est parvenue oans l'éducation, dans less sciences, dans les arts, dans l'industrie et dans les inventions, c'est aux resources créées par leur labeur qu'elle le doit.

Les visiteurs de l'Exposition universelle columbienne qui sont au courant de ces faits, les étrangers suitout, vont naturellement demandor: Pourquoi donc la classe de couleur, qui constitue unélément si considérable de la population américaine, et qui ont largement contribué à la grandeur de l'Amérique n'est elle pas mieux representé et ne paraitelle pas plus visiblement dans cette Exposition? Pourquoi ces hommes ne prennent ils point part à cette glorieuse célébration du quatre-centième anniversaire de la Découverte de leur pays? Sont ils donc d'une incapacité et d'une stupidité telles qu'ils ne sentent aucun intérêt pour eux dans ce grand évènement? C'est pour répondre à cesquestions et suppléer autant que possible à notre oubli de représentation à l'Exposition que la race noire d'Amérique a publié ce livre.

VORWORT

An Alle, dieWahrheit suchen:

Columbus hat die civilisirte Welt eingeladen, sich an der vierhundertjährigen Feier der Entdeckung Amerika's zu betheiligen; diese Einladung ist angenommen worden. Im Jackson-Park befinden sich Ausstellungsgegenstände, die von seinem Naturreichthum zeugen, vom dem Fortschritte in Kunst und Wissenschaft, wahrend indessen Eines, das seine moralische Größe am besten bezeugen wurde, vollständig außer Acht gelassen worden ist.

Die Darstellung des Fortschrittes gemacht von einer Rasse
während fünfundzwanzigjähriger Freiheit, gegenüber dem
einer zewihundertundfünfzigjährigen Sklaverei, würde den
besten Beweis für die Größe und den Fortschritt Amerika's
geliefert haben. Die farbige Bevölkerung dieser großen Re-
publik beläuft sich auf acht Millionen—mehr als ein Zehntel
der Gesammtbevölkerung der Vereinigten Staaten. Die Farbigen waren unter den frühesten Ansiedlern dieses Conti-
nents, da sie bereits im Jahre 1619 in Jamestown, Virginien
landeten und zwar als Sklaven, noch ehe die Puritaner ihr
Erscheinen machten, die in 1620 landeten. Sie haben einen
beträchtlichen Theil für das allgemeine Wohl und Civilisation
beigetragen; die Hälfte der Arbeit des ganzen Landes wurde
und wird jetzt noch von ihnen verrichtet. Das Produkt,
durch welches Amerika im Verkehr mit den übrigen Nationen
zuerst Bedeutung gewonnen, war erzeugt durch ihre Arbeit.
Der durch ihren Fleiß erzeugte Reichthum hat der weißen
Bevölkerung die Muße gegeben, die zu einem Fortschritte
auf den Gebieten der Bildung, Kunst und Wissenschaft,
Industrie und Erfindung nöthig ist.

Jene Besucher der Weltaustellung, welchen diese That-
sachen bekannt sind und vorzüglich Fremde werden natürlich
fragen: Warum sind die Farbigen, sie einen so bedeutenden
Theil der amerikanischen Bevölkerung ausmachen und so viel
zur Größe Amerika's beigetragen haben, nicht besser auf der
Ausstellung vertreten? Warum betheiligen sie sich nicht an
der vierhundertjährigen Feier der Entdeckung ihres Landes?
Sind sie so beschränkt und unwissend, daß sie kein Intere-
sse an diesem wichtigen Ereigniß nehmen? Es ist mit Hins-
icht auf die Antwort zu diesen Fragen und auf eine bes-
sere Vertretung auf der Ausstellung, daß der Afrikanisch-
Amerikaner den vorliegenden Band veröffentlicht.

PREFACE

To the Seeker After Truth:

Columbia has bidden the civilized world to join with her in celebrating the four-hundredth anniversary of the discovery of America, and the invitation has been accepted. At Jackson Park are displayed exhibits of her natural resources, and her progress in the arts and sciences, but that which would best illustrate her moral grandeur has been ignored.

The exhibit of the progress made by a race in 25 years of freedom as against 250 years of slavery, would have been the greatest tribute to the greatness and progressiveness of American institutions which could have been shown the world. The colored people of this great Republic number eight millions— more than one-tenth the whole population of the United States. They were among the earliest settlers of this continent, landing at Jamestown, Virginia in 1619 in a slave ship, before the Puritans, who landed at Plymouth in 1620. They have contributed a large share to American prosperity and civilization. The labor of one-half of this country has always been, and is still being done by them. The first credit this country had in its commerce with foreign nations was created by productions resulting from their labor. The wealth created by their industry has afforded to the white people of this country the leisure essential to their great progress in education, art, science, industry and invention.

Those visitors to the World's Columbian Exposition who know these facts, especially foreigners will naturally ask: Why are not the colored people, who constitute so large an element of the American population, and who have contributed so large a share to American greatness,—more visibly present and better represented in this World's Exposition? Why are they not taking part in this glorious celebration of the four-hundredth anniversary of the discovery of their country? Are they so dull and stupid as to feel no interest in this great event? It is to answer these questions and supply as far as possible our lack of representation at the Exposition that the Afro-American has published this volume.

CHAPTER I
INTRODUCTION
Frederick Douglass

The colored people of America are not indifferent to the good opinion of the world, and we have made every effort to improve our first years of freedom and citizenship. We earnestly desired to show some results of our first thirty years of acknowledged manhood and womanhood. Wherein we have failed, it has been not our fault but our misfortune, and it is sincerely hoped that this brief story, not only of our successes, but of trials and failures, our hopes and disappoint-ments will relieve us of the charge of indifference and indolence. We have deemed it only a duty to ourselves, to make plain what might otherwise be misunderstood and misconstrued concerning us. To do this we must begin with slavery. The duty undertaken is far from a welcome one.

It involves the necessity of plain speaking of wrongs and outrages endured, and of rights withheld, and withheld in flagrant contradiction to boasted American Republican liberty and civilization. It is always more agreeable to speak well of one's country and its institutions than to speak otherwise; to tell of their good qualities rather than of their evil ones.

There are many good things concerning our country and

countrymen of which we would be glad to tell in this pamphlet, if we could do so, and at the same time tell the truth.
We would like for instance to tell our visitors that the moral
progress of the American people has kept even pace with their
enterprise and their material civilization; that practice by the
ruling class has gone on hand in hand with American professions; that two hundred and sixty years of progress and
enlightenment have banished barbarism and race hate from
the United States; that the old things of slavery have entirely
passed away, and that all things pertaining to the colored
people have become new; that American liberty is now the
undisputed possession of all the American people; that American law is now the shield alike of black and white; that the
spirit of slavery and class domination has no longer any
lurking place in any part of this country; that the statement
of human rights contained in its glorious Declaration of
Independence, including the right to life, liberty and the
pursuit of happiness is not an empty boast nor a mere
rhetorical flourish, but a soberly and honestly accepted truth,
to be carried out in good faith; that the American Church
and clergy, as a whole, stand for the sentiment of universal
human brotherhood and that its Christianity is without par-
tiality and without hypocrisy; that the souls of Negroes are
held to be as precious in the sight of God, as are the souls of
white men; that duty to the heathen at home is as fully
recognized and as sacredly discharged as is duty to the heathen
abroad; that no man on account of his color, race, or condition, is deprived of life, liberty or property without due
process of law; that mobs are not allowed to supersede courts
of law or usurp the place of government; that here Negroes
are not tortured, shot, hanged or burned to death, merely on
suspicion of crime and without ever seeing a judge, a jury or
advocate; that the American Government is in reality a Gov-

ernment of the people, by the people and for the people, and
for all the people; that the National Government is not a rope
of sand, but has both the power and the disposition to protect
the lives and liberties of American citizens of whatever color,
at home, not less than abroad; that it will send its men-of-
war to chastise the murder of its citizens in New Orleans or
in any other part of the south, as readily as for the same
purpose it will send them to Chili, Hayti, or San Domingo;
that our national sovereignty, in its rights to protect the lives
of American citizens is ample and superior to any right or
power possessed by the individual states; that the people of
the United States are a nation in fact as well as in name; that
in time of peace as in time of war, allegiance to the nation is
held to be superior to any fancied allegiance to individual
states; that allegiance and protection are here held to be
reciprocal; that there is on the statute books of the nation no
law for the protection of personal or political rights, which
the nation may not or can not enforce, with or without the
consent of individual states; that this World's Columbian
Exposition, with its splendid display of wealth and power, its
triumphs of art and its multitudinous architectural and other
attractions, is a fair indication of the elevated and liberal
sentiment of the American people, and that to the colored
people of America, morally speaking, the World's Fair now
in progress, is not a whited sepulcher.

All this, and more, we would gladly say of American laws,
manners, customs and Christianity. But unhappily, nothing
of all this can be said, without qualification and without
flagrant disregard of the truth. The explanation is this: We
have long had in this country, a system of iniquity which
possessed the power of blinding the moral perception, stifling
the voice of conscience, blunting all human sensibilities and
perverting the plainest teaching of the religion we have here

professed, a system which John Wesley truly characterized as the sum of all villanies, and one in view of which Thomas Jefferson, himself a slaveholder, said he "trembled for his country" when he reflected "that God is just and that His justice cannot sleep forever." That system was American slavery. Though it is now gone, its asserted spirit remains.

The writer of the initial chapter of this pamphlet, having himself been a slave, knows the slave system both on the inside and outside. Having studied its effects not only upon the slave and upon the master, but also upon the people and institutions by which it has been surrounded, he may there-fore, without presumption, assume to bear witness to its malign agency in explaining the present condition of the colored people of the United States, who were its victims; and to the sentiment held toward them both by the people who held them in slavery, and the people of the country who tolerated and permitted their enslavement, and the bearing it has upon the relation which we the colored people sustain to the World's Fair. What the legal and actual condition of the colored people was previous to emancipation is easily told.

It should be remembered by all who would entertain just views and arrive at a fair estimate of our character, our attainments and our worth in the scale of civilization, that prior to the slave-holder's rebellion thirty years ago, our legal condition was simply that of dumb brutes. We were classed as goods and chattels, and numbered on our master's ledgers with horses, sheep and swine. We were subject to barter and sale, and could be bequeathed and inherited by will, like real estate or any other property. In the language of the law: A slave was one in the power of his master to whom he belonged. He could acquire nothing, have nothing, own nothing that did not belong to his master. His time and talents, his mind and muscle, his body and soul, were the property of the master. He, with all that could be predicated of him as a human being, was simply the property of his master. He was a marketable commodity. His money value was regulated like any other article; it was increased or diminished according to his perfections or imperfections as a beast of burden.

Chief Justice Taney truly described the condition of our people when he said in the infamous Dred Scott decision, that they were supposed to have no rights which white men were bound to respect. White men could shoot, hang, burn, whip and starve them to death with impunity. They were made to feel themselves as outside the pale of all civil and political institutions. The master's power over them was complete and absolute. They could decide no question of pursuit or condition for themselves. Their children had no parents, their mothers had no husbands and there was no marriage in a legal sense.

But I need not elaborate the legal and practical definition of slavery. What I have aimed to do, has not only been to show the moral depths, darkness and destitution from which we are still emerging, but to explain the grounds of the prejudice, hate, and contempt in which we are still held by the people, who for more than two hundred years doomed us to this cruel and degrading condition. So when it is asked why we are excluded from the World's Columbian Exposition, the answer is Slavery.

Outrages upon the Negro in this country will be narrated in these pages. They will seem too shocking for belief. This doubt is creditable to human nature, and yet in view of the education and training of those who inflict the wrongs complained of, and the past condition of those upon whom they were inflicted as already described, such outrages are not only credible but entirely consistent and logical. Why should not these outrages be inflicted?

The life of a Negro slave was never held sacred in the estimation of the people of that section of the country in the time of slavery, and the abolition of slavery against the will of the enslavers did not render a slave's life more sacred. Such a one could be branded with hot irons, loaded with chains, and whipped to death with impunity when a slave. It only needed be said that he or she was impudent or insolent to a white man, to excuse or justify the killing of him or her. The people of the south are with few exceptions but slightly improved in their sentiments towards those they once held as slaves. The mass of them are the same to-day that they were in the time of slavery, except perhaps that now they think they can murder with a decided advantage in point of economy. In the time of slavery if a Negro was killed, the owner sustained a loss of property. Now he is not restrained by any fear of such loss.

The crime of insolence for which the Negro was formerly killed and for which his killing was justified, is as easily pleaded in excuse now, as it was in the old time and what is worse, it is sufficient to make the charge of insolence to provoke the knife or bullet. This done, it is only necessary to say in the newspapers, that this dead Negro was impudent and about to raise an insurrection and kill all the white people, or that a white woman was insulted by a Negro, to lull the conscience of the north into indifference and reconcile its people to such murder. No proof of guilt is required. It is enough to accuse, to condemn and punish the accused with death. When he is dead and silent, and the murderer is alive and at large, he has it all his own way. He can tell any story he may please and will be believed. The popular ear is open to him, and his justification is sure. At the bar of public opinion in this country all presumptions are against the Negro accused of crime.

The crime to which the Negro is now said to be so generally and specially addicted, is one of which he has been heretofore, seldom accused or supposed to be guilty. The importance of this fact cannot be over estimated. He was formerly accused of petty thefts, called a chicken thief and the like, but seldom or never was he accused of the atrocious crime of feloniously assaulting white women. If we may believe his accusers this is a new development. In slaveholding times no one heard of any such crime by a Negro. During all the war, when there was the fullest and safest opportunity for such assaults, nobody ever heard of such being made by him. Thousands of white women were left for years in charge of Negroes, while their fathers, brothers and husbands were absent fighting the battles of the rebellion; yet there was no assault upon such women by Negroes, and no accusation of such assault. It is only since the Negro has become a citizen and a voter that this charge has been made. It has come along with the pretended and baseless fear of Negro supremacy. It is an effort to divest the Negro of his friends by giving him a revolting and hateful reputation. Those who do this would make the world believe that freedom has changed the whole character of the Negro, and made of him a moral monster.

This is a conclusion revolting alike to common sense and common experience. Besides there is good reason to suspect a political motive for the charge. A motive other than the one they would have the world believe. It comes in close connection with the effort now being made to disfranchise the colored man. It comes from men who regard it innocent to lie, and who are unworthy of belief where the Negro is concerned. It comes from men who count it no crime to falsify the returns of the ballot box and cheat the Negro of his lawful vote. It comes from those who would smooth the way for the Negro's disfranchisement in clear defiance of the

constitution they have sworn to support—men who are per-
jured before God and man.

We do not deny that there are bad Negroes in this country
capable of committing this, or any other crime that other
men can or do commit. There are bad black men as there are
bad white men, south, north and everywhere else, but when
such criminals, or alleged criminals are found, we demand
that their guilt shall be established by due course of law.
When this will be done, the voice of the colored people
everywhere will then be "Let no guilty man escape." The
man in the South who says he is for Lynch Law because he
honestly believes that the courts of that section are likely to
be too merciful to the Negro charged with this crime, either
does not know the South, or is fit for prison or an insane
asylum.

Not less absurd is the pretense of these law breakers that
the resort to Lynch Law is made because they do not wish
the shocking details of the crime made known. Instead of a
jury of twelve men to decently try the case, they assemble a
mob of five hundred men and boys and circulate the story of
the alleged outrage with all its concomitant, disgusting detail.
If they desire to give such crimes the widest publicity they
could adopt no course better calculated to secure that end than
by a resort to lynch law. But this pretended delicacy is
manifestly all a sham, and the members of the blood-thirsty
mob bent upon murder know it to be such. It may deceive
people outside of the sunny south, but not those who know
as we do the bold and open defiance of every sentiment of
modesty and chastity practiced for centuries on the slave
plantations by this same old master class.

We know we shall be censured for the publication of this
volume. The time for its publication will be thought to be
ill chosen. America is just now, as never before, posing

before the world as a highly liberal and civilized nation, and in many important respects she has a right to this reputation. She has brought to her shores and given welcome to a greater variety of mankind than were ever assembled in one place since the day of Penticost. Japanese, Javanese, Soudanese, Chinese, Cingalese, Syrians, Persians, Tunisians, Algerians, Egyptians, East Indians, Laplanders, Esquimoux, and as if to shame the Negro, the Dahomians are also here to exhibit the Negro as a repulsive savage.

It must be admitted that, to outward seeming, the colored people of the United States have lost ground and have met with increased and galling resistance since the war of the rebellion. It is well to understand this phase of the situation. Considering the important services rendered by them in suppressing the late rebellion and the saving of the Union, they were for a time generally regarded with a sentiment of gratitude by their loyal white fellow citizens. This sentiment however, very naturally became weaker as, in the course of events, those services were retired from view and the memory of them became dimmed by time and also by the restoration of friendship between the north and the south. Thus, what the colored people gained by the war they have partly lost by peace.

Military necessity had much to do with requiring their services during the war, and their ready and favorable response to that requirement was so simple, generous and patriotic, that the loyal states readily adopted important amendments to the constitution in their favor. They accorded them freedom and endowed them with citizenship and the right to vote and the right to be voted for. These rights are now a part of the organic law of the land, and as such, stand to-day on the national statue book. But the spirit and purpose of these have been in a measure defeated by state legislation and by judicial decisions. It has nevertheless been found impossible to defeat them entirely and to relegate colored citizens to their former condition. They are still free.

The ground held by them to-day is vastly in advance of that they occupied before the war, and it may be safely predicted that they will not only hold this ground, but that they will regain in the end much of that which they seem to have lost in the reaction. As to the increased resistance met with by them of late, let us use a little philosophy. It is easy to account in a hopeful way for this reaction and even to regard it as a favorable symptom. It is a proof that the Negro is not standing still. He is not dead, but alive and active. He is not drifting with the current, but manfully resisting it and fighting his way to better conditions that those of the past, and better than those which popular opinion prescribes for him. He is not contented with his surroundings, but nobly dares to break away from them and hew out a way of safety and happiness for himself in defiance of all opposing forces.

A ship rotting at anchor meets with no resistance, but when she sets sail on the sea, she has to buffet opposing billows. The enemies of the Negro see that he is making progress and they naturally wish to stop him and keep him in just what they consider his proper place.

They have said to him "you are a poor Negro, be poor still," and "you are an ignorant Negro, be ignorant still and we will not antagonize you or hurt you." But the Negro has said a decided no to all this, and is now by industry, economy and education wisely raising himself to conditions of civili-zation and comparative well being beyond anything formerly thought possible for him. Hence, a new determination is born to keep him down. There is nothing strange or alarming about this. Such aspirations as his when cherished by the lowly are always resented by those who have already reached

the top. They who aspire to higher grades than those fixed
for them by society are scouted and scorned as upstarts for
their presumptions.

In their passage from an humble to a higher position, the
white man in some measure, goes through the same ordeal.
This is in accordance with the nature of things. It is simply
an incident of a transitional condition. It is not the fault of
the Negro, but the weakness, we might say the depravity, of
human nature. Society resents the pretensions of those it
considers upstarts. The new comers always have to go through
with this sort of resistance. The old and established are ever
adverse to the new and aspiring. But the upstarts of to-day
are the elite of tomorrow. There is no stopping any people
from earnestly endeavoring to rise. Resistance ceases when
the prosperity of the rising class becomes pronounced and
permanent.

The Negro is just now under the operation of this law of
society. If he were white as the driven snow, and had been
enslaved as we had been, he would have to submit to this
same law in his progress upward. What the Negro has to do
then, is to cultivate a courageous and cheerful spirit, use
philosophy and exercise patience. He must embrace every
avenue open to him for the acquisition of wealth. He must
educate his children and build up a character for industry,
economy, intelligence and virtue. Next to victory is the glory
and happiness of manfully contending for it. Therefore,
contend! contend!

That we should have to contend and strive for what is
freely conceded to other citizens without effort or demand
may indeed be a hardship, but there is compensation here as
elsewhere. Contest is itself ennobling. A life devoid of purpose and earnest effort, is a worthless life. Conflict is better
than stagnation. It is bad to be a slave, but worse to be a

willing and contented slave. We are men and our aim is perfect manhood, to be men among men. Our situation demands faith in ourselves, faith in the power of truth, faith in work and faith in the influence of manly character. Let the truth be told, let the light be turned on ignorance and prejudice, let lawless violence and murder be exposed.

The Americans are a great and magnanimous people and this great exposition adds greatly to their honor and renown, but in the pride of their success they have cause for repentence as well as complaisance, and for shame as well as for glory, and hence we send forth this volume to be read of all men.

CHAPTER II
CLASS LEGISLATION

The Civil War of 1861–5 ended slavery. It left us free, but it also left us homeless, penniless, ignorant, nameless and friendless. Life is derived from the earth, and the American Government is thought to be more humane than the Russian. Russia's liberated serf was given three acres of land and agricultural implements with which to begin his career of liberty and independence. But to us no foot of land nor implement was given. We were turned loose to starvation, destitution and death. So desperate was our condition that some of our statesmen declared it useless to try to save us by legislation as we were doomed to extinction.

The original fourteen slaves which the Dutch ship landed at Jamestown, Virginia in 1619, had increased to four millions by 1865, and were mostly in the southern states. We were liberated not only empty-handed but left in the power of a people who resented our emancipation as an act of unjust punishment to them. They were therefore armed with a

motive for doing everything in their power to render our
freedom a curse rather than a blessing. In the halls of National
legislation the Negro was made a free man and citizen. The
southern states, which had seceded from the Union before
the war, regained their autonomy by accepting these amendments and promising to support the constitution. Since "reconstruction" these amendments have been largely nullified
in the south, and the Negro vote reduced from a majority to
a cipher. This has been accomplished by political massacres,
by midnight outrages of Ku Klux Klans, and by state legislative enactment. That the legislation of the white south is
hostile to the interests of our race is shown by the existence
in most of the southern states of the convict lease system, the
chain-gang, vagrant laws, election frauds, keeping back laborers' wages, paying for work in worthless script instead of
lawful money, refusing to sell land to Negroes and the many
political massacres where hundreds of black men were murdered for the crime (?) of casting the ballot. These were some
of the means resorted to during our first years of liberty to
defeat the little beneficence comprehended in the act of our
emancipation.

The South is enjoying to-day the results of this course
pursued for the first fifteen years of our freedom. The solid
South means that the South is a unit for white supremacy,
and that the Negro is practically disfranchised through intimidation. The large Negro population of that section gives the
South thirty-nine more votes in the National Electoral College
which elects the President of the United States, than she
would otherwise have. These votes are cast by white men who
represent the Democratic Party, while the Negro vote has
heretofore represented the entire Republican Party of the
South. Every National Congress has thirty-nine more white
members from the South in the House of Representatives

than there would be, were it not for the existence of her voiceless and unrepresented Negro vote and population. One Representative is allowed to every 150,000 persons. What other States have usurped, Mississippi made in 1892, a part of her organic law.

The net result of the registration under the educational and poll tax provision of the new Mississippi Constitution is as follows.

Over 21 years		Registered votes
Whites	110,100	68,127
Negroes	147,205	8,615
Total	257,305	76,742

In 1880 there were 130,278 colored voters a colored majority of 22,024. Every county in Mississippi now has a white majority. Thirty-three counties have less than 100 Negro votes.

Yazoo county, with 6,000 Negroes of voting age, has only nine registered votes, or one to each 666. Noxubee has four colored voters or one to each 150 colored men. In Lowndes there is one colored voter to each 310 men. In the southern tier counties on the Gulf about one Negro man in eight or ten is registered, which is the best average.

Depriving the Negro of his vote leaves the entire political, legislative, executive and judicial machinery of the country in the hands of the white people. The religious, moral and financial forces of the country are also theirs. This power has been used to pass laws forbidding intermarriage between the races, thus fostering immorality. The union, which the law forbids, goes on without its sanction in dishonorable alliances.

Sec. 3291 M. & V. Code Tennessee, provides that: The intermarriage of white persons with Negroes, Mulattoes or persons of mixed blood descended from a Negro to the third generation inclusive, or their living together as man and wife in this State, is hereby forbidden.

Sec. 3292, M. & V. Code, Tenn., provides that: The persons knowingly violating the provisions in above Section shall be deemed guilty of a felony, and upon conviction thereof shall undergo imprisonment in the penitentiary not less than one nor more than five years; and the court may, in the event of conviction, on the recommendation of the jury, substitute in lieu of punishment in the penitentiary, fine and imprisonment in the county jail.

NOTES:—It need not charge the act to have been done knowingly. Such persons may be indicted for living together as man and wife though married in another state where such marriages are lawful. 7 Bok. 9. This law is constitutional. 3 Hill's 287.

Out of 44 states only twenty-three states and territories allow whites and Negroes to marry if they see fit to contract such alliances, vis: Louisiana, Illinois, Kansas, Connecticut, Iowa, Maine, Massachusetts, Michigan, Minnesota, Montana, New Hampshire, New Jersey, New York, North Dakota, Ohio, Oklahoma, Pennsylvania, Rhode Island, South Dakota, Vermont, Washington, Wisconsin, and Wyoming. All of these are northern states and territories except one— Louisiana.

The others, especially Virginia, Maryland, W. Virginia, Delaware, North Carolina, South Carolina, Georgia, Florida, Alabama, Mississippi, Arkansas, Kentucky, Missouri, Indiana, Tennessee, and Texas, have laws similar to the Tennessee Statute. Under these laws men and women are prosecuted and punished in the courts of these states for inter-marrying, but not for unholy alliances.

"The Thirteenth amendment to the Constitution making the race citizens, was virtually made null and void by the legislatures of the re-constructed states. So it became necessary to pass the Civil Rights Bill giving colored people the right to enter public places and ride on first-class railroad cars.”— Johnson’s History of the Negro race in America. This Bill passed Congress in 1875. For nearly ten years it was the Negro’s only protection in the south. In 1884 the United States Supreme Court declared the Civil Rights Bill unconstitutional. With “state’s rights,” doctrine once more supreme and this last barrier removed, the southern states are enacting separate car laws. Mississippi, Louisiana, Texas, Arkansas, Tennessee, Alabama, Georgia and Kentucky have each passed a law making it punishable by fine and imprisonment for colored persons to ride in the same railway carriage with white persons unless as servants to white passengers. These laws have all been passed within the past 6 years. Kentucky passed this law last year (1892). The legislatures of Missouri, West Virginia and North Carolina had such bills under consideration at the sessions this year, but they were defeated.

Aside from the inconsistency of class legislation in this country, the cars for colored persons are rarely equal in point of accommodation. Usually one-half the smoking car is reserved for the “colored car.” Many times only a cloth curtain or partition run half way up, divides this “colored car” from the smoke, obscene language and foul air of the smokers’ end of the coach. Into this “separate but equal(?)” half-carriage are crowded all classes and conditions of Negro humanity, without regard to sex, standing, good breeding, or ability to pay for better accommodation. White men pass through these “colored cars” and ride in them whenever they feel inclined to do so, but no colored woman however refined, well educated or well dressed may ride in the ladies, or first-class coach, in any of these states unless she is a nurse-maid traveling with a white child. The railroad fare is exactly the same in all cases however. There is no redress at the hands of the law. The men who execute the law share the same prejudices as those who made these laws, and the courts rule in favor of the law. A colored young school teacher was dragged out of the only ladies coach on the train in Tennessee by the conductor and two trainmen. She entered suit in the state courts as directed by the United States Supreme Court. The Supreme Court of the State of Tennessee, although the lower courts had awarded damages to the plaintiff, reversed the decision of those courts and ruled that the smoking car into which the railway employees tried to force the plaintiff was a first-class car, equal in every respect to the one in which she was seated, and as she was violating the law, she was not entitled to damages.

The Tennessee law is as follows,

———Chapter 52———Page 135—An Act to promote the comfort of passengers on railroad trains by regulating separate accommodations for the white and colored races.

SECTION 1. Be it enacted by the General Assembly of the State of Tennessee—That all railroads carrying passengers in the State (other than street railroads) shall provide equal but separate accommodations for the white and colored races, by providing two or more passenger cars for each passenger train, or by dividing the passenger cars by a partition so as to secure separate accommodations; PROVIDED, that any person may be permitted to take a nurse in the car or compartment set aside for such persons; PROVIDED, that this Act shall not apply to mixed and freight trains which only carry one passenger or combination passenger and baggage; PROVIDED, always that in such cases the one passenger car so carried shall be partitioned into apartments, one apartment for the whites and one for the colored.

SEC. 2. Be it further enacted: That the conductors of such passenger trains shall have power and are hereby required to assign to the car or compartments of the car (when it is divided by a partition) used for the race to which such passengers belong, and should any passenger refuse to occupy the car to which he or she is assigned by such conductor, said conductor shall have power to refuse to carry such passenger on his train, and for such neither he nor the railroad company shall be liable for any damages in any court in this State.

Sec. 3. Be it further enacted: That all railroad companies that shall fail, refuse or neglect to comply with the requirements of section 1, of this Act shall be deemed guilty of a misdemeanor, and, upon conviction in a court of competent jurisdiction, be fined not less than one hundred, nor more than four hundred dollars, and any conductor that shall fail, neglect or refuse to carry out the provisions of this Act shall, upon conviction, be fined not less than twenty-five, nor more than fifty dollars for each offense.

Sec. 4. Be it further enacted: That this Act take effect ninety days from and after its passage, the public welfare requiring it.

Passed March 11, 1891.
Thomas R. Myers.
Speaker of the House of Representatives.
Approved March 27, 1891.
W. C. Dismukes,
Speaker of Senate.
John P. Buchanan,
Governor.

CHAPTER III
THE CONVICT LEASE SYSTEM

The Convict Lease System and Lynch Law are twin infamies which flourish hand in hand in many of the United States. They are the two great outgrowths and results of the class legislation under which our people suffer to-day. Alabama, Arkansas, Florida, Georgia, Kentucky, Louisiana, Mississippi, Nebraska, North Carolina, South Carolina, Tennessee and Washington claim to be too poor to maintain state convicts within prison walls. Hence the convicts are leased out to work for railway contractors, mining companies and those who farm large plantations. These companies assume charge of the convicts, work them as cheap labor and pay the states a handsome revenue for their labor. Nine-tenths of these convicts are Negroes. There are two reasons for this.

(1) The religious, moral and philanthropic forces of the country—all the agencies which tend to uplift and reclaim the degraded and ignorant, are in the hands of the Anglo-Saxon. Not only has very little effort been made by these forces to reclaim the Negro from the ignorance, immorality and shiftlessness with which he is charged, but he has always been and is now rigidly excluded from the enjoyment of those elevating influences toward which he felt voluntarily drawn. In communities where Negro population is largest and these counteracting influences most needed, the doors of churches, schools, concert halls, lecture rooms, Young Men's Christian Associations, and Women's Christian Temperance Unions, have always been and are now closed to the Negro who enters on his own responsibility. Only as a servant or inferior being placed in one corner is he admitted. The white Christian and moral influences have not only done little to prevent the Negro becoming a criminal, but they have deliberately shut him out of everything which tends to make for good citizenship.

To have Negro blood in the veins makes one unworthy of consideration, a social outcast, a leper, even in the church. Two Negro Baptist Ministers, Rev. John Frank, the pastor of the largest colored church in Louisville, Ky., and Rev.

C. H. Parish, President of Extein Norton University at Cane Spring, Ky., were in the city of Nashville, Tennessee, in May when the Southern Baptist Convention was in session. They visited the meeting and took seats in the body of the church. At the request of the Association, a policeman was called and escorted these men out because they would not take the seats set apart for colored persons in the back part of the Tabernacle. Both these men are scholarly, of good moral character, and members of the Baptist denomination. But they were Negroes, and that eclipsed everything else. This spirit is even more rampant in the more remote, densely populated plantation districts. The Negro is shut out and ignored—left to grow up in ignorance and vice. Only in the gambling dens and saloons does he meet any sort of welcome. What wonder that he falls into crime?

(2) The second reason our race furnishes so large a share of the convicts is that the judges, juries and other officials of the courts are white men who share these prejudices. They also make the laws. It is wholly in their power to extend clemency to white criminals and mete severe punishment to black criminals for the same or lesser crimes. The Negro criminals are mostly ignorant, poor and friendless. Possessing neither money to employ lawyers nor influential friends, they are sentenced in large numbers to long terms of imprisonment for petty crimes. The *People's Advocate*, a Negro journal, of Atlanta, Georgia, has the following observation on the prison showing of that state for 1892. "It is an astounding fact that 90 per cent of the state's convicts are colored. 194 white males and 2 white females; 1710 colored males and 44 colored females. Is it possible that Georgia is so color prejudiced that she won't convict her white law breakers. Yes, it is just so, but we hope for a better day."

George W. Cable, author of *The Grandissimes, Dr. Sevier,*

etc., in a paper on "The Convict Lease System," read before a Prison Congress in Kentucky says: "In the Georgia penitentiary in 1880, in a total of nearly 1200 convicts, only 22 prisoners were serving as low a term as one year, only 52 others as low as two years, only 76 others as low a term as three years; while those who were under sentences of ten years and *over* numbered 538, although ten years, as the rolls show, is the *utmost* length of time that a convict can be expected to remain alive in a Georgia penitentiary. Six men were under sentence for simple assault and battery—mere fisticuffing— one of two years, two of five years, one of six years, one of seven and one of eight. For larceny, three men were serving under sentence of twenty years, five were sentenced each for fifteen years: one for fourteen years, six for twelve years; thirty-five for ten years, and 172 from one year up to nine years. In other words, a large majority of these 1200 convicts had for simple stealing, without breaking in or violence, been virtually condemned to be worked and misused to death. One man was under a twenty years' sentence for hog-stealing. Twelve men were sentenced to the South Carolina penitentiary on no other finding but a misdemeanor commonly atoned for by a fine of a few dollars, and which thousands of the state's inhabitants (white) are constantly committing with impunity—the carrying of concealed weapons. Fifteen others were sentenced for mere assault and battery. In Louisiana a man was sentenced to the penitentiary for 12 months for stealing five dollars worth of gunnysacks! Out of 2378 convicts in the Texas prison in 1882, only two were under sentence of less than two years length, and 509 of these were under twenty years of age. Mississippi's penitentiary roll for the same year showed 70 convicts between the ages of 12 and 18 years of age serving long terms. Tennessee showed 12 boys under 18 years of age, under sentences of more than a year; and the

North Carolina penitentiary had 234 convicts under 20 years of age serving long terms."

Mr. Cable goes on to say in another part of his admirable paper: "In the Georgia convict force only 15 were whites among 215 who were under sentences of more than ten years." What is true of Georgia is true of the convict lease system everywhere. The details of vice, cruelty and death thus fostered by the states whose treasures are enriched thereby, equals anything from Siberia. Men, women and children are herded together like cattle in the filthiest quarters and chained together while at work. The Chicago *Inter-Ocean* recently printed an interview with a young colored woman who was sentenced six months to the convict farm in Mississippi for fighting. The costs etc., lengthened the time to 18 months. During her imprisonment she gave birth to two children, but lost the first one from premature confinement, caused by being tied up by the thumbs and punished for failure to do a full day's work. She and other women testified that they were forced to criminal intimacy with the guards and cook to get food to eat.

Correspondence to the Washington D.C. *Evening Star* dated Sept. 27, 1892, on this same subject has the following:

> The fact that the system puts a large number of criminals afloat in the community from the numerous escapes is not its worst feature. The same report shows that the mortality is fearful in the camps. In one camp it is stated that the mortality is 10 per cent per month, and in another even more than that. In these camps men and women are found chained together, and from twenty to twenty-five children have been born in captivity in the convicts camps.
>
> Some further facts are cited with reference to the system in use in Tennessee. The testimony of a guard at the Coal

Creek prison in Tennessee shows that prisoners, black and dirty from their work in the mines, were put into their rooms in the stockades without an opportunity to change their clothing or sufficient opportunity for cleanliness. Convicts were whipped, a man standing at the head and another at the feet, while a third applied the lash with both hands. Men who failed to perform their task of mining from two to four tons of coal per day were fastened to planks by the feet, then bent over a barrel and fastened by the hands on the other side, stripped and beaten with a strap. Out of the fifty convicts worked in the mines from one to eight were whipped per day in this manner. There was scarcely a day, according to the testimony of the witness, James Frazier, in which one or more were not flogged in this manner for failure to perform their day's task. The work in the mines was difficult and the air sometimes so bad that the men felt insensible and had to be hauled out. Their beds he describes as "dirty, black and nasty looking." One of the convicts, testifying as to the kind of food given them, said that the pea soup was made from peas containing weevils and added: "I have got a spoonful of weevils off a cup of soup." In many cases convicts were forced to work in water six inches deep for weeks at a time getting out coal with one-fourth of the air necessary for a healthy man to live in, forced to drink water from stagnant pools when mountain springs were just outside of the stockades, and the reports of the prison officials showing large numbers killed in attempting to escape.

The defense of this prison is based wholly upon its economy to the state. It is argued that it would cost large sums of money to build penitentiaries in which to confine and work the prisoners as is done in the Northern States, while the lease system brings the state a revenue and relieves it of the cost of building and maintaining prisons. The fact that the convicts labor is in this way brought into direct competition with free labor does not seem to be taken into account. The contractors, who get these laborers for 30 or 40 cents per day, can drive out of the market the man who employs free labor at $1 a day.

This condition of affairs briefly alluded to in detail in Tennessee and Georgia exists in other Southern States. In North Carolina the same system exists, except that only able-bodied convicts are farmed out. The death rates among the convicts is reported as greater than the death rate of New Orleans in the greatest yellow fever epidemic ever known. In Alabama a new warden with his natural instincts unblunted by familiarity with the situation wrote of it: "The system is a better training school for criminals than any of the dens of iniquity in our large cities. The system is a disgrace to the state and the reproach of the civilization and Christian sentiment of the age."

Every Negro so sentenced not only means able-bodied men to swell the state's number of slaves, but every Negro so convicted is thereby *disfranchised*.

It has been shown that numbers of Negro youths are sentenced to these penitentiaries every year and there mingle with the hardened criminals of all ages and both sexes. The execution of law does not cease with the incarceration of those of tender years for petty crimes. In the state of South Carolina last year Mildred Brown, a little thirteen year old colored girl was found guilty of murder in the first degree on the charge of poisoning a little white infant that she nursed. She was sentenced to be hanged. The Governor refused to commute her sentence, and on October 7th, 1892, at Columbia, South Carolina, she was hanged on the gallows. This made the second colored female hanged in that state within one month. Although tried, and in rare cases convicted for murder and other crimes, no white girl in this country ever met the same fate. The state of Alabama in the same year hanged a ten year old Negro boy. He was charged with the murder of a peddler.

CHAPTER IV
LYNCH LAW
Ida B. Wells

"Lynch Law," says the *Virginia Lancet,*"as known by that appellation, had its origin in 1780 in a combination of citizens of Pittsylvania County, Virginia, entered into for the purpose of suppressing a trained band of horse-thieves and counter-feiters whose well concocted schemes had bidden defiance to the ordinary laws of the land, and whose success encouraged and emboldened them in their outrages upon the community. Col. Wm. Lynch drafted the constitution for this combination of citizens, and hence 'Lynch Law' has ever since been the name given to the summary infliction of punishment by private and unauthorized citizens."

This law continues in force to-day in some of the oldest states of the Union, where courts of justice have long been established, whose laws are executed by white Americans. It flourishes most largely in the states which foster the convict lease system, and is brought to bear mainly, against the Negro. The first fifteen years of his freedom he was murdered by masked mobs for trying to vote. Public opinion having made lynching for that cause unpopular, a new reason is given to justify the murders of the past 15 years. The Negro was first charged with attempting to rule white people, and hundreds were murdered on that pretended supposition. He is now charged with assaulting or attempting to assault white women. This charge, as false as it is foul, robs us of the sympathy of the world and is blasting the race's good name.

The men who make these changes encourage or lead the mobs which do the lynching. They belong to the race which holds Negro life cheap, which owns the telegraph wires, newspapers, and all other communication with the outside world. They write the reports which justify lynching by painting the Negro as black as possible, and those reports are accepted by the press associations and the world without question or investigation. The mob spirit has increased with alarming frequency and violence. Over a thousand black men, women and children have been thus sacrificed the past ten years. Masks have long since been thrown aside and the lynchings of the present day take place in broad daylight. The sheriffs, police and state officials stand by and see the work well done. The coroner's jury is often formed among those who took part in the lynching and a verdict, "Death at the hands of parties unknown to the jury" is rendered. As the number of lynchings have increased, so has the cruelty and barbarism of the lynchers. Three human beings were burned alive in civilized America during the first six months of this year (1893). Over one hundred have been lynched in this half year. They were hanged, then cut, shot and burned.

The following table published by the Chicago *Tribune* January, 1892, is submitted for thoughtful consideration.

1882,	52	Negroes	murdered	by	mobs
1883,	39	"	"	"	"
1884,	53	"	"	"	"
1885,	77	"	"	"	"
1886,	73	"	"	"	"
1887,	70	"	"	"	"
1888,	72	"	"	"	"
1889,	95	"	"	"	"
1890,	100	"	"	"	"
1891,	169	"	"	"	"

Of this number

269	were charged with		rape.
253	"	" "	murder.
44	"	" "	robbery.
37	"	" "	incendiarism.
4	"	" "	burglary.
27	"	" "	race prejudice.
13	"	" "	quarreling with white men.
10	"	" "	making threats.
7	"	" "	rioting.
5	"	" "	miscegenation.
32	"	" "	no reasons given.

This table shows (1) that only one-third of nearly a thousand murdered black persons have been even charged with the crime of outrage. This crime is only so punished when white women accuse black men, which accusation is never proven. The same crime committed by Negroes against Negroes, or by white men against black women is ignored even in the law courts.

(2) That nearly as many were lynched for murder as for the above crime, which the world believes is the cause of all the lynchings. The world affects to believe that *white* womanhood and childhood, surrounded by their lawful protectors, are not safe in the neighborhood of the black man, who protected and cared for them during the four years of civil war. The husbands, fathers and brothers of those white women were away for four years, fighting to keep the Negro in slavery, yet not one case of assault has ever been reported!

(3) That "robbery, incendiarism, race prejudice, quarreling with white men, making threats, rioting, miscegenation (marrying a white person), and burglary," are capital offences

punishable by death when committed by a black against a white person. Nearly as many blacks were lynched for these charges (and unproven) as for the crime of rape.

(4) That for nearly fifty of these lynchings no reason is given. There is no demand for reasons, or need of concealment for what no one is held responsible. The simple word of any white person against a Negro is sufficient to get a crowd of white men to lynch a Negro. Investigation as to the guilt or innocence of the accused is never made. Under these conditions, white men have only to blacken their faces, commit crimes against the peace of the community, accuse some Negro, nor rest till he is killed by a mob. Will Lewis, an 18 year old Negro youth was lynched at Tullahoma, Tennessee, August, 1891, for being "drunk and saucy to white folks."

The women of the race have not escaped the fury of the mob. In Jackson, Tennessee, in the summer of 1886, a white woman died of poisoning. Her black cook was suspected, and as a box of rat poison was found in her room, she was hurried away to jail. When the mob had worked itself to the lynching pitch, she was dragged out of jail, every stitch of clothing torn from her body, and she was hung in the public courthouse square in sight of everybody. Jackson is one of the oldest towns in the State, and the State Supreme Court holds its sittings there; but no one was arrested for the deed—not even a protest was uttered. The husband of the poisoned woman has since died a raving maniac, and his ravings showed that he, and not the poor black cook, was the poisoner of his wife. A fifteen year old Negro girl was hanged in Rayville, Louisiana, in the spring of 1892, on the same charge of poisoning white persons. There was no more proof or investigation of this case than the one in Jackson. A Negro woman, Lou Stevens, was hanged from a railway bridge in Hollendale, Mississippi, in 1892. She was charged with being accessory to the murder of her white paramour, who had shamefully abused her.

In 1892 there were 241 persons lynched. The entire number is divided among the following states.

Alabama	22	Montana	4
Arkansas	25	New York	1
California	3	North Carolina	5
Florida	11	North Dakota	1
Georgia	17	Ohio	3
Idaho	8	South Carolina	5
Illinois	1	Tennessee	28
Kansas	3	Texas	15
Kentucky	9	Virginia	7
Louisiana	29	West Virginia	5
Maryland	1	Wyoming	9
Mississippi	16	Arizona Ter.	3
Missouri	6	Oklahoma	2

Of this number 160 were of Negro descent. Four of them were lynched in New York, Ohio and Kansas; the remainder were murdered in the south. Five of this number were females. The charges for which they were lynched cover a wide range. They are as follows:

Rape	46	Attempted Rape	11
Murder	58	Suspected Robbery	4
Rioting	3	Larceny	1
Race prejudice	6	Self-defense	1
No cause given	4	Insulting women	2
Incendiarism	6	Desperadoes	6
Robbery	6	Fraud	1
Assault and Battery	1	Attempted murder	2
No offense stated, boy and girl.			2

In the case of the boy and girl above referred to, their father, named Hastings, was accused of the murder of a white man; his fourteen year old daughter and sixteen year old son were hanged and their bodies filled with bullets. Then the father was also lynched. This was in November, 1892, at Jonesville, Louisiana.

A lynching equally as cold-blooded took place in Memphis, Tennessee, March 1892. Three young colored men in an altercation at their place of business, fired on white men in self-defense. They were imprisoned for three days, then taken out by the mob and horribly shot to death. Thomas Moss, Will Stewart and Calvin McDowell, were energetic business men who had built up a flourishing grocery business. This business had prospered and that of a rival white grocer named Barrett had declined. Barrett led the attack on their grocery which resulted in the wounding of three white men. For this cause were three innocent men barbarously lynched, and their families left without protectors. Memphis is one of the leading cities of Tennessee, a town of seventy-five thousand inhabitants! No effort whatever was made to punish the murderers of these three men. It counted for nothing that the victims of this outrage were three of the best known young men of a population of thirty thousand colored people of Memphis. They were the officers of the company which conducted the grocery. Moss being the President, Stewart the Secretary of the Company and McDowell the Manager. Moss was in the Civil Service of the United States as letter carrier, and all three were men of splendid reputation for honesty, integrity and sobriety. But their murders, though well known, have never been indicted, were not even troubled with a preliminary examination.

With law held in such contempt, it is not a matter of surprise that the same city—one of the so-called queen cities of the South, should again give itself over to a display of almost indescribable barbarism. This time the mob made no attempt to conceal its identity, but reveled in the contemplation of its feast of crime. Lee Walker, a colored man was the victim. Two white women complained that while driving to town, a colored man jumped from a place of concealment and dragged one of the two women from the wagon, but their screams frightened him away. Alarm was given that a Negro had made an attempted assault upon the women and bands of men set out to run him down. They shot a colored man who refused to stop when called. It was fully ten days before Walker was caught. He admitted that he did attack the women, but that he made no attempt to assault them; that he offered them no indecency whatever, of which as a matter of fact, they never accused him. He said he was hungry and he was determined to have something to eat, but after throwing one of the women out of the wagon, became frightened and ran away. He was duly arrested and taken to the Memphis jail. The fact that he was in prison and could be promptly tried and punished did not prevent the good citizens of Memphis from taking the law in their own hands, and Walker was lynched.

The *Memphis Commercial* of Sunday, July 23, contains a full account of the tragedy from which the following extracts are made.

> At 12 o'clock last night, Lee Walker, who attempted to outrage Miss Millie McCadden last Tuesday morning, was taken from the county jail and hanged to a telegraph pole just north of the prison. All day rumors were afloat that with nightfall an attack would be made upon the jail, and as everyone anticipated that a vigorous resistance would be made, a conflict between the mob and the authorities was feared.
>
> At 10 o'clock Capt. O'Haver, Sergt. Horan and several patrol men were on hand, but they could do nothing with the

crowd. An attack by the mob was made on the door in the south wall and it yielded. Sheriff McLendon and several of his men threw themselves into the breach, but two or three of the storming party shoved by. They were seized by the police but were not subdued, the officers refraining from using their clubs. The entire mob might at first have been dispersed by ten policemen who would use their clubs, but the sheriff insisted that no violence be done.

The mob got an iron rail and used it as a battering ram against the lobby doors. Sheriff McLendon tried to stop them, and some one of the mob knocked him down with a chair. Still he counseled moderation and would not order his deputies and the police to disperse the crowd by force. The pacific policy of the sheriff impressed the mob with the idea that the officers were afraid, or at least would do them no harm, and they redoubled their efforts, urged on by a big switchman. At 12 o'clock the door of the prison was broken in with a rail.

As soon as the rapist was brought out of the door, calls were heard for a rope; then some one shouted "Burn him!" But there was no time to make a fire. When Walker got into the lobby a dozen of the men began beaten and stabbing him. He was half dragged, half carried to the corner of Front street and the alley between Sycamore and Mill, and hung to a telephone pole.

Walker made a desperate resistance. Two men entered his cell first and ordered him to come forth. He refused and they failing to drag him out, others entered. He scratched and bit his assailants, wounding several of them severely with his teeth. The mob retaliated by striking and cutting him with fists and knives. When he reached the steps leading down to the door he made another stand and was stabbed again and again. By the time he reached the lobby his power to resist was gone, and he was shoved along through the mob of yelling, cursing men and boys, who beat, spat upon and slashed the wretch-like demon. One of the leaders of the mob fell, and the crowd walked ruthlessly over him. He was badly hurt—a jawbone fractured and internal injuries inflicted. After the lynching friends took charge of him.

The mob proceeded north on Front street with the victim, stopping at Sycamore street to get a rope from a grocery. "Take him to the iron bridge on Main street," yelled several men. The men who had hold of the Negro were in a hurry to finish the job, however, and when they reached the telephone pole at the corner of Front street and the first alley north of Sycamore they stopped. A hastily improvised noose was slipped over the Negro's head and several young men mounted a pile of lumber near the pole and threw the rope over one of the iron stepping pins. The Negro was lifted up until his feet were three feet above the ground, the rope was made taut, and a corpse dangled in midair. A big fellow who helped lead the mob pulled the Negro's legs until his neck cracked. The wretch's clothes had been torn off, and, as he swung, the man who pulled his legs mutilated the corpse.

One or two knife cuts, more or less, made little difference in the appearance of the dead rapist, however, for before the rope was around his neck his skin was cut almost to ribbons. One pistol shot was fired while the corpse was hanging. A dozen voices protested against the use of firearms, and there was no more shooting. The body was permitted to hang for half an hour, then it was cut down and the rope divided among those who lingered around the scene of the tragedy. Then it was suggested that the corpse be burned, and it was done. The entire performance, from the assault on the jail to the burning of the dead Negro was witnessed by a score or so of policemen and as many deputy sheriffs, but not a hand was lifted to stop the proceedings after the jail door yielded.

As the body hung to the telegraph pole, blood streaming down from the knife wounds in his neck, his hips and lower part of his legs also slashed with knives, the crowd hurled expletives at him, swung the body so that it was dashed against the pole, and, so far from the ghastly sight proving trying to the nerves, the crowd looked on with complaisance, if not with real pleasure. The Negro died hard. The neck was not broken, as the body was drawn up without being given a fall, and death came by strangulation. For fully ten minutes after he was strung up the chest heaved occasionally and there were convulsive movements of the limbs. Finally he was pronounced dead, and a few minutes later Detective Richardson climbed on a pile of staves and cut the rope. The body fell in a ghastly heap, and the crowd laughed at the sound and crowded around the prostrate body, a few kicking the inanimate carcass.

Detective Richardson, who is also a deputy coroner, then proceeded to impanel the following jury of inquest J. S. Moody, A. C. Waldran, B. J. Childs, J. N. House, Nelson Bills, T. L. Smith, and A. Newhouse. After viewing the body the inquest was adjourned without any testimony being taken until 9 o'clock this morning. The jury will meet at the coroner's office, 51 Beale street, upstairs, and decide on a verdict. If no witnesses are forthcoming, the jury will be able to arrive at a verdict just the same, as all members of it saw the lynching. Then some one raised the cry of, "Burn him!" It was quickly taken up and soon resounded from a hundred throats. Detective Richardson for a long time, single handed, stood the crowd off. He talked and begged the men not to bring disgrace on the city by burning the body, arguing that all the vengeance possible had been wrought.

While this was going on a small crowd was busy starting a fire in middle of the street. The material was handy. Some bundles of staves were taken from the adjoining lumber yard for kindling. Heavier wood was obtained from the same source, and coal oil from a neighboring grocery. Then the cries of "Burn him!" Burn him!" were redoubled.

Half a dozen men seized the naked body. The crowd cheered. They marched to the fire, and giving the body a swing, it was landed in the middle of the fire. There was a cry for more wood, as the fire had begun to die owing to the long delay. Willing hands procured the wood, and it was piled up on the Negro, almost, for a time, obscuring him from view. The head was in plain view, as also were the limbs, and one arm which stood out high above the body, the elbow crooked, held in that position by a stick of wood. In a few moments the hands began to swell, then came great blisters over all the exposed parts of the body; then in places the flesh was burned away and the bones began to show through. It was a horrible sight, one which perhaps none there had ever witnessed before. It proved too much for a large part of the crowd and the majority of the mob left very shortly after the burning began.

But a large number stayed, and were not a bit set back by the sight of a human body being burned to ashes. Two or three white women, accompanied by their escorts, pushed to the front to obtain an unobstructed view, and looked on with astonishing coolness and nonchalance. One man and woman brought a little girl, not over 12 years old, apparently their daughter, to view a scene which was calculated to drive sleep from the child's eyes for many nights, if not to produce a permanent injury to her nervous system. The comments of the crowd were varied. Some remarked on the efficacy of this style of cure for rapists, others rejoiced that men's wives and daughters were now safe from the wretch. Some laughed as the flesh cracked and blistered, and while a large number pronounced the burning of a dead body as an useless episode, not in all that throng was a word of sympathy heard for the wretch himself.

The rope that was used to hang the Negro, and also that which was used to lead him from the jail, were eagerly sought by relic hunters. They almost fought for a chance to cut off a piece of rope, and in an incredibly short time both ropes had disappeared and were scattered in the pockets of the crowd in sections of from an inch to six inches long. Others of the relic hunters remained until the ashes cooled to obtain such ghastly relics as the teeth, nails and bits of charred skin of the immolated victim of his own lust. After burning the body the mob tied a rope around the charred trunk and dragged it down Main street to the court house, where it was hanged to a center pole. The rope broke and the corpse dropped with a thud, but it was again hoisted, the charred legs barely touching the ground. The teeth were knocked out and the finger nails cut off as souvenirs. The crowd made so much noise that the police interfered. Undertaker Walsh was telephoned for, who took charge of the body and carried it to his establishment, where it will be prepared for burial in the potter's field today.

A prelude to this exhibition of 19th century barbarism was the following telegram received by the Chicago *Inter-Ocean*, at 2 o'clock, Saturday afternoon—ten hours before the lynching:

"MEMPHIS, TENN, July 22, To *Inter-Ocean*, Chicago.

"Lee Walker, colored man, accused of raping white women, in jail here, will be taken out and burned by whites to-night. Can you send Miss Ida Wells to write it up? Answer. R. M. Martin, with Public Ledger"

The *Public Ledger* is one of the oldest evening daily papers in Memphis, and this telegram shows that the intentions of the mob were well known long before they were executed. The personnel of the mob is given by the Memphis *Appeal-Avalanche*. It says, "At first it seemed as if a crowd of roughs were the principals, but as it increased in size, men in all walks of life figured as leaders, although the majority were young men."

This was the punishment meted out to a Negro, charged, not with rape, but attempted assault, and without any proof as to his guilt, for the women were not given a chance to identify him. It was only a little less horrible than the burning alive of Henry Smith, at Paris, Texas, February 1st, 1893, or that of Edward Coy, in Texarkana, Texas, February 20, 1892. Both were charged with assault on white women, and both were tied to the stake and burned while yet alive, in the presence of ten thousand persons. In the case of Coy, the white woman in the case, applied the match, even while the victim protested his innocence.

The cut which is here given is the exact reproduction of the photograph taken at the scene of the lynching at Clanton, Alabama, August 1891. The cause for which the man was hanged is given in the words of the mob which were written on the back of the photograph, and they are also given. This photograph was sent to Judge A. W. Tourgee, of Mayville, N.Y.

In some of these cases the mob affects to believe in the Negro's guilt. The world is told that the white woman in the case identifies him, or the prisoner "confesses." But in the lynching which took place in Barnwell County, South Carolina, April 24, 1893, the mob's victim, John Peterson escaped and placed himself under Governor Tillman's protection; not only did he declare his innocence, but offered to prove an alibi, by white witnesses. Before his witnesses could be brought, the mob arrived at the Governor's mansion and demanded the prisoner. He was given up, and although the white woman in the case said he was *not* the man, he was hanged 24 hours after, and over a thousand bullets fired into his body, on the declaration that "a crime had been committed and some one had to hang for it."

The lynching of C. J. Miller, at Bardwell, Kentucky, July 7, 1893, was on the same principle. Two white girls were found murdered near their home on the morning of July 5th; their bodies were horribly mutilated. Although their father had been instrumental in the prosecution and conviction of one of his white neighbors for murder, that was not considered as a motive. A hue and cry was raised that some Negro had committed rape and murder, and a search was immediately begun for a Negro. A bloodhound was put on the trail which he followed to the river and into the boat of a fisherman named Gordon. This fisherman said he had rowed a white man, or a very fair mulatto across the river at six o'clock the evening before. The bloodhound was carried across the river, took up the trail on the Missouri side, and ran about two hundred yards to the cottage of a white farmer, and there lay down refusing to go further.

Meanwhile a strange Negro had been arrested in Sikes-town, Missouri, and the authorities telegraphed that fact to Bardwell, Kentucky. The sheriff, without requisition, escorted the prisoner to the Kentucky side and turned him over to the authorities who accompanied the mob. The prisoner was a man with dark brown skin; he said his name was Miller and that he had never been in Kentucky. The fisherman who had said the man he rowed over was white, when told by the sheriff that he would be held responsible as knowing the guilty man, if he failed to identify the prisoner, said Miller was the man. The mob wished to burn him then, about ten o'clock in the morning, but Mr. Ray, the father of the girls, with great difficulty urged them to wait till three o'clock that afternoon. Confident of his innocence, Miller remained cool, while hundreds of drunken, heavily armed men raged about him. He said: "My name is C. J. Miller, I am from Springfield, Ill., my wife lives at 716 North Second Street. I am here among you to-day looked upon as one of the most brutal men before the people. I stand here surrounded by men who are excited; men who are not willing to let the law take its course, and as far as the law is concerned, I have committed no crime, and certainly no crime gross enough to deprive me of my life or liberty to walk upon the green

Scene of lynching at Clanton, Alabama, Aug. 1891.

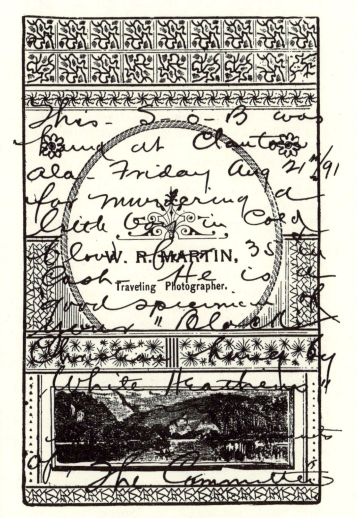

Facsimile of back of photograph.

earth. I had some rings which I bought in Bismarck of a Jew peddler. I paid him $4.50 for them. I left Springfield on the first day of July and came to Alton. From Alton I went to East St. Louis, from there to Jefferson Barracks, thence to Desoto, thence to Bismarck; and to Piedmont, thence to Poplar Bluff, thence to Hoxie, to Jonesboro, and then on a local freight to Malden, from there to Sikeston. On the 5th day of July, the day I was supposed to have committed the offense, I was at Bismarck."

Failing in any way to connect Miller with the crime, the mob decided to give him the benefit of the doubt and *hang, instead of burn him,* as was first intended. At 3 o'clock, the hour set for the execution, the mob rushed into the jail, tore off Miller's clothing and tied his shirt around his loins. Some one said the rope was "a white man's death," and a log-chain nearly a hundred feet in length, weighing nearly a hundred pounds was placed about his neck. He was led through the street in that condition and hanged to a telegraph pole. After a photograph of him was taken as he hung, his fingers and toes cut off, and his body otherwise horribly mutilated, it was burned to ashes. This was done within twelve hours after Miller was taken prisoner. Since his death, his assertions regarding his movements have been proven true. But the mob refused the necessary time for investigation.

No more appropriate close for this chapter can be given than an editorial quotation from that most consistent and outspoken journal the *Inter-Ocean.* Commenting on the many barbarous lynchings of these two months (June and July) in its issue of August 5th, 1893, it says:

"So long as it is known that there is one charge against a man which calls for no investigation before taking his life there will be mean men seeking revenge ready to make that charge. Such a condition would soon destroy all law. It would

Hanging of C. J. Miller, at Bardwell, Kentucky,
July 7th, 1893.

not be tolerated for a day by white men. But the Negroes have been so patient under all their trials that men who no longer feel that they can safely shoot a Negro for attempting to exercise his right as a citizen at the polls are ready to trump up any other charge that will give them the excuse for their crime. It is a singular coincidence that as public sentiment has been hurled against political murders there has been a corresponding increase in lynchings on the charge of attacking white women. The lynchings are conducted in much the same way that they were by the Ku Klux Klans when Negroes were mobbed for attempting to vote. The one great difference is in the cause which the mob assigns for its action.

"The real need is for a public sentiment in favor of enforcing the law and giving every man, white and black, a fair hearing before the lawful tribunals. If the plan suggested by the Charleston *News and Courier* will do this let it be done at once. No one wants to shield a fiend guilty of these brutal attacks upon unprotected women. But the Negro has as good a right to a fair trial as the white man, and the South will not be free from these horrible crimes of mob law so long as the better class of citizens try to find excuse for recognizing Judge Lynch."

CHAPTER V
THE PROGRESS OF THE AFRO-AMERICAN SINCE EMANCIPATION
J. Garland Penn

That the Afro-American has made some progress in education, in the professions, in the accumulation of wealth and literature, and how much, this chapter will show. To determine the progress of the race in education it is necessary to know the relative progress in the increase of population since Emancipation, the number who could read and write, and the number who were in school. According to the census report there were in this country in

1850,	3,638,808	Afro-Americans.
1860,	4,441,830	"
1870,	4,880,009	"
1880,	6,580,793	"
1890,	7,470,040	"

The census of 1860 shows an increase of 703,022 in ten years, that of 1870 shows an increase of 438,179 in ten years, that of 1880 shows an increase of 1,700,784 in ten years; that of 1890 shows an increase of 889,247 in ten years. From 1850 to 1890 the race increased 3,831,232 persons.

It was hardly considered probable that any considerable number of the freedmen would at once seize the opportunity for immediate education as they did when the first ray of hope and light beamed upon them from the philanthropic north. Yet the Afro-American, as upon a moment's thought availed himself of the opportunities which were offered under the Freedmens' Bureau, the first organized effort to educate the freedmen. With this effort came in close succession efforts of the church and those of a general character, so that we now have the following schools for the training of Afro-American youth: The American Baptist Home Mission Society; the American Missionary Association; the Presbyterian Board of Missions for Freedmen; the Freedmen's Aid and Southern Education Society; the Colored Evangelistic Fund (Southern Presbyterian Church); Negro Education and Evangelization Society (Christian Church); the Educational Society in the United Presbyterian Church; the Protestant Episcopal

Commission; the African Methodist Episcopal Church; the African Methodist Episcopal Zion Church; the Colored Methodist Episcopal Church in America; the Colored Baptist Church. In the non-denominational schools of the United States the number of schools for the Higher, Secondary Normal, Graded and Common Schools' training is 379. Number of teachers 1775, of which 646 are Afro-Americans, number of students in 1892, 52,443.

The number of teachers in the Public School system of the United States reported by the United States Census in 1890 were 23,866, and the number of pupils seeking education under the free school system were 1,460,447. These figures reported in 1890 can safely be relied upon as an approximation for 1892, since year by year the Afro-American is becoming more awakened to a sense of duty in respect to the training of his offspring. Taking the census figures of '90 as a basis of '92, and adding the 646 Afro-American teachers in de-nominational and non-denominational schools, we have a sum total approximation of 24,510 Afro-American teachers in the United States with 1,512,890 pupils. The showing as to teachers is a bright ray of hope for the Afro-American's future when the fact is considered in all of its bearings that these 24,510, or in round numbers 25,000 (if the reader will allow 490 teachers graduated and obtaining employment dur-ing '90 and '92), have been prepared and put into the field during a quarter of a century, very little more than the school life allotted an individual.

As to pupils the showing is more remarkable. Five years after the surrender, in 1870, only a tenth of the Afro-American children eligible to school opportunities were ac-tually reported therein. In 1890 we find that within a fraction, ONE-HALF of the eligibles are reported in school. Figures can be given to authenticate this statement upon application, as they are only omitted for sake of space which is precious.

In 1870 there were according to census figures 2,789,679 persons of color above the age of ten years who could not read nor write. If we should make an approximation of a million for persons of color under ten years (which we think every fair minded reader will accept as just) we should have 3,789,679 who could not read or write twenty years ago. With a population of 4,880,009 we should have one and a tenth million of people of African descent who could read and write in '70. It is unfair to say that the increase from '70 to '93 should be less than four times that of '70 under great and constantly increasing educational facilities in all the departments of state and church education.

If the reader accepts the statement that the great educational endeavors of twenty years in all departments and all lines justify an increase four times as large as that of '70 we shall have four and four-tenth millions of Afro-Americans who can now read and write. The writer maintains that of this balance of illiteracy, a majority are ex-slaves; elderly persons who may not read the letter but who are yet intelligent by contact and association. At least two hundred thousand boys and girls of the race to-day are private students. In a certain city there are ten private night schools in which an aggregate of 300 boys are training in the light of knowledge and education by night, wealth and habits of industry by day.

Bishop Atticus G. Haygood says, "The most unique and altogether wonderful chapter in the history of education is that which tells the story of the education of the Negroes of the south since 1865."

Rev. C. C. Smith, D. D., Cor. Secretary of the "Negro Education and Evangelization Society" of the Christian Church, carefully studies the problem and awakes to find himself making this admission that "The Negroes desire for education considering his past environments is 'The Eighth Wonder.' "

THE PROFESSIONS

The black man's desire for professional training has been a subject for adverse criticism. It has been alleged that he is acquiring too much professional training for the support which conditions among the race offer him. The professions in which he is most largely represented, are the ministry and teaching. These claim our largest numbers for many reasons, prominent among them is the patent fact that a people who would rise must have religious and secular training. An admission that these professions for the first few years after the Civil War were besieged because of the ease by which employment could be obtained in them is perhaps just, but for the past ten years these charges are met with the declarations of Conferences, Conventions, Associations, Presbyteries, Synods, Superintendents, School Boards, etc., that none need apply except the well equipped. Of the 23,866 common school teachers in the Union, two-thirds are Normal and High School Graduates. The Theological institutions have graduated over 500 preachers and five times as many left school in their second and third years, who are now in the ministry doing yeoman service.

These professions have been again most largely followed for the reason that the facilities were greater, help larger and such training more easily obtained. Since and prior to the organization of schools for training of Afro-American physicians 417 graduates in the practice of Medicine have come forth occupying to-day honorable station in the medical jurisprudence of our common country. There are not twenty-five Afro-American physicians who are failures either as to their knowledge of medicine or financial condition. Their practice takes the wide range of from $1,000 to $5,000 per annum. Their residences are generally the finest and most representative in the towns in which they are located, and they rapidly accumulate wealth because they are skillful and successful in their profession. The Medical Afro-Americans are yearly organizing state associations and bringing their interests closer together. A graduate of Meharry Medical School, now practicing physician at Jackson, Tennessee, publishes a Medical Magazine, known as the Medical and Surgical Observer. While a staff of colored physicians and trained nurses manages one of the best hospitals in Chicago—the Provident Hospital. In dentistry there are 33 practicing physicians in the south, and nearly the same number in the north. In Pharmacy over 75 have been graduated. The profession in which Afro-Americans have met the sharpest opposition and the strongest competition has been the law. There have been graduated from the Law Schools together with those who have taken private courses, about 300, among whom we find men of eminent legal ability, one a Circuit Court Commissioner, several Judges, numbers of Clerks of Courts, several District Commonwealth and City Attorneys. They are also Deans and Professors of Law in their legal schools, the students of which have not been turned down by any Court or Board in examination. Greater credit, perhaps, is due these advocates for a successful stand maintained, than is due those of any other profession. Besides sharp competition with white lawyers, open and free before a white jury in a land pregnant with prejudice, the Afro-American lawyer has had also to contend with his black fellow citizens whose lack of confidence in the black laywer is evident for the reason that prejudice, fear and oppression have been elements sufficient in themselves to arouse and determine a pre-judgment.

An eminent newspaper of the south makes the statement that 250 black lawyers in the Union have practice ranging from $1,000 to $20,000 per annum. The writer knows a black lawyer in his own city who handles $150,000 annually. As in medicine so in law. State Bar Associations are being formed in almost every state of the south for legal advice, union and strength.

IN LITERATURE

Our history shows that prior to 1861, there had been thirty-five works of Afro-American authorship published and sold. In the earlier days of 1792, America's first poet was Phillis Wheatley, a little black girl, who was brought to this country in a slave ship. After careful education by her white friends, she published a book of poems. The purity of style, simplicity of expression, and refinement of feeling shown in these poems, caused many to doubt their authorship. This doubt was set at rest by her master John Wheatley of Boston, and the leading ministers of the city. They wrote a letter in which they declared Phillis to be the author of the poems published by her. Near the same time Benjamin Banneker, a Negro of Virginia, made his own measurements and calculations, and published an almanac. Since 1865 over 100 books have been published by Afro-American writers. They have been mainly histories of the race, autobiographies, poems, and works on science, fiction, religion and general literature. A Greek Grammar for beginners, by W. S. Scarborough, of Wilberforce Ohio, is in use in the schools of Ohio.

IN JOURNALISM

The first journal published in race interest was Freedom's Journal, issued in 1827, in New York City. At the present time there are 206 journals and four magazines published by the colored people of the country. At a recent meeting of the State Press Association of Virginia, the statement was made that the Afro-American newspapers of that state owned property amounting to $25,000. At least two-thirds of these publications are made in their own offices and on their own presses. Several of our journalists hold responsible positions on the leading dailies as editors of departments and reporters. Essays, short stories and poems by race writers have appeared in the North American Review, Arena, Harper's, Forum, Atlantic Monthly, Frank Leslie, Our Day, The Independent, The Sunday School Journal of the Methodist Church, and other magazines of the country.

IN CHURCH

Bishop Haygood, of M. E. Church South, very truthfully writes in one of his books that all of the Negro's interest, particularly his social life, centers in his church. The denominations in which the Afro-American is most largely found are: Methodist Episcopal, African Methodist Episcopal, African Methodist Episcopal Zion, Colored Methodist Episcopal Church in America, the Methodist Protestant, the African Union Methodist Protestant, the Union American Methodist Episcopal Church, the Zion Union American Methodist Episcopal Church, the Zion Union Apostolic Church, the Evangelist Missionary Church in America, Congregational Methodist Church, Christian Church, Protestant Episcopal, Cumberland Presbyterian, Presbyterian Church in America, Presbyterian Church in the United States, United Presbyterian Church, Lutherans, Congregationalist and Regular Baptist Churches.

The numbers in these denominations are some very large and some small. The division and separation, particularly in the Methodist Churches, are upon very slight and inconsequential grounds. Of these denominations there are about 21,801 organizations, 22,153 church edifices with a seating capacity of perhaps 6 millions, (since an estimate cannot be made in some cases on account of the absence of separate statistics on this last item.) The African Methodist Episcopal, African Methodist Episcopal Zion, the Colored Methodist Episcopal Church in America, the African Union Methodist Protestant Church, the Union American Methodist Episcopal Church, The Zion Union Apostolic, the Evangelist Missionary Church in America, the Congregational Methodist Church, the Cumberland Presbyterian Church and regular Colored Baptist Church, own 920 halls with a seating capacity of 78,289. The value of the Afro-Americans, church property may be approximated at $22,570,882; the number of church members, 2,613,154. This estimate exceeds that of Dr. H. K. Carroll, Special Agent for the U.S. Census Bureau on Churches, in the Sept. *Forum* by over two thousand members, for the reason that special care was taken in the separation of Afro-American membership from those of the whites, where no separate returns are given in the U.S. Census bulletins. The churches built by Afro-Americans are very fine. The Afro-American who makes five dollars per week, usually contributes a fifth of that to his church.

There are 26 bishops in the distinctively Afro-American Methodist bodies. The general officers are men of ability. Their colleges, normal schools and academies are manned by Afro-American presidents, principals, professors and instructors. Their members contributed for eight years ending in 1892, over $600,000 for the cause of education, in churches where the Anglo-Saxon and Afro-American are still blending their interests. Four Afro-Americans are at the head of four of the Methodist Episcopal schools, Professors hold responsible chairs, and writers are being recognized in the literary channels of the church. In the Presbyterian church a similiar condition prevails. At the General Assembly, which met during April in Washington, an Afro-American President, Dr. D. J. Saunders, was heard in behalf of his school and its endowment, etc. He was there and then pledged $400,000 for the benefit of Biddle University, Charlotte, N.C. There are 57 Afro-American Presidents of Afro-American colleges, denominational and otherwise. For the scholastic year, 1891–2, of the $834,646.41 contributed or expended in Afro-American education by various societies, denominations, etc., $316,446.92 was contributed by the Afro-American himself, being nearly one-half of the entire expenditure. Many of the largest edifices and finest church buildings are those owned by Afro-American congregations. "In three large cities of the South (said a Southern man in the writer's presence) the finest churches are 'Nigger' churches," One of the seven finest Sunday-schools in the 27,493 of the great Methodist Episcopal Church is an Afro-American School, the plan of which has been adopted by several leading Anglo-Saxon Sunday Schools.

HIS WEALTH AND BUSINESS INTERESTS

The wealth of the Afro-American has been fixed by statisticians at the following figures:

Alabama	$9,200,125	North Carolina	$11,010,652
Oregon	85,000	Nevada	250,000
Connecticut	500,155	Arkansas	8,100,315
Delaware	1,200,179	California	4,006,209
North Dakota	76,459	Colorado	3,100,472
Florida	7,900,040	Dist. Columbia	5,300,633
Utah	75,000	South Dakota	175,225
Iowa	2,500,372	Georgia	10,415,330
Chicago alone	2,500,000	Illinois	8,300,511
Indiana	4,004,113	Indian Territory	600,000

Kentucky	5,900,000	Kansas	3,900,222
Maine	175,211	Louisiana	18,100,528
Missouri	6,600,340	Mississippi	13,400,213
Minnesota	1,100,236	Maryland	9,900,735
Montana	120,000	Michigan	4,800,000
New York	17,400,756	New Jersey	3,300,185
New Mexico	290,000	New Hampshire	300,125
Nebraska	2,500,000	Virginia	4,900,000
Massachusetts	9,004,122	Ohio	7,800,325
Rhode Island	3,400,000	Pennsylvania	15,300,648
South Carolina	12,500,000	Texas	18,010,545
Tennessee	10,400,211	Vermont	1,100,371
West Virginia	5,600,721	Washington	573,000
		Wyoming	231,115

The total amount of property owned by the race is $263,000,000.

This report, which is an under-estimate, has been going the rounds and accepted as a most remarkable showing. It is an underestimate by at least ten millions. For instance in the state of Virginia, according to the report of the Auditor of Public Accounts, the Afro-American property in the state was valued at $9,425,578. This is over four million and a half more than the above table. In Texas the property interests of the Afro-American are estimated at twenty millions, two millions more than the above table gives. The Comptroller of South Carolina informs the writer that the figures above given for South Carolina are very much below the real estimate. With these corrections and one or two exceptions, the figures are in the main correct. With these corrections, we should have an estimated wealth of not less than $275,000,000 for the Afro-American population of the United States. This added to Church property would give $300,000,000.

Until the recent failure of the Penny Savings Bank of Chattanooga, due to money loaned and inability to make collections, the Afro-American had five banking institutions. The remaining four are doing a splendid business. There are not less than thirty-five Building, Loan and Co-operative Associations on a firm footing and doing legitimate business subject to the regular state and municipal investigation. Lack of space prevents the details of the operations, assets and liabilities of each of these efforts.

This has been accumulated in spite of the failure of the Freedman's Savings Bank. This bank was established under the National Government in 1866, with branch offices in the different states. In this bank the colored people deposited in the five years succeeding the war, nearly fifty-seven million dollars. As the result of bad management it failed in 1871, and the savings from the Negro's scanty wages were thus largely swept away. The confidence thus shaken in the outset has never been entirely restored.

AS TRADESMEN AND GENERAL LABORERS

Until recent years the Afro-American has had a monopoly of the general and trade labor of the south. Recent times skilled labor has been the demand, and in many instances he has been driven out of the field, but in every southern city there are Afro-Americans who can do the best work in all trades. The writer knows of an instance not two weeks from date of this writing. A very large church is being remodeled and a handsome pressed brick front is a part of the improvement. There could not be found in a city of 22,000 inhabitants masons who could lay these brick satisfactorily. In response to a telegram four Afro-Americans were secured, and at this writing, August 2nd, 1893, the front is nearing completion. A more beautiful piece of work of its kind has not been done in the city. One of these men is a graduate of one of our best industrial schools.

The dearth in recent years of our mechanics is due to age, infirmities and each of those who were taught the trades in slavery; but the large and intelligent class of mechanics, who are being sent out from our mechanical schools, men whose head, heart and hands are trained, is remedying the deficiency. Nearly 6,000 of our young people were enrolled in the Industrial departments of Afro-American schools last year, and it is a fortunate thing that nearly all of the large schools of the south now have their industrial departments.

Rev. J. C. Hartzell, D. D., Secretary of the Freedman's Aid and Southern Education Society was heard once to say "A man said to me 'I will tell you one thing you cannot make a mechanic out of a Negro.' I took a wheel out of my pocket and showed it to him. I said 'there came into our shop at Central Tennessee College a black young man with no white blood in his veins, who had never seen such a machine before as that required to make this wheel. The manager had a lot of these wheels to make. This wheel must be made very exact; there must not be the least variation in any of its parts. The manager asked the young man if he could make wheels, and he said he would try; he did try and cut twenty-six hundred of these cogs before he made a variation.' I wonder if there is any other wheel of the kind ever made by a Negro. We are proud, first, that we have such places, and second, because such places are filled up with black boys." This was done in the school of Mechanic Arts, at Central Tennessee College, Nashville, Tennessee. From the same school the writer saw a ten inch telescope exhibited at the General Conference of the Methodist Episcopal church at Omaha, Neb., May, 1892. This telescope is now in the observatory at Laurence University, Appleton, Wisconsin, having been built for that purpose. Three of the Professors' homes at Clark University, Atlanta, Ga., were built by the industrial students.

The largest agricultural and industrial features are connected with the following schools: Hampton Normal and Agricultural Institute, Tuskegee Normal and Industrial Institute, Bishop College, Central Tennessee, Claflin University, Clark University, Shaw University, Spellman Female Institute, Straight University, Talladega College, Tougaloo University, State Normal and Industrial School (Alabama) and others. These with others are yearly sending forth skilled labor which demands a consideration and can easily compete in all lines of industry, where prejudice does not debar them. Tuskegee Institute, situated in the heart of the "black belt" in Alabama was founded by Booker T. Washington, an Afro-American. From a small one-room beginning twelve years ago, he has a school property there of 21 buildings and 1,400 acres of land, and this property is valued at $180,000.

Phelps' Hall—used as
a Bible-training department.

Porter Hall—one of the main buildings containing office and recitation rooms, of Tuskegee Institute.

Of this school, Mrs. A. J. Cooper, in "A Voice from the South," the ablest book yet written by a Negro, on the Negro, says: "In the heart of what is known as the "Black Belt," of Alabama and within easy reach of the great cotton plantations of Georgia, Mississippi and Florida, a devoted young colored man ten years ago started a school with about thirty Negro children assembled in a comical looking shanty at Tuskegee. His devotion was contagious and his work grew; an abandoned farm of 100 acres was secured and that gradually grew to 640 acres, largely woodland, on which a busy and prosperous school is located; and besides, a supply farm was added, of heavy rich land, 800 acres, from which grain and sugar cane are the main products. Since 1881 2,947 students have been taught here, of whom 102 have graduated, while 200 more have received training to fit them to do good work as teachers, intelligent farmers and mechanics. The latest enrollment shows girls 247; boys, 264. Of the 102 graduates, 70 per cent are teachers, ministers and farmers. They usually combine teaching and farming. Three are printers (learned the trades at school), one is a tinner, one a blacksmith, one a wheelwright, three are merchants, three are carpenters, others are in the professions or filling miscellaneous positions.

Another institution founded by the race, is the Provident Hospital, of Chicago. Prejudice because of color has denied our doctors opportunity for practical surgical work, and refused our young women who wish to become trained nurses, admittance to the hospital training schools of the country. Out of this necessity grew the Provident Hospital, which is owned and managed by colored men. It has been in operation a little over two years; patients of every color and all creeds are treated by Afro-American nurses and physicians, and the cures there effected have attracted more than local attention in the medical world. One of the most recent cases was by a knife wound in the pericardium which was sewed up after the removal of a section of the ribs. The patient has since recovered. The training school has graduated four nurses, and has many more applicants for training than can be accommodated.

As a general laborer, the Negro needs no introduction. He has built the railroads of the South, watered and nurtured its fields, reclaimed its swamps, beautified its cities, and caused

Provident Hospital and Training School.

the waste places to blossom as a rose. Besides general laborers and skilled artizans, the race has made some record in inventions. The following list is taken from the columns of *The Colored American*, July 8th, 1893, of Washington, D.C. A partial list of patents granted by the United States for inventions by colored persons.

Improved Gridiron—Joseph Hawkins, West Windsor, N. J., March 26, 1845. No. 3,973.

Animal Trap—Henry Lee, Richmond, Va., Feb. 12, 1867. 61,941.

Shoe—W. A. Dietz, Albany, N. Y., April 30, 1867. 64,205.

Corn-stalk Harvester—Wm. Murray, Alexandria, Va., Feb. 1, 1870. 99,463.

Shield for Infantry and Artillerymen—Hardy Spears, Snow Hill, N. C., Dec. 27, 1870. 110,599.

Locomotive Smoke-stack—Landrow Bell, Washington, D. C., May 23, 1871. 115,153.

Fire Extinguisher—T. J. Martin, Dowagiac, Mich., March 26, 1872. 125,063.

Dough Kneader—Landrow Bell, Washington, D. C., Dec. 10, 1872. 133,823.

Cotton Cultivator—E. H. Sutton, Edenton, N. C., April 7, 1874. 149,543.

Joiners' Clamp—David A. Fisher, Jr., Washington, D. C. April 20, 1875. 162,281.

Process for Preparing Cocoanut for Domestic Use—Alex. P. Ashbourne, Oakland, Cal., June 1, 1875. 163,962.

Life-Preserving Stool—Henry H. Nash, Baltimore, Md., Oct. 5, 1875. 168,519.

Biscuit Cutter—Alex. P. Ashbourne, Oakland, Cal., Nov. 30, 1875. 170,460.

Furniture Castor—David A. Fisher, Jr., Washington, D. C., March 14, 1876. 174,794.

Range—T. A. Carrington, Baltimore, Md., July 25, 1876. 180,323.

Treating Cocoanut—Alex. P. Ashbourne, Oakland, Cal., Aug. 21, 1877. 184,287.

Rotary Engines—B. H. Taylor, Rosedale, Miss., April 23, 1878. 202,888.

Fire Escape Ladder—J. R. Winters, Chambersburg, Pa., May 7, 1878. 203,517.

Printing Press—W. A. Lavelette, Washington, D. C., Sept. 17, 1878. 208,184.

Library Table—W. R. Davis, Jr., New York City, Sept. 24, 1873. 208,378.

Fire Escape Ladder—Jos. R. Winters, Chambersburg, Pa., April 8, 1879. 214,224.

Ladder Scaffold Support—Wm. Bailis, Princeton, N. J., Aug. 5, 1879. 218,154.

Refining Cocoanut Oil—A. P. Ashbourne, Boston, Mass., July 17, 1880. 230,518.

File Holder—Traverse B. Pinn, Alexandria, Va., Aug. 17, 1880. 231,355.

Eye Protector—Powell Johnson, Barton, Ala., Nov. 2, 1880. 234,039.

Life Saving Apparatus—J. Wormley, Washington, D. C., May 24, 1881. 242,091.

Corn Planter Check Row—R. W. Alexander, Galesburg, Ill., April 18, 1882. 256,610.

Lasting Machine for Shoes—J. E. Matzeliger, Lynn Mass., (Cuban), March 20, 1883. 274,207.

Ventilator for Railroad Cars—H. H. Reynolds, Detroit, Mich., April 3, 1883. 275,271.

Shutter and Fastening therefor—Jonas Cooper, Washington, D. C., May 1, 1883. 276,563.

Combined Truss and Bandage—Leonard D. Bailey. Washington, D.C., Sept. 25, 1883. 285,545.

Hand Corn-Shelling Device—Lockrum Blue, Washington, D. C., May 20, 1884. 298,937.

Steam Boiler Furnace—Granville T. Woods, Cincinnati, Ohio, June 3, 1884. 399,894.

Telephone Transmitter—Granville T. Woods, Cincinnati, Ohio, Dec. 2, 1884. 308,817.

Apparatus for Transmission of Messages by Electricity—Granville T. Woods, Cincinnati, Ohio, April 7, 1885; assigned to the American Bell Telephone Co., Boston, Mass. 315,368.

Horse Shoe—J. Ricks, Washington, D. C., March 30, 1886. 338,781.

Receptacle for Storing and Preserving Papers—Henry Brown, Washington, D. C., Nov. 2, 1886. 352,036.

Gate Latch—Samuel Pugsley, New Rochelle, N. Y. Feb. 15, 1887. 357,787.

Motor—Joseph Gregory, Bogensville, S. C., April 26, 1887. 361,937.

Game Table—Wm. R. Davis, New York City, N. Y., May 10, 1887. 362,611.

Gong and Signal Chairs for Hotels—Miss Mariam E. Benjamin, Washington, D. C. July 17, 1888. 396,289.

Spring Horse Shoe—Moses Payne, Bellevue, Ky., Dec. 11, 1888. 394,398.

Instantaneous Detachment for Harnesses—J. S. Coolidge, Washington, D. C., Nov. 13, 1888. 392,908.

Folding Chair—Sadgwar & Purdy, Washington, D. C., June 11, 1889. 405,117.

Device for Preventing Back Flow of Water in Cellars—
Hugh M. Browne, Washington, D. C., April 29, 1890.
426,429.

Electric Switch for Railroads—Philip B. Downing, Boston, Mass., July 17, 1890. 430,118.

Blind Stop—Abram Pugsley, Jamestown, R. I., July 29, 1890. 433,306.

Shutter Worker—Abram Pugsley, Jamestown, R. I., Aug. 5, 1890.

Water Evaporators for Hot Air Registers—Andrew F. Hilyer, Washington, D. C., Aug. 26, 1890. 435,095.

Safety Gate for Bridges—H. H. Reynolds, Detroit, Mich., Oct. 7, 1890. 437,937.

Drill for Boring and Reaming—J. R. Watts, Springfield, Ill., May 5, 1891. 451,789.

Lasting Machine—Sept. 22, 1891—Jean Earnest Matzeliger (dec'd), Lynn, Mass., (Cuban). 459,899.

Car Coupling—James Dixon, Cincinnati, Ohio., March 29, 1892.

Bracket for Miners' Lamps—J. R. Watts, Springfield, Ill., March 7, 1893. 493,137.

Railroad Signal—A. B. Blackburn, Springfield, Ohio, Dec. 23, 1884. 309,517.

Railway Signal—A. B. Blackburn, Springfield, Ohio, Jan. 10, 1888. 376,362.

Spring Seat for Chairs—A. B. Blackburn, Springfield, Ohio, April 3, 1888. 380,420.

Cash Carrier—A. B. Blackburn, Springfield, Ohio, Oct. 23, 1888. 391,577.

Also fifteen (15) patents as follows to Elijah McCoy, of Detroit, Mich., for his inventions in Steam Engine and Railway Lubricating Cups: Nos. 129,843; 139,407; 173,032; 179,585; 255,443; 261,166; 270,238; 320,379; 357,491;

283,745; 383,746; 418,130; 465,875; 470,263; and 472,066.

Propeller for Vessels—Geo. Toliver, Philadelphia, Pa., April 28, 1891. 451,086.

L. W. Benjamin, Boston, Mass. 497,747.

IN THE REALM OF ART

With most meagre incentive, our race has many amateur artists who possess great native talent, and several who have won recognition for their ability as professionals. E. N. Bannister, of Providence, Rhode Island, had a picture in the Centennial Exposition, of Philadelphia, in 1876, which was awarded one of the medals of the first class. This picture "Under the Oaks" was purchased for fifteen hundred dollars by a wealthy Boston gentleman. C. E. Porter of Hartford, Connecticut exhibits in the National Academy of Design of New York, in which city he has a studio. H. O. Tanner of Philadelphia, studied in his native city at the Academy of Fine Arts and has exhibited in the art galleries of New York, Chicago, Louisville, Cincinnati, Washington and Paris. He has spent the past two years abroad prosecuting his studies under Benjamin Constant and Jean Paul Laurens, in the Institute of France. On his return to this country they gave him a letter of recommendation. He belongs to the American Art Association in Paris and won the prize for a sketch of "The Deluge," from the Julian School of Art in 1892, and another for a sketch of "Peasant Life in Brittany." Mr. Tanner thinks the picturesque in our own race life can best be interpreted by one of ourselves and will exhibit this winter a picture representing one phase of Negro life. He has called it "The First Lesson." As a study it is regarded by art critics as the best thing he has done. Mr. Tanner is not yet thirty-five years of age.

We have a number of excellent crayon portrait painters

who have made little effort to acquaint the world with their gifts. We also have a representative in

THE ART OF SCULPTURE

Miss Edmonia Lewis, a young, ignorant girl, saw the statue of Benjamin Franklin on a first visit to Boston and exclaimed, "I can make a stone man!" Wm. Lloyd Garrison introduced her to a leading Boston sculptor, who gave her some clay and the model of a human foot, which she copied. From this beginning, Miss Lewis has now a studio of her own in Rome. Here she has executed work which has brought her the patronage of noted men and women. Her best works are busts of Charles Sumner, and Abraham Lincoln, "Hiawatha's Wooing," "Forever Free," Hagar in the Wilderness and the Madonna.

IN MUSIC

"Blind Tom" our musical prodigy imitates on the piano all sounds, and plays the most difficult classical music after hearing it once rendered. He has composed the "Battle of Manasses," in which the firing of cannon, marching of troops and playing of the bands are perfectly reproduced. Madame Selika, "The Black Patti," (Madame Jones) and Mrs. Nellie Brown Mitchell are the best of numbers of splendid vocalists who are training every year in the art the race loves best. Gussie L. Davis is one of the most popular song writers of the day. The Fisk Jubilee Singers have made the music of the American Negro known throughout the world. So eminent an authority as Dr. Antonin Dvorak, the great Bohemian composer, voluntarily says: "I am now satisfied that the future music of this country must be founded upon what are called the Negro melodies. This must be the real foundation of any serious and original school of composers to be developed in the United States. When I first came here last year I was impressed with this idea and it has developed into a settled conviction. These beautiful and varied themes are the product of the soil. They are American. I would like to trace out the individual authorship of the Negro melodies, for it would throw a great deal of light upon the question I am deeply interested in at present.

"These are the folk songs of America and your composers must turn to them. All of the great musicians have borrowed from the songs of the common people. Beethoven's most charming scherzo is based upon what might now be considered a skillfully handled Negro melody. I have myself gone to the simple, half forgotten tunes of the Bohemian peasants for hints in my most serious work. Only in this way can a musician express the true sentiment of his people. He gets into touch with the common humanity of his country.

"In the Negro melodies of America I discover all that is needed for a great and noble school of music. They are pathetic, tender, passionate, melancholy, solemn, religious, bold, merry, gay or what you will. It is music that sets itself to any mood or any purpose. There is nothing in the whole range of composition that cannot be supplied with themes from this source. The American musician understands these tunes, and they move sentiment in him. They appeal to his imagination because of their associations.

"When I was in England one of the ablest musical critics in London complained to me that there was no distinctively English school of music, nothing that appealed particularly to the British mind and heart. I replied to him that the composers of England had turned their backs upon the fine melodies of Ireland and Scotland instead of making them the essence of an English school. It is a great pity that English musicians have not profited out of this rich store. Somehow the old Irish and Scotch ballads have not seized upon or appealed to them. I hope it will not be so in this country, and I intend to do all in my power to call attention to these treasures of melody which you have.

"Among my pupils in the National Conservatory of Music I have discovered strong talents. There is one young man upon whom I am building strong expectations. His compositions are based upon Negro melodies, and I have encouraged him in this direction. The other members in the composition class seem to think that it is not in good taste to get ideas from the old plantation songs, but they are wrong, and I have tried to impress upon their minds the fact that the greatest composers have not considered it beneath their dignity to go to the humble folk songs for motifs.

"I did not come to America to interpret Beethoven or Wagner for the public. That is not my work and I would not waste any time on it. I came to discover what young Americans had in them and help them to express it. When the Negro minstrels are here again I intend to take my young composers with me and have them comment on the melodies."

CHAPTER VI
THE REASON WHY
F. L. Barnett

The celebration of the four hundredth anniversary of the discovery of America is acknowledged to be our greatest National enterprise of the century. From the inception of the plan down to the magnificent demonstration of the opening day, every feature has had for its ultimate attainment the highest possible degree of success. The best minds were called upon to plan a work which should not only exceed all others in the magnitude of its scope, but which should at the same time surpass all former efforts in the excellence and completion of every detail.

No such enthusiasm ever inspired the American people to any work. From the humblest citizen to the Chief Magistrate of the Nation, the one all absorbing question seemed to be, "How shall America best present its greatness to the civilized world?" Selfishness abated its conflicting interests, rivalry merged itself into emulation and envy lost its tongue. An "era of good feeling" again dawned upon the land and with "Malice towards none and charity to all" the Nation moved to the work of preparing for the greatest Exposition the world has ever known.

The enthusiasm for the work which permeated every phase of our National life, especially inspired the colored people who saw in this great event their first opportunity to show what freedom and citizenship can do for a slave. Less than thirty years have elapsed since "Grim visaged war smoothed its wrinkled front," and left as a heritage of its short but eventful existence four millions of freedmen, now the Nation's wards. In its accounting to the world, none felt more keenly than the colored man, that America could not omit from the record the status of the former slave. He hoped that the American people with their never failing protestation of justice and fair play, would gladly respond to this call, and side by side with the magnificence of its industry, intelligence and wealth give evidence of its broad charity and splendid humane impulses. He recognized that during the twenty-five years past the United States in the field of politics and economics has had a work peculiar to itself. He knew that achievements of his country would interest the world, since no event of the century occurred in the life of any nation, of greater importance than the freedom and enfranchisement of the American slaves. He was anxious to respond to this interest by showing to the world, not only what America has done for the Negro, but what the Negro has done for himself.

It had been asserted that slavery was a divine institution, that the Negro, in the economy of nature, was predestinated to be a slave, and that he was so indolent and ignorant that his highest good could be attained only under the influence of a white master. The Negro wanted to show by his years of freedom, that his industry did not need the incentive of a master's whip, and that his intelligence was capable of successful self direction. It had been said that he was improvident and devoid of ambition, and that he would gradually lapse into barbarism. He wanted to show that in a quarter of a century, he had accumulated property to the value of two hundred million dollars, that his ambition had led him into every field of industry, and that capable men of his race had served his Nation well in the legislatures of a dozen states in both Houses of the Nation's Congress and as National Representatives abroad.

It had been said that the Negro was fit only for a "hewer of wood and a drawer of water" and that he could not be educated. In answer to this, the Negro wanted to show, that in a quarter of a century after emancipation, nearly one half of the race had learned to read and that in schools of higher education colored scholars had repeatedly won highest honors in contest with scholars of the dominant race. In a word, the Negro wanted to avail himself of the opportunity to prove to his friends that their years of unselfish work for him, as a slave, had been appreciated by him in his freedom, and that he was making every possible effort to gratify the sanguine expectations of his friends and incidentally to confound the wisdom of those who justified his oppression on the ground that God cursed Ham.

But herein he was doomed to be disappointed. In the very first steps of the Exposition work, the colored people were given to understand that they were *persona non grata*, so far as any participation in the directive energy of the Exposition was concerned. In order to Nationalize the Exposition the United States Congress by legislation in its behalf, provided for the appointment of a National Board of Commissioners, which Board should be constituted by the appointment of two Commissioners from each state, one from each territory and ten Commissioners at large. It was further provided that one alternate should be named for every commissioner. These appointments were made by the President of the United States (Benjamin Harrison) who thus had the appointment of a Board of National Commissioners numbering two hundred and eight members to represent the sixty millions of our population.

The colored people of our country number over seven and one half millions. In two of the states of the south the colored population exceeds the white population, and so far as the productive energy of the southern states is concerned, almost the entire output of agricultural products is the work of Negro labor. The colored people therefore thought that their numbers, more than one eighth of the entire population of the country, would entitle them to one Commissioner at Large, and that their importance as a labor factor in the South would secure for them fair representation among the Commissioners appointed from the states. But it was not so. President Harrison appointed his entire list of Commissioners, and their alternates, and refused to name one colored man. The President willfully ignored the millions of colored people in the country and thus established a precedent which remained inviolate through the entire term of Exposition work.

Finding themselves with no representation on the National Board, a number of applications were made to the direct management of the Exposition through the Director General, Hon. George R. Davis, for the appointment of some capable colored person, in some representative capacity to the end that the intelligent and enthusiastic co-operation of the colored people might be secured. The Director General declined to make any such appointment.

Prominent colored men suggested the establishment of a Department of Colored Exhibits in the Exposition. It was urged by them that nothing would so well evidence the progress of the colored people as an exhibit made entirely of the products of skill and industry of the race since emancipation. This suggestion was considered by the National Directors and it was decided that no separate exhibit for the colored people be permitted.

Recognizing that there was not much hope for successful work under authority of the Board of Directors, there was still a hope that in the work undertaken by the women there would be sympathy and a helpful influence for colored women. Unprecedented importance had been given to woman's work by the Congress of the United States, which in its World's Fair legislation provided for a Board of Lady Managers and set aside for their exclusive use sufficient money to make a most creditable exhibit of women's work. It was hoped that this Board would take especial interest in helping all aspiring womankind to show their best possible evidence of thrift and intelligent labor. It was therefore decided by colored women in various parts of the country to secure, if possible, means for making an exhibit that would partly compensate for the failure made in the attempt with the National Board of Directors. An idea of the plan of work suggested by these colored organizations can be had from one petition, addressed to the Lady Managers, from Chicago. It is as follows:

To the Board of Lady Managers,
World's Columbian Exposition,
Chicago, Illinois.

The Women's Columbian Auxiliary Association desires to bring its work properly before your honorable body, with a few suggestions which we hope may be of assistance in promoting the cause of woman's work among our colored citizens.

The above organization is working under a charter granted by the State of Illinois, and has perfected plans upon which it is working with the most gratifying success. Our membership in Chicago numbers nearly one hundred active, earnest workers, who have at heart the success of the women's department, and a creditable display of the skill and energy of the colored people.

Besides our city organization, the work has had the endorsement of two National Orders of a benevolent nature, and its work is being especially urged in that direction.

Much more will be done when we find that our plan of work meets the approval and has the endorsement of the Board of Lady Managers. To that end we desire to be accorded an audience with this body, or some representative of this body, who will give our work the consideration we believe its merits.

In the prosecution of our work, we have consulted some of the best minds of our race. We do not in any way suggest a separate department in the coming exposition for colored people, but we do believe there is a field of labor among the colored people, in which members of the race can serve with special effectiveness and success.

Our ideas and plans in this connection are carefully outlined in a published prospectus for use of societies co-operating with us. We enclose a copy for your consideration.

Hoping to render you a service, in which we will gladly
engage, We remain, respectfully,
Women's Columbian Auxiliary Association,
Mrs. R. D. Boone, Pres.

Prior to this movement, another society, by name the
Woman's Columbian Association had filed a similar petition,
through Mrs. Lettie Trent, its president. The two associations
suggested work on nearly the same general plan, and contemplated work through various channels, such as secret societies,
private schools and church organizations, which particularly
reach the colored people. Naturally the two organizations had
different leaders whom they endorsed and supported for the
work, with more or less earnestness, fidelity and sometimes
acerbity of temper, each of course, desiring its plans to succeed
through the success of its representative. But both failed as
the Board of Lady Managers eagerly availed itself of the
opportunity to say that the colored people were divided into
factions and it would be impolitic to recognize either faction.

The promptness which marked their assumption of this
position, is fairly indicative of the hypocrisy and duplicity
which the colored people met in every effort made. In
refusing to give the colored people any representation whatever, upon the ground that they were not united, the Board
made an excuse which was wholly unworthy of itself. The
failure of the few colored people of Chicago to agree, could
not by any kind of logic, justify the Board in ignoring the
seven and one half millions outside of the city. A number of
colored women in other sections of the country were highly
endorsed and commended to the Board as capable, earnest
and efficient representatives of the race. Because the few
people here in Chicago did not agree upon the same person
for their support the Board of Lady Managers ignored the
plea of the entire race.

If in a reflective mood, the Lady Managers had read the minutes of their own organization, punctured as they are with points of order, cries of "shame," "shame," enlivened frequently with hysterics and bathed at times in tears, their sisterly love and sweetness of temper, marking a rose wreathed way through the law courts into Congress itself, possibly they would have been better able to realize that all people are liable to differ, and that colored people are not alone in their failure to agree upon the same person, to do a designated work.

But they never thought of such a possibility at that time. They dismissed the entire matter by referring the petitions of the colored people to the various State Boards.

With but a single exception the State Boards refused to take any action calculated to enlist the interest of the colored people. The State of New York, the exception referred to, appointed a capable and worthy colored woman, Miss Imogene Howard, as a member of the Board of Lady Managers. In the short period of her service she worked earnestly in behalf of her race, but met only with indifferent success.

The relegation of the interests of the colored people to the State Boards plainly proved that the Board of Lady Managers did not desire to have anything to do with the colored people. Still something was needed to be done and thousands of capable and conscientious colored men and women were waiting patiently for some suggestion of the work they might attempt to do. No suggestions came however, and renewed efforts were exerted.

Miss Hallie Q. Brown, a teacher of Wilberforce College, Ohio, concluded to secure, if possible, from the several Lady Managers an expression of their views upon the subject of enlisting the interest and co-operation of the colored people in the formative work of the Fair. In pursuance of her plans,

Miss Brown sent a letter of inquiry to each member of the Board of Lady Managers asking the personal consideration of her plan of appointing some colored person who would make this work a special care. The letter of Miss Brown reads as follows:

Chicago, Illinois, April 8, 1892.

Mrs. _____

Lady Manager of the Columbian Exposition for ———

Dear Madam:

It seems to be a settled conviction among the colored people, that no adequate opportunity is to be offered them for proper representation in the World's Fair. A circular recently issued and widely distributed makes that charge direct. That there is an element of truth in it seems apparent, since neither recognition has been granted, nor opportunity offered.

And further it is shown that the intercourse between the two races, particularly in the southern states, is so limited that the interchange of ideas is hardly seriously considered. If, therefore, the object of the Woman's Department of the Columbian Exposition is to present to the world the industrial and educational progress of the breadwinners—the wage women—how immeasurably incomplete will that work be without the exhibit of the thousands of the colored women of this country.

The question naturally arises, who is awakening an interest among our colored women, especially in the South where the masses are, and how many auxiliaries have been formed through which they may be advised of the movement that is intended to be so comprehensive and all inclusive? Considering the peculiar relation that the Negro sustains in this country, is it less than fair to request for him a special representation?

Presuming that such action would be had, several colored men and women, including the writer, have endorsements of unquestionable strength from all classes of American citizens.

These endorsements are on file in the President's office of the Woman's Commission in this city.

It is urged at headquarters that the Lady Managers would seriously object to the appointment of a special representative to canvass the various states. Permit me to emphasize the fact, that this matter is in earnest discussion, among the representatives of eight millions of the population of the United States.

I address this circular to you, kindly requesting your opinion upon the suggestions made herein, and solicit a reply at your earliest convenience.

> Yours respectfully,
> (Miss) Hallie Q. Brown.
> 4440 Langley Ave.,
> Chicago, Illinois.

The inquiry of Miss Brown received answers from less than one-half of the Lady Managers and in not more than three cases was any endorsement given to her suggestion to appoint some colored person to give especial attention to the work of securing exhibits from the colored people. In most of the answers received, the writers said that the appointment of a colored person could not be made without interfering with the work already assigned to the respective states. Several members excused the action of the Exposition Managers in refusing representation to the colored people among the promoters of the Exposition, by stating that the colored people themselves were divided upon the character of the exhibit which should be made; some declaring in favor of a separate colored exhibit, and others opposing it. Great emphasis was placed upon this statement and the further specious argument that colored people are citizens, and that it was against the policy of the Exposition to draw any distinction between different classes of American citizens. These arguments upon the first thought appear reasonable, but a slight consideration shows that they were made only as a subterfuge to compass the discrimination already planned.

The majority of the Lady Managers ignored the letters of inquiry entirely, while some were frank enough to speak their pronounced opposition to any plan which would bring them in contact with a colored representative and to emphasize the opposition by a declaration that they would resign in case such an appointment was made.

So far as the character of the exhibit was concerned there was an honest difference of opinion among both white and colored people, as to the manner of making the exhibit, some declaring in favor of a separate exhibit to be composed exclusively of products of the skill, ingenuity and industry of the colored people, others quite as earnestly opposed to any color line exhibit and insisted upon placing exhibits furnished by colored people in the classes to which they respectively belonged.

In support of the plan for the separate exhibit it was urged:

First: That the exhibits by the colored people would be so few in number, that when installed in their places as classified they would be almost unnoticed and as there would be no way of ascertaining that they were products of our skill and industry, the race would lose the credit of their production.

Second: That while the exhibits made by colored people would not compare favorably with the general exhibits of the white people, still in number, variety and excellence they would give most gratifying evidence of the capacity, industry and ambition of the race, showing what it had accomplished in the first third of a century of freedom.

The opponents to the separate exhibit, both colored and white, based their opposition upon the broad principle that merit knows no color line, and that colored people should be willing to be measured by the same rule which was applied to other people. The colored people asked that no special grade of merit be established for them; but held that the race was willing to accept whatever place was accorded it by virtue of the measure of merit shown. They asked that colored persons specially interested in the cause be appointed to promote the work among colored people, but that the exhibits when received, should be impartially judged and assigned to their places as classified.

But this was a question of method rather than action. The colored people were untiring in their demands for some responsible work, and were perfectly willing to allow the arrangement of details with the exposition management. But they earnestly maintained that whether the colored exhibits be installed in bulk or placed as properly classified, there was no doubt that the existing condition of public sentiment warranted the active assistance of colored representatives in promoting the work among colored people.

The fact patent to all thinking people that, in the first steps of exposition work they had been purposely ignored together with the equally apparent fact that the various State Boards, with one exception, had emphasized this slight by refusing to give any representation whatever to colored people, gave good ground for the belief that colored people were not wanted in any responsible connection with the Exposition work. But the demands for a separate exhibit and for the appointment of colored persons to assist in promoting the work of the exposition were all fruitless. They were met always with the statement that the exposition authorities had considered it best to act entirely without reference to any color line, that all citizens of all classes stood on the same plane, that no distinctions should be drawn between any classes and special work extended to none. This position which has every indication of justice would still be inequitable even if fairly maintained.

It may have been strictly just but it was certainly not equitable to compel the colored people who have been emancipated but thirty years to stand on the same plane with their masters who for two and one half centuries had enslaved them. Had the colored people of America enjoyed equal opportunities with the people they would have asked in the Exposition no favor of any kind. But when it is remembered that only a few years ago the statutes of many of the states made it a misdemeanor to teach a colored person to read, it must be conceded that in no competition with the white man is it possible for the former slave to stand upon the same plane.

But the position taken was not only inequitable but was a false and shallow pretense. If no distinctions were to be drawn in favor of the colored man, then it was only fair that none should be drawn against him. Yet the whole history of the exposition is a record of discrimination against the colored people. President Harrison began it when with the appointment of more than two hundred and eight national commissioners and their alternates to represent the several states, he refused to appoint a single representative of seven and one half millions of colored people, more than one-eighth of the entire population of the United States.

When it was ascertained that the seals and glaciers of Alaska had been overlooked in the appointment of National Commissioners, it was a comparatively easy task for the President to manipulate matters so that he could give that far away land a representative of the National Board. It was entirely different, however, with the colored people. When the fact was laid before the President that they had been ignored and were entirely unrepresented, he found his hands tied and the best he was ever willing to do thereafter to remedy the matter, was to appoint a colored man, Mr. Hale G. Parker, as alternate commissioner from the State of Missouri.

In the appointments made on the Board of Lady Managers the discrimination was equally apparent, not a single colored woman being named on the Board proper and only one named on the entire list of members of the State Boards of management.

Taking these precedents for aid and comfort, the management of the Exposition found it easy to refuse to employ colored men or women in places of honor or emolument. Hundreds of clerks were necessary to carry on the work of preparation for the Exposition but all applications by colored men or women for clerical positions were politely received and tenderly pigeon-holed. Of the entire clerical force of the Exposition, only one colored man, Mr. J. E. Johnson ever received a clerical appointment. A clerical position was filled for a few months by Mrs. A. M. Curtis and soon after her resignation a similar place was filled by Mrs. Fannie B. Williams who was appointed only two months before the Exposition opened. These three clerical places constitute the best representation accorded the colored people during the entire Exposition period. This, in spite of the fact, that the propriety and justice of their employment was freely recognized and admitted. By vote of the Board of Reference and Control, the Director General was requested to report on the expediency of giving colored people a place in the great work. The minutes of the above Board show, that after a clear and forceful presentation of the claims of the colored people by Mrs. F. B. Williams the following resolution was adopted:

"*Resolved:* That the Director General be requested to lay before the Local Directory the expediency of having the department of Publicity and Promotion employ a colored man and a colored woman to promote the interests of the World's Columbian Exposition throughout the United States."

Whether the Board really meant anything by the resolution or not it is difficult to say, but certain it is that nothing was done. The expediency of the appointments was not questioned, but claim was made that there was not money to pay for the service. In fact, a standing reply to suggestions for the employment of colored persons was the assertion that the Exposition had no fund which it could use for that purpose. It had no funds to meet the expenses contemplated in the suggestion made in the above quoted resolution of the Board of Control, yet it had actually and wantonly wasted nearly ninety thousand dollars in the construction of floats for use on opening day; which floats were discarded before they were finished and never used at all, their entire cost being an absolute and total loss of the entire sum of money used in their construction. The management readily found ninety thousand dollars to waste in this child's play, but could not find a fraction of that sum to meet a demand which was just, urgent and plainly apparent.

A final effort was made to secure the service of a good statistician whose duty it would be to prepare a statistical exhibit of the Negro since emancipation. The work mentioned could be done by colored people and would have contributed helpfully to the effort of proving our ability in all lines of thought and action. The appropriation asked for was only two thousand dollars, but the Board refused to allow that sum, and the plan was abandoned.

This unwritten law of discrimination was felt not only in higher places but its effects were seen in the employment of persons for positions of no more importance than the Columbian Guards. These were selected for duty on the Exposition grounds. The Commander, Col. Rice, requested a blank to be used in making applications, the questions asked being as carefully framed as those found upon the application blanks of an insurance company. It was noted that all colored applicants had some defect which disqualified them for service. This was more marked when so many colored persons were rejected who appeared to be eligible from every point of view, and from the further fact that many of the guards who were chosen clearly failed to meet the printed requirements, and a number of them could scarcely speak English. The rumor soon ripened into conviction, and it was generally understood that so far as the Columbian Guards were concerned, "No Negro need apply."

A sample of the treatment accorded colored applicants will serve to show that discrimination was undoubtedly practiced and was plainly intentional. The applicant in this case was Wm. J. Crawford of Chicago. He filled out his application blank and was soon ordered for examination. He reported and the examiner deliberately falsified the record and returned his report rejecting the applicant upon the ground that his chest measurement was only thirty-four inches, (the requirement being thirty-six inches) a report which he knew to be false. This action of the medical examiner was so clearly unjust that the applicant concluded to appeal to the Commander for a redress of the wrong. He prepared his appeal of which the following is a copy.

Chicago, Ill., March 5, 1893.
Col. Edward Rice,
     Commander Columbian Guards,
          World's Columbian Exposition.
Dear Sir:
    I desire to ask your consideration of a matter, which I think, belongs to your department of the World's Fair. On the first day of the present month, I made an application for appointment on the force of guards for the exposition. My

application was made on a blank furnished by Capt. Farnham, and I was ordered for examination.

The physician who examined me gave my height five feet eleven and one eighth inches; my weight one hundred and sixty-five and one half pounds, which was declared satisfactory. Upon examination for chest measurement, however, the examiner said that I measured thirty-four inches. He then said that this was too small and that I could not be accepted. He wrote on my application—"Rejected," adding "not on account of color, but because chest measurement not thirty-six inches."

I knew at the time that his mark was incorrect and as soon as I left the grounds, went to a reputable physician, who gave me a certificate of measurement of thirty-six and one half inches. As I was rejected because the examiner made my measurement thirty-four inches, I respectfully appeal to you for a reversal of that finding and an appointment upon the force of the Columbian Guards.

Obediently Yours,
W. J. Crawford.

This appeal was sent by registered letter to Commander Rice, and was receipted for by G. N. Farnham, his chief assistant. But the Commander gave no reply whatever to the appeal. Still determined to have a hearing, the applicant, after waiting ten days for an answer made an appeal to the President of the Board of Control. This second appeal was as follows:

Chicago, Ill., March 15, 1893.
To the President of the
    Board of Control of the
        World's Columbian Exposition,
            Chicago, Illinois.
Dear Sir:

I have the honor to appeal to you for a consideration of my rejected application for a position as one of the Columbian Guards of the World's Columbian Exposition.

I have been a resident of Chicago for seven years and on the first day of March, 1893, I made a formal application and was subjected to the required examination by the medical examiner. At the conclusion of my examination, I was told by the examining surgeon that I had met every requirement and was in every way qualified except in the single point of chest measurement; the rule of the department requires a chest measurement of thirty-six inches, but the said medical examiner stated in his certificate of examination that my chest measurement was less than thirty-five inches, and further marked on said certificate the gratuitous information "not rejected on account of color."

I appeal to your honorable board for a reopening of my application for appointment as a Columbian Guard on the following grounds:

I am satisfied that my application was rejected solely on account of my color. I have been especially convinced that it is a case of mean and unjust discrimination against me, because, after leaving the World's Fair Grounds and the regular medical examiner in the employment of the Columbian Guard authority, I went to no less eminent physician than Dr. S. N. Davis of this city, and requested him to give me a careful and impartial examination as to my chest. I would respectfully refer you to Dr. Davis' certificate attached hereto. It will be seen that the finding of Dr. Davis' examination is in direct contradiction to the alleged measurement of the medical examiner at the World's Fair Grounds.

Although the said medical examiner at the World's Fair grounds laboriously stretched his tape measure and compressed my chest in every possible way, so as to force a short measurement, and in other ways aroused my suspicions as to his willingness to give me a fair examination, I did not feel justified in questioning his findings and appealing to you, until I had obtained an impartial examination from a physician, who could have no interest in me and my plans.

A further reason for this appeal to you is to call your attention to the fact that it is the settled policy on the part of the authorities in charge to make it impossible for any American Negro, however well qualified, to become a member of the force of Columbian Guards. It is a significant fact that every colored applicant, thus far, has been rejected for causes more or less trivial, or, as in my case, false.

I would respectfully state that before submitting this appeal to your Honorable Board, I duly applied to Colonel Rice, Commander in Chief of said Columbian Guards. Attached hereto please find a copy of the letter sent to Colonel Rice, but from which I received no reply. I also appealed to the Council of Administration and Control for a consideration of my claim, but I was refused a hearing.

It is believed by many of our people that this fixed policy of discrimination against us, is without the sanction and knowledge of the Board of Control, and as I have no means of redress from the injustice done me, as above set forth, I have determined to lay the matter before you, hoping that my appeal will be justly considered, and that I will be given a chance to win the position for which I have made due application, if I am qualified therefor.

Obediently yours,
W. J. Crawford.
No. 400 27th street.

It was merely an indication of the plan and policy of the Exposition Management that no notice whatever was taken of the respectful but, at the same time, convincing appeal made by Mr. Crawford. It had been determined that no colored man should be employed on the force of the Columbian Guards and that determination was not to be varied. The fact that one colored man had succeeded in discovering the contemptible duplicity and falsehood used to compass that purpose, made no difference in the plan, nor affected in any way its promoters. Theoretically open to all Americans, the Exposition practically is, literally and figuratively, a "White

City," in the building of which the Colored American was allowed no helping hand, and in its glorious success he has no share.

Recognizing that the spirit and purpose of the local management of the Exposition were inimical to the interests of the colored people, leaders of the race made effective appeals to Congress and asked that the general government reserve out of its appropriation to the Exposition a sum of money to be used in making a Statistical Exhibit which should show the moral, educational and financial growth of the American Negro since his emancipation. The colored people recognized that the discrimination which prevented their active participation in the Exposition work could not be remedied, but they hoped that the Nation would take enough interest in its former slaves to spend a few thousand dollars in making an exhibit which would tell to the world what they as freedmen had done.

But here they were disappointed again. Congress refused to act. One appropriation bill passed the Senate and at another time an appropriation was made by the House of Representatives, but at no time did both bodies agree upon the same measure. The help that was expected from Congress failed and having failed in every other quarter to secure some worthy place in this great National undertaking the Colored American recognized the inevitable and accepted with the best grace possible one of the severest disappointments which has fallen to his lot.

In consideration of the color proof character of the Exposition Management it was the refinement of irony to set aside August 25th to be observed as "Colored People's Day." In this wonderful hive of National industry, representing an outlay of thirty million dollars, and numbering its employees by the thousands, only two colored persons could be found whose occupations were of a higher grade than that of janitor, laborer and porter, and these two only clerkships. Only as a menial is the Colored American to be seen—the Nation's deliberate and cowardly tribute to the Southern demand "to keep the Negro in his place." And yet in spite of this fact, the Colored Americans were expected to observe a designated day as their day—to rejoice and be exceeding glad. A few accepted the invitation, the majority did not. Those who were present, by the faultless character of their service showed the splendid talent which prejudice had led the Exposition to ignore; those who remained away evinced a spirit of manly independence which could but command respect. They saw no reason for rejoicing when they knew that America could find no representative place for a colored man, in all its work, and that it remained for the Republic of Hayti to give the only acceptable representation enjoyed by us in the Fair. That republic chose Frederick Douglass to represent it as Commissioner through which courtesy the Colored American received from a foreign power the place denied to him at home.

That we are not alone in the conviction that our country should have accorded an equal measure of recognition to one of its greatest citizens is evidenced by the following editorial in the Chicago *Herald* of Sunday, August 27th, 1893: "That a colored man, Douglass, Langston or Bruce, should have been named a National Commissioner, will be admitted by fair-minded Americans of all political parties. That President Harrison should have omitted to name one of them is apparently inexplicable. That the race has made extraordinary progress will also be conceded."

The World's Columbian Exposition draws to a close and that which has been done is without remedy. The colored people have no vindictiveness actuating them in this presentation of their side of this question, our only desire being to tell the reason why we have no part nor lot in the Exposition. Our failure to be represented is not of our own working and we can only hope that the spirit of freedom and fair play of which some Americans so loudly boast, will so inspire the Nation that in another great National endeavor the Colored American shall not plead for a place in vain.

TO THE PUBLIC

This pamphlet is published by contribution from colored people of the United States. The haste necessary for the press, prevents the incorporation of interesting data showing the progress of the colored people in commercial lines.

Besides the cuts of a school and hospital it was desired to have a cut of the Capital Savings Bank, a flourishing institution conducted by the colored people of Washington, D. C. The cut, however, did not arrive in time for the press.

Twenty thousand copies of THE REASON WHY are now ready for gratuitous distribution. Applications by mail will enclose three cents for postage. All orders addressed to the undersigned will be promptly acknowledged.

IDA B. WELLS,
Room 9, 128 Clark St., Chicago, Ill.
AUGUST 30, 1893.

A RED RECORD

Tabulated Statistics and Alleged Causes of Lynchings in the United States, 1892–1893–1894

Respectfully submitted to the Nineteenth Century civilization in "the Land of the Free and the Home of the Brave."

PREFACE

DEAR MISS WELLS:

Let me give you thanks for your faithful paper on the lynch abomination now generally practiced against colored people in the South. There has been no word equal to it in convincing power. I have spoken, but my word is feeble in comparison. You give us what you know and testify from actual knowledge. You have dealt with the facts with cool, painstaking fidelity, and left those naked and uncontradicted facts to speak for themselves.

Brave woman! you have done your people and mine a service which can neither be weighed nor measured. If the American conscience were only half alive, if the American church and clergy were only half Christianized, if American moral sensibility were not hardened by persistent infliction of outrage and crime against colored people, a scream of horror, shame, and indignation would rise to heaven wherever your pamphlet shall be read.

But alas! even crime has power to reproduce itself and create conditions favorable to its own existence. It sometimes seems we are deserted by earth and Heaven—yet we must still think, speak and work, and trust in the power of a merciful God for final deliverance

Very truly and gratefully yours,
FREDERICK DOUGLASS.
Cedar Hill, Anacostia, D. C.

Originally published in 1895 by Donohue & Henneberry, Chicago.

CHAPTER I

THE CASE STATED

The student of American sociology will find the year 1894 marked by a pronounced awakening of the public conscience to a system of anarchy and outlawry which had grown during a series of ten years to be so common, that scenes of unusual brutality failed to have any visible effect upon the humane sentiments of the people of our land.

Beginning with the emancipation of the Negro, the inevitable result of unbridled power exercised for two and a half centuries, by the white man over the Negro, began to show itself in acts of conscienceless outlawry. During the slave regime, the Southern white man owned the Negro body and soul. It was to his interest to dwarf the soul and preserve the body. Vested with unlimited power over his slave, to subject him to any and all kinds of physical punishment, the white man was still restrained from such punishment as tended to injure the slave by abating his physical powers and thereby reducing his financial worth. While slaves were scourged mercilessly, and in countless cases inhumanly treated in other respects, still the white owner rarely permitted his anger to go so far as to take a life, which would entail upon him a loss of several hundred dollars. The slave was rarely killed, he was too valuable; it was easier and quite as effective, for discipline or revenge, to sell him "Down South."

But Emancipation came and the vested interests of the white man in the Negro's body were lost. The white man had no right to scourge the emancipated Negro, still less has he a right to kill him. But the Southern white people had been educated so long in that school of practice, in which might makes right, that they disdained to draw strict lines of action in dealing with the Negro. In slave times the Negro was kept subservient and submissive by the frequency and severity of the scourging, but, with freedom, a new system of intimidation came into vogue; the Negro was not only whipped and scourged; he was killed.

Not all nor nearly all of the murders done by white men, during the past thirty years in the South, have come to light, but the statistics as gathered and preserved by white men, and which have not been questioned, show that during these years more than ten thousand Negroes have been killed in cold blood, without the formality of judicial trial and legal execution. And yet, as evidence of the absolute impunity with which the white man dares to kill a Negro, the same record shows that during all these years, and for all these murders only three white men have been tried, convicted, and executed. As no white man has been lynched for the murder of colored people, these three executions are the only instances of the death penalty being visited upon white men for murdering Negroes.

Naturally enough the commission of these crimes began to tell upon the public conscience, and the Southern white man, as a tribute to the nineteenth century civilization, was in a manner compelled to give excuses for his barbarism. His excuses have adapted themselves to the emergency, and are aptly outlined by that greatest of all Negroes, Frederick Douglass, in an article of recent date, in which he shows that there have been three distinct eras of Southern barbarism, to account for which three distinct excuses have been made.

The first excuse given to the civilized world for the murder of unoffending Negroes was the necessity of the white man to repress and stamp out alleged "race riots." For years immediately succeeding the war there was an appalling slaughter of colored people, and the wires usually conveyed to northern people and the world the intelligence, first, that an insurrection was being planned by Negroes, which, a few hours later, would prove to have been vigorously resisted by white men, and controlled with a resulting loss of several killed and wounded. It was always a remarkable feature in these insurrections and riots that only Negroes were killed during the rioting, and that all white men escaped unharmed.

From 1865 to 1872, hundreds of colored men and women were mercilessly murdered and the almost invariable reason assigned was that they met their death by being alleged participants in an insurrection or riot. But this story at last wore itself out. No insurrection ever materialized; no Negro rioter was ever apprehended and proven guilty, and no dynamite ever recorded the black man's protest against oppression and wrong. It was too much to ask thoughtful people to believe this transparent story, and the southern white people at last made up their minds that some other excuse must be had.

Then came the second excuse, which had its birth during the turbulent times of reconstruction. By an amendment to the Constitution the Negro was given the right of franchise, and, theoretically at least, his ballot became his invaluable emblem of citizenship. In a government "of the people, for the people, and by the people," the Negro's vote became an important factor in all matters of state and national politics. But this did not last long. The southern white man would not consider that the Negro had any right which a white man was bound to respect, and the idea of a republican form of government in the southern states grew into general contempt. It was maintained that 'This is a white man's government," and regardless of numbers the white man should rule. "No Negro domination" became the new legend on the sanguinary banner of the sunny South, and under it rode the Ku Klux

Klan, the Regulators, and the lawless mobs, which for any cause chose to murder one man or a dozen as suited their purpose best. It was a long, gory campaign; the blood chills and the heart almost loses faith in Christianity when one thinks of Yazoo, Hamburg, Edgefield, Copiah, and the countless massacres of defenseless Negroes, whose only crime was the attempt to exercise their right to vote.

But it was a bootless strife for colored people. The government which had made the Negro a citizen found itself unable to protect him. It gave him the right to vote, but denied him the protection which should have maintained that right. Scourged from his home; hunted through the swamps; hung by midnight raiders, and openly murdered in the light of day, the Negro clung to his right of franchise with a heroism which would have wrung admiration from the hearts of savages. He believed that in that small white ballot there was a subtle something which stood for manhood as well as citizenship, and thousands of brave black men went to their graves, exemplifying the one by dying for the other.

The white man's victory soon became complete by fraud, violence, intimidation and murder. The franchise vouchsafed to the Negro grew to be a "barren ideality," and regardless of numbers, the colored people found themselves voiceless in the councils of those whose duty it was to rule. With no longer the fear of "Negro Domination" before their eyes, the white man's second excuse became valueless. With the Southern governments all subverted and the Negro actually eliminated from all participation in state and national elections, there could be no longer an excuse for killing Negroes to prevent "Negro Domination."

Brutality still continued; Negroes were whipped, scourged, exiled, shot and hung whenever and wherever it pleased the white man so to treat them, and as the civilized world with increasing persistency held the white people of the South to account for its outlawry, the murderers invented the third excuse—that Negroes had to be killed to avenge their assaults upon women. There could be framed no possible excuse more harmful to the Negro and more unanswerable if true in its sufficiency for the white man.

Humanity abhors the assailant of womanhood, and this charge upon the Negro at once placed him beyond the pale of human sympathy. With such unanimity, earnestness and apparent candor was this charge made and reiterated that the world has accepted the story that the Negro is a monster which the Southern white man has painted him. And to-day, the Christian world feels, that while lynching is a crime, and lawlessness and anarchy the certain precursors of a nation's fall, it can not by word or deed, extend sympathy or help to a race of outlaws, who might mistake their plea for justice and deem it an excuse for their continued wrongs.

The Negro has suffered much and is willing to suffer more. He recognizes that the wrongs of two centuries can not be righted in a day, and he tries to bear his burden with patience for to-day and be hopeful for to-morrow. But there comes a time when the veriest worm will turn, and the Negro feels to-day that after all the work he has done, all the sacrifices he has made, and all the suffering he has endured, if he did not, now, defend his name and manhood from this vile accusation, he would be unworthy even of the contempt of mankind. It is to this charge he now feels he must make answer.

If the Southern people in defense of their lawlessness, would tell the truth and admit that colored men and women are lynched for almost any offense, from murder to a mis-demeanor, there would not now be the necessity for this defense. But when they intentionally, maliciously and constantly belie the record and bolster up these falsehoods by the words of legislators, preachers, governors and bishops, then the Negro must give to the world his side of the awful story.

A word as to the charge itself. In considering the third reason assigned by the Southern white people for the butchery of blacks, the question must be asked, what the white man means when he charges the black man with rape. Does he mean the crime which the statutes of the civilized states describe as such? Not by any means. With the Southern white man, any mesalliance existing between a white woman and a colored man is a sufficient foundation for the charge of rape. The Southern white man says that it is impossible for a voluntary alliance to exist between a white woman and a colored man, and therefore, the fact of an alliance is a proof of force. In numerous instances where colored men have been lynched on the charge of rape, it was positively known at the time of lynching, and indisputably proven after the victim's death, that the relationship sustained between the man and woman was voluntary and clandestine, and that in no court of law could even the charge of assault have been successfully maintained.

It was for the assertion of this fact, in the defense of her own race, that the writer hereof became an exile; her property destroyed and her return to her home forbidden under penalty of death, for writing the following editorial which was printed in her paper, the Free Speech, in Memphis, Tenn., May 21, 1892:

"Eight Negroes lynched since last issue of the 'Free Speech' one at Little Rock, Ark., last Saturday morning where the citizens broke (?) into the penitentiary and got their man; three near Anniston, Ala., one near New Orleans; and three at Clarksville, Ga., the last three for killing a white man, and five on the same old racket—the new alarm about raping

white women. The same programme of hanging, then shooting bullets into the lifeless bodies was carried out to the letter.
Nobody in this section of the country believes the old thread-
bare lie that Negro men rape white women. If Southern
white men are not careful, they will over-reach themselves
and public sentiment will have a reaction; a conclusion will
then be reached which will be very damaging to the moral
reputation of their women."

But threats cannot suppress the truth, and while the Negro
suffers the soul deformity, resultant from two and a half
centuries of slavery, he is no more guilty of this vilest of all
vile charges than the white man who would blacken his name.

During all the years of slavery, no such charge was ever
made, not even during the dark days of the rebellion, when
the white man, following the fortunes of war went to do
battle for the maintenance of slavery. While the master was
away fighting to forge the fetters upon the slave, he left his
wife and children with no protectors save the Negroes themselves. And yet during those years of trust and peril, no
Negro proved recreant to his trust and no white man returned
to a home that had been dispoiled.

Likewise during the period of alleged "insurrection," and
alarming "race riots," it never occurred to the white man,
that his wife and children were in danger of assault. Nor in
the Reconstruction era, when the hue and cry was against
"Negro Domination," was there ever a thought that the
domination would ever contaminate a fireside or strike to
death the virtue of womanhood. It must appear strange
indeed, to every thoughtful and candid man, that more than
a quarter of a century elapsed before the Negro began to
show signs of such infamous degeneration.

In his remarkable apology for lynching, Bishop Haygood,
of Georgia, says: "No race, not the most savage, tolerates the

rape of woman, but it may be said without reflection upon any other people that the Southern people are now and always have been most sensitive concerning the honor of their women— their mothers, wives, sisters and daughters." It is not the purpose of this defense to say one word against the white women of the South. Such need not be said, but it is their misfortune that the chivalrous white men of that section, in order to escape the deserved execration of the civilized world, should shield themselves by their cowardly and infamously false excuse, and call into question that very honor about which their distinguished priestly apologist claims they are most sensitive. To justify their own barbarism they assume a chivalry which they do not possess. True chivalry respects all womanhood, and no one who reads the record, as it is written in the faces of the million mulattoes in the South, will for a minute conceive that the southern white man had a very chivalrous regard for the honor due the women of his own race or respect for the womanhood which circumstances placed in his power. That chivalry which is "most sensitive concerning the honor of women" can hope for but little respect from the civilized world, when it confines itself entirely to the women who happen to be white. Virtue knows no color line, and the chivalry which depends upon complexion of skin and texture of hair can command no honest respect.

When emancipation came to the Negroes, there arose in the northern part of the United States an almost divine sentiment among the noblest, purest and best white women of the North, who felt called to a mission to educate and Christianize the millions of southern ex-slaves. From every nook and corner of the North, brave young white women answered that call and left their cultured homes, their happy associations and their lives of ease, and with heroic determination went to the South to carry light and truth to the benighted blacks. It was a heroism no less than that which calls for volunteers for India, Africa and the Isles of the sea. To educate their unfortunate charges; to teach them the Christian virtues and to inspire in them the moral sentiments manifest in their own lives, these young women braved dangers whose record reads more like fiction than fact. They became social outlaws in the South. The peculiar sensitiveness of the southern white men for women, never shed its protecting influence about them. No friendly word from their own race cheered them in their work; no hospitable doors gave them the companionship like that from which they had come. No chivalrous white man doffed his hat in honor or respect. They were "Nigger teachers"—unpardonable offenders in the social ethics of the South, and were insulted; persecuted and ostracised, not by Negroes, but by the white manhood which boasts of its chivalry toward women.

And yet these northern women worked on, year after year, unselfishly, with a heroism which amounted almost to martyrdom. Threading their way through dense forests, working in schoolhouse, in the cabin and in the church, thrown at all times and in all places among the unfortunate and lowly Negroes, whom they had come to find and to serve, these northern women, thousands of them, have spent more than a quarter of a century in giving to the colored people their splendid lessons for home and heart and soul. Without protection, save that which innocence gives to every good woman, they went about their work, fearing no assault and suffering none. Their chivalrous protectors were hundreds of miles away in their northern homes, and yet they never feared any "great dark faced mobs," they dared night or day to "go beyond their own roof trees." They never complained of assaults, and no mob was ever called into existence to avenge crimes against them. Before the world adjudges the Negro a moral monster, a vicious assailant of womanhood and a menace to the sacred precincts of home, the colored people ask the consideration of the silent record of gratitude, respect, protection and devotion of the millions of the race in the South, to the thousands of northern white women who have served as teachers and missionaries since the war.

The Negro may not have known what chivalry was, but he knew enough to preserve inviolate the womanhood of the South which was entrusted to his hands during the war. The finer sensibilities of his soul may have been crushed out by years of slavery, but his heart was full of gratitude to the white women of the North, who blessed his home and inspired his soul in all these years of freedom. Faithful to his trust in both of these instances, he should now have the impartial ear of the civilized world, when he dares to speak for himself as against the infamy wherewith he stands charged.

It is his regret, that, in his own defense, he must disclose to the world that degree of dehumanizing brutality which fixes upon America the blot of a national crime. Whatever faults and failings other nations may have in their dealings with their own subjects or with other people, no other civilized nation stands condemned before the world with a series of crimes so peculiarly national. It becomes a painful duty of the Negro to reproduce a record which shows that a large portion of the American people avow anarchy, condone murder and defy the contempt of civilization.

These pages are written in no spirit of vindictiveness, for all who give the subject consideration must concede that far too serious is the condition of that civilized government in which the spirit of unrestrained outlawry constantly increases in violence, and casts its blight over a continually growing area of territory. We plead not for the colored people alone, but for all victims of the terrible injustice which puts men and women to death without form of law. During the year 1894, there were 132 persons executed in the United States by due form of law, while in the same year, 197 persons were put to death by mobs who gave the victims no opportunity to make a lawful defense. No comment need be made upon a condition of public sentiment responsible for such alarming results.

The purpose of the pages which follow shall be to give the record which has been made, not by colored men, but that which is the result of compilations made by white men, of reports sent over the civilized world by white men in the South. Out of their own mouths shall the murderers be condemned. For a number of years the Chicago Tribune, admittedly one of the leading journals of America, has made a specialty of the compilation of statistics touching upon lynching. The data compiled by that journal and published to the world January 1st, 1894, up to the present time has not been disputed. In order to be safe from the charge of exaggeration, the incidents hereinafter reported have been confined to those vouched for by the Tribune.

CHAPTER II
LYNCH LAW STATISTICS

From the record published in the Chicago Tribune, January 1, 1894, the following computation of lynching statistics is made referring only to the colored victims of Lynch Law during the year 1893:

ARSON

Sept. 15, Paul Hill, Carrollton, Ala.; Sept. 15, Paul Archer, Carrollton, Ala.; Sept. 15, William Archer, Carrollton, Ala.; Sept. 15, Emma Fair, Carrollton, Ala.

SUSPECTED ROBBERY

Dec. 23, unknown Negro, Fannin, Miss.

ASSAULT

Dec. 25, Calvin Thomas, near Brainbridge, Ga.

ATTEMPTED ASSAULT

Dec. 28, Tillman Green, Columbia, La.

INCENDIARISM

Jan. 26, Patrick Wells, Quincy, Fla.; Feb. 9, Frank Harrell, Dickery, Miss.; Feb. 9, William Filder, Dickery, Miss.

ATTEMPTED RAPE

Feb. 21, Richard Mays, Springville, Mo.; Aug. 14, Dug Hazleton, Carrollton, Ga.; Sept. 1, Judge McNeil, Cadiz, Ky.; Sept. 11, Frank Smith, Newton, Miss.; Sept. 16, William Jackson, Nevada, Mo.; Sept. 19, Riley Gulley, Pine Apple, Ala.; Oct. 9, John Davis, Shorterville, Ala.; Nov. 8, Robert Kennedy, Spartansburg, S. C.

BURGLARY

Feb. 16, Richard Forman, Granada, Miss.

WIFE BEATING

Oct. 14, David Jackson, Covington, La.

ATTEMPTED MURDER

Sept. 21, Thomas Smith, Roanoke, Va.

ATTEMPTED ROBBERY

Dec. 12, four unknown negroes, near Selma, Ala.

RACE PREJUDICE

Jan. 30, Thomas Carr, Kosciusko, Miss.; Feb. 7, William Butler, Hickory Creek, Texas; Aug. 27, Charles Tart, Lyons Station, Miss.; Dec. 7, Robert Greenwood, Cross county, Ark,; July 14, Allen Butler, Lawrenceville, Ill.

THIEVES

Oct. 24, two unknown negroes, Knox Point, La.

ALLEGED BARN BURNING

Nov. 4, Edward Wagner, Lynchburg, Va.; Nov. 4, William Wagner, Lynchburg, Va.; Nov. 4, Samuel Motlow, Lynchburg, Va.; Nov. 4, Eliza Motlow, Lynchburg, Va.

ALLEGED MURDER

Jan. 21, Robert Landry, St. James Parish, La.; Jan. 21, Chicken George, St. James Parish, La.; Jan. 21, Richard Davis, St. James Parish, La.; Dec. 8, Benjamin Menter, Berlin, Ala.; Dec. 8, Robert Wilkins, Berlin, Ala.; Dec. 8, Joseph Gevhens, Berlin, Ala.

ALLEGED COMPLICITY IN MURDER

Sept. 16, Valsin Julian, Jefferson Parish, La.; Sept. 16, Basil Julian, Jefferson Parish, La.; Sept. 16, Paul Julian, Jefferson Parish, La.; Sept. 16, John Willis, Jefferson Parish, La.

MURDER

June 29, Samuel Thorp, Savannah, Ga.; June 29, George S. Riechen, Waynesboro, Ga.; June 30, Joseph Bird, Wilberton, I. T.; July 1, James Lamar, Darlen Ga.; July 28, Henry Miller, Dallas, Texas; July 28, Ada Hiers, Walterboro, S. C.; July 28, Alexander Brown, Bastrop, Texas; July 30, W.

G. Jamison, Quincy, Ill.; Sept. 1, John Ferguson, Lawrens, S. C.; Sept. 1, Oscar Johnston, Berkeley, S. C.; Sept. 1, Henry Ewing, Berkeley, S. C.; Sept. 8, William Smith, Camden, Ark.; Sept. 15, Staples Green, Livingston, Ala.; Sept. 29, Hiram Jacobs, Mount Vernon, Ga.; Sept. 29, Lucien Mannet, Mount Vernon, Ga.; Sept. 29, Hire Bevington, Mount Vernon, Ga.; Sept. 29, Weldon Gordon, Mount Vernon, Ga.; Sept. 29, Parse Strickland, Mount Vernon, Ga.; Oct. 20, William Dalton, Cartersville, Ga.; Oct. 27, M. B. Taylor, Wise Court House, Va.; Oct. 27, Isaac Williams, Madison, Ga.; Nov. 10, Miller Davis, Center Point, Ark.; Nov. 14, John Johnston, Auburn, N. Y.

Sept. 27, Calvin Stewart, Langley, S. C.; Sept. 29, Henry Coleman, Benton, La.; Oct. 18, William Richards, Summerfield, Ga.; Oct. 18, James Dickson, Summerfield, Ga.; Oct. 27, Edward Jenkins, Clayton county, Ga.; Nov. 9, Henry Boggs, Fort White, Fla.; Nov. 14, three unknown negroes, Lake City Junction, Fla.; Nov. 14, D. T. Nelson, Varney, Ark.; Nov. 29, Newton Jones, Baxley, Ga.; Dec. 2, Lucius Holt, Concord, Ga.; Dec. 10, two unknown negroes, Richmond, Ala.; July 12, Henry Fleming, Columbus, Miss.; July 17, unknown negro, Briar Field, Ala.; July 18, Meredith Lewis, Roseland, La.; July 29, Edward Bill, Dresden, Tenn.; Aug. 1, Henry Reynolds, Montgomery, Tenn.; Aug. 9, unknown negro, McCreery, Ark.; Aug. 12, unknown negro, Brantford, Fla.; Aug. 18, Charles Walton, Morganfield, Ky.; Aug. 21, Charles Tait, near Memphis, Tenn.; Aug. 28, Leonard Taylor, New Castle, Ky.; Sept. 8, Benjamin Jackson, Quincy, Miss.; Sept. 14, John Williams, Jackson, Tenn.

SELF DEFENSE

July 30, unknown negro, Wingo, Ky.

POISONING WELLS

Aug. 18, two unknown negroes, Franklin Parish, La.

ALLEGED WELL POISONING

Sept. 15, Benjamin Jackson, Jackson, Miss.; Sept. 15, Mahala Jackson, Jackson, Miss.; Sept. 15, Louisa Carter, Jackson, Miss.; Sept. 15, W. A. Haley, Jackson, Miss.; Sept. 15, Rufus Bigley, Jackson, Miss.

INSULTING WHITES

Feb. 18, John Hughes, Moberly, Mo.; June 2, Isaac Lincoln, Fort Madison, S. C.

MURDEROUS ASSAULT

April 20, Daniel Adams, Selina, Kan.

NO OFFENSE

July 21, Charles Martin, Shelby Co., Tenn.; July 30, William Steen, Paris, Miss.; August 31, unknown negro, Yarborough, Tex.; Sept. 30, unknown negro, Houston, Tex.; Dec. 28, Mack Segars, Brantley, Ala.

ALLEGED RAPE

July 7, Charles T. Miller, Bardwell, Ky.; Aug. 10, Daniel Lewis, Waycross, Ga.; Aug. 10, James Taylor, Waycross, Ga.; Aug. 10, John Chambers, Waycross, Ga.

ALLEGED STOCK POISONING

Dec. 16, Henry G. Givens, Nebro, Ky.

SUSPECTED MURDER

Dec. 23, Sloan Allen, West Mississippi.

SUSPICION OF RAPE

Feb. 14, Andy Blount, Chattanooga, Tenn.

TURNING STATE'S EVIDENCE

Dec. 19, William Ferguson, Adele, Ga.

RAPE

Jan. 19, James Williams, Pickens Co., Ala.; Feb. 11, unknown negro, Forest Hill, Tenn.; Feb. 26, Joseph Hayne, or Paine, Jellico, Tenn.; Nov. 1, Abner Anthony, Hot Springs, Va.; Nov. 1, Thomas Hill, Spring Place, Ga.; April 24, John Peterson, Denmark, S. C.; May 6, Samuel Gaillard,———, S. C.; May 10, Haywood Banks, or Marksdale, Columbia, S. C.; May 12, Israel Halliway, Napoleonville, La.; May 12, unknown negro, Wytheville, Va.; May 31, John Wallace, Jefferson Springs, Ark.; June 3, Samuel Bush, Decatur, Ill.; June 8, L. C. Dumas, Gleason, Tenn.; June 13, William Shorter, Winchester, Va.; June 14, George Williams, near Waco, Tex.; June 24, Daniel Edwards, Selina or Selma, Ala.; June 27, Ernest Murphy, Daleville, Ala.; July 6, unknown negro, Poplar Head, La.; July 6, unknown negro, Poplar Head, La.; July 12, Robert Larkin, Oscola, Tex.; July 17, Warren Dean, Stone Creek, Ga.; July 21, unknown negro, Brantford, Fla.; July 17, John Cotton, Connersville, Ark.; July 22, Lee Walker, New Albany, Miss.; July 26,———Handy, Suansea, S. C.; July 30, William Thompson, Columbia, S. C.; July 28, Isaac Harper, Calera, Ala.; July 30, Thomas Preston, Columbia, S. C.; July 30, Handy Kaigler, Columbia, S. C.; Aug. 13, Monroe Smith,

Springfield, Ala.; Aug. 19, negro tramp, near Paducah, Ky.; Aug. 21, John Nilson, near Leavenworth, Kan.; Aug. 23, Jacob Davis, Green Wood, S. C.; Sept. 2, William Arkinson, McKenney, Ky.; Sept. 16, unknown negro, Centerville, Ala.; Sept. 16, Jessie Mitchell, Amelia C. H., Va.; Sept. 25, Perry Bratcher, New Boston, Tex.; Oct. 9, William Lacey, Jasper, Ala.; Oct. 22, John Gamble, Pikesville, Tenn.

OFFENSES CHARGED ARE AS FOLLOWS

Rape, 39; attempted rape, 8; alleged rape, 4; suspicion of rape, 1; murder, 44; alleged murder, 6; alleged complicity in murder, 4; murderous assault, 1; attempted murder, 1; attempted robbery, 4; arson, 4; incendiarism, 3; alleged stock poisoning, 1; poisoning wells, 2; alleged poisoning wells, 5; burglary, 1; wife beating, 1; self defense, 1; suspected robbery, 1; assault and battery, 1; insulting whites, 2; malpractice, 1; alleged barn burning, 4; stealing, 2; unknown offense, 4; no offense, 1; race prejudice, 4; total, 159.

LYNCHINGS BY STATES

Alabama, 25; Arkansas, 7; Florida, 7; Georgia, 24; Indian Territory, 1; Illinois, 3; Kansas, 2; Kentucky, 8; Louisiana, 18; Mississippi, 17; Missouri, 3; New York, 1; South Carolina, 15; Tennessee, 10; Texas, 8; Virginia, 10.

RECORD FOR THE YEAR 1892

While is it intended that the record here presented shall include specially the lynchings of 1893, it will not be amiss to give the record for the year preceding. The facts contended for will always appear manifest—that not one-third of the victims lynched were charged with rape, and further that the charges made embraced a range of offenses from murders to misdemeanors.

In 1892 there were 241 persons lynched. The entire number is divided among the following states:

Alabama, 22; Arkansas, 25; California, 3; Florida, 11; Georgia, 17; Idaho, 8; Illinois, 1; Kansas, 3; Kentucky, 9; Louisiana, 29; Maryland, 1; Mississippi, 16; Missouri, 6; Montana, 4; New York, 1; North Carolina, 5; North Dakota, 1; Ohio, 3; South Carolina, 5; Tennessee, 28; Texas, 15; Virginia, 7; West Virginia, 5; Wyoming, 9; Arizona Territory, 3; Oklahoma, 2.

Of this number 160 were of Negro descent. Four of them were lynched in New York, Ohio and Kansas; the remainder were murdered in the South. Five of this number were females. The charges for which they were lynched cover a wide range. They are as follows:

Rape, 46; murder, 58; rioting, 3; race prejudice, 6; no cause given, 4; incendiarism, 6; robbery, 6; assault and battery, 1; attempted rape, 11; suspected robbery, 4; larceny, 1; self defense, 1; insulting women, 2; desperadoes, 6; fraud, 1; attempted murder, 2; no offense stated, boy and girl, 2.

In the case of the boy and girl above referred to, their father, named Hastings, was accused of the murder of a white man; his fourteen-year-old daughter and sixteen-year-old son were hanged and their bodies filled with bullets, then the father was also lynched. This was in November, 1892, at Jonesville, Louisiana.

CHAPTER III
LYNCHING IMBECILES

(AN ARKANSAS BUTCHERY)

The only excuse which capital punishment attempts to find is upon the theory that the criminal is past the power of

reformation and his life is a constant menace to the community. If, however, he is mentally unbalanced, irresponsible
for his acts, there can be no more inhuman act conceived of
than the wilful sacrifice of his life. So thoroughly is that
principle grounded in the law, that all civilized society
surrounds human life with a safeguard, which prevents the
execution of a criminal who is insane, even if sane at the time
of his criminal act. Should he become insane after its commission the law steps in and protects him during the period
of his insanity. But Lynch Law has no such regard for human
life. Assuming for itself an absolute supremacy over the law
of the land, it has time and again dyed its hands in the blood
of men who were imbeciles. Two or three noteworthy cases
will suffice to show with what inhuman ferocity irresponsible
men have been put to death by this system of injustice.

An instance occurred during the year 1892 in Arkansas, a
report of which is given in full in the Arkansas Democrat,
published at Little Rock, in that state, on the 11th day of
February of that year. The paper mentioned is perhaps one
of the leading weeklies in that state and the account given in
detail has every mark of a careful and conscientious investigation. The victims of this tragedy were a colored man,
named Hamp Biscoe, his wife and a thirteen year-old son.
Hamp Biscoe, it appears, was a hard working, thrifty farmer,
who lived near England, Arkansas, upon a small farm with
his family. The investigation of the tragedy was conducted
by a resident of Arkansas named R. B. Carlee, a white man,
who furnished the account to the Arkansas Democrat over his
own signature. He says the original trouble which led to the
lynching was a quarrel between Biscoe and a white man about
a debt. About six years after Biscoe pre-empted his land, a
white man made a demand of $100 upon him for services in
showing him the land and making the sale. Biscoe denied the

service and refused to pay the demand. The white man, however, brought suit, obtained judgment for the hundred dollars and Biscoe's farm was sold to pay the judgment.

The suit, judgment and subsequent legal proceedings appear to have driven Biscoe almost crazy and brooding over his wrongs he grew to be a confirmed imbecile. He would allow but few men, white or colored, to come upon his place, as he suspected every stranger to be planning to steal his farm. A week preceding the tragedy, a white man named Venable, whose farm adjoined Biscoe's, let down the fence and proceeded to drive through Biscoe's field. The latter saw him; grew very excited, cursed him and drove him from his farm with bitter oaths and violent threats. Venable went away and secured a warrant for Biscoe's arrest. This warrant was placed in the hands of a constable named John Ford, who took a colored deputy and two white men out to Biscoe's farm to make the arrest. When they arrived at the house Biscoe refused to be arrested and warned them he would shoot if they persisted in their attempt to arrest him. The warning as unheeded by Ford, who entered upon the premises, when Biscoe, true to his word, fired upon him. The load tore a part of his clothes from his body, one shot going through his arm and entering his breast. After he had fallen, Ford drew his revolver and shot Biscoe in the head and his wife through the arm. The Negro deputy then began firing and struck Biscoe in the small of the back. Ford's wound was not dangerous and in a few days he was able to be around again. Biscoe, however, was so severely shot that he was unable to stand after the firing was over.

Two other white men hearing the exchange of shots went to the rescue of the officers, forced open the door of Biscoe's cabin and arrested him, his wife and thirteen-year-old son, and took them, together with a babe at the breast, to a small frame house near the depot and put them under guard. The subsequent proceedings were briefly told by Mr. Carlee in the columns of the Arkansas Democrat above mentioned, from whose account the following excerpt is taken:

"It was rumored here that the Negroes were to be lynched that night, but I do not think it was generally credited, as it was not believed that Ford was greatly hurt and the Negro was held to be fatally injured and crazy at that. But that night, about 8 o'clock, a party of perhaps twelve or fifteen men, a number of whom were known to the guards, came to the house and told the Negro guards they would take care of the prisoners now, and for them to leave; as they did not obey at once they were persuaded to leave with words that did not admit of delay.

"The woman began to cry and said, 'You intend to kill us to get our money.' They told her to hush (she was heavy with child and had a child at her breast) as they intended to give her a nice present. The guards heard no more, but hastened to a Negro church near by and urged the preacher to go up and stop the mob. A few minutes after, the shooting began, perhaps about forty shots being fired. The white men left rapidly and the Negroes went to the house. Hamp Biscoe and his wife were killed, the baby had a slight wound across the upper lip; the boy was still alive and lived until after midnight, talking rationally and telling who did the shooting.

"He said when they came in and shot his father, he attempted to run out of doors and a young man shot him in the bowels and that he fell. He saw another man shoot his mother and a taller young man, whom he did not know, shoot his father. After they had killed them, the young man who had shot his mother pulled off her stockings and took $220 in currency that she had hid there. The men then came to the door where the boy was lying and one of them turned him over and put his pistol to his breast and shot him again. This is the story the dying boy told as near as I can get it. It is quite singular that the guards and those who had conversed with him were not required to testify. The woman was known to have the money as she had exposed it that day. She also had $36 in silver, which the plunderer of the body did not get. The Negro was undoubtedly insane and had been for several years. The citizens of this community condemn the murder and have no sympathy with it. The Negro was a well to do farmer, but had become crazed because he was convinced some plot had been made to steal his land and only a few days ago declared that he expected to die in defense of his home in a short time and he did not care how soon. The killing of a woman with the child at her breast and in her condition, and also a young boy, was extremely brutal. As for Hamp Biscoe he was dangerous and should long have been confined in the insane asylum. Such were the facts as near as I can get them and you can use them as you see fit, but I would prefer you would suppress the names charged by the Negroes with the killing."

Perhaps the civilized world will think, that with all these facts laid before the public, by a writer who signs his name to his communication, in a land where grand juries are sworn to investigate, where judges and juries are sworn to administer the law and sheriffs are paid to execute the decrees of the courts, and where, in fact, every instrument of civilization is supposed to work for the common good of all citizens, that this matter was duly investigated, the criminals apprehended and the punishment meted out to the murderers. But this is a mistake; nothing of the kind was done or attempted. Six months after the publication, above referred to, an investigator, writing to find out what had been done in the matter, received the following reply:

OFFICE OF
S. S. GLOVER,
SHERIFF AND COLLECTOR,
LONOKE COUNTY.

Lonoke, Ark., 9-12-1892.

Geo. Washington, Esq.,
Chicago, Ill.

DEAR SIR:—The parties who killed Hamp Briscoe February the 9th, have never been arrested. The parties are still
in the county. It was done by some of the citizens, and those
who know will not tell.

S. S. GLOVER, Sheriff.

Thus acts the mob with the victim of its fury, conscious
that it will never be called to an account. Not only is this
true, but the moral support of those who are chosen by the
people to execute the law, is frequently given to the support
of lawlessness and mob violence. The press and even the
pulpit, in the main either by silence or open apology, have
condoned and encouraged this state of anarchy.

TORTURED AND BURNED IN TEXAS

Never in the history of civilization has any Christian people
stooped to such shocking brutality and indescribable barbarism as that which characterized the people of Paris, Texas,
and adjacent communities on the 1st of February, 1893. The
cause of this awful outbreak of human passion was the murder
of a four year old child, daughter of a man named Vance.
This man, Vance, had been a police officer in Paris for years,
and was known to be a man of bad temper, overbearing
manner and given to harshly treating the prisoners under his
care. He had arrested Smith and, it is said, cruelly mistreated
him. Whether or not the murder of his child was an act of
fiendish revenge, it has not been shown, but many persons

who know of the incident have suggested that the secret of the attack on the child lay in a desire for revenge against its father.

In the same town there lived a Negro, named Henry Smith, a well known character, a kind of roustabout, who was generally considered a harmless, weak-minded fellow, not capable of doing any important work, but sufficiently able to do chores and odd jobs around the houses of the white people who cared to employ him. A few days before the final tragedy, this man, Smith, was accused of murdering Myrtle Vance. The crime of murder was of itself bad enough, and to prove that against Smith would have been amply sufficient in Texas to have committed him to the gallows, but the finding of the child so exasperated the father and his friends, that they at once shamefully exaggerated the facts and declared that the babe had been ruthlessly assaulted and then killed. The truth was bad enough, but the white people of the community made it a point to exaggerate every detail of the awful affair, and to inflame the public mind so that nothing less than immediate and violent death would satisfy the populace. As a matter of fact, the child was not brutally assaulted as the world has been told in excuse for the awful barbarism of that day. Persons who saw the child after its death, have stated, under the most solemn pledge to truth, that there was no evidence of such an assault as was published at that time, only a slight abrasion and discoloration was noticeable and that mostly about the neck. In spite of this fact, so eminent a man as Bishop Haygood deliberately and, it must also appear, maliciously falsified the fact by stating that the child was torn limb from limb, or to quote his own words, "First outraged with demoniacal cruelty and then taken by her heels and torn asunder in the mad wantonness of gorilla ferocity."

Nothing is farther from the truth than that statement. It is a cold blooded, deliberate, brutal falsehood which this Christian (?) Bishop uses to bolster up the infamous plea that the people of Paris were driven to insanity by learning that the little child had been viciously assaulted, choked to death, and then torn to pieces by a demon in human form. It was a brutal murder, but no more brutal than hundreds of murders which occur in this country, and which have been equalled every year in fiendishness and brutality, and for which the death penalty is prescribed by law and inflicted only after the person has been legally adjudged guilty of the crime. Those who knew Smith, believe that Vance had at some time given him cause to seek revenge and that this fearful crime was the outgrowth of his attempt to avenge himself of some real or fancied wrong. That the murderer was known as an imbecile, had no effect whatever upon the people who thirsted for his blood. They determined to make an example of him and proceeded to carry out their purpose with unspeakably greater ferocity than that which characterized the half crazy object of their revenge.

For a day or so after the child was found in the woods, Smith remained in the vicinity as if nothing had happened, and when finally becoming aware that he was suspected, he made an attempt to escape. He was apprehended, however, not far from the scene of his crime and the news flashed across the country that the white Christian people of Paris, Texas and the communities thereabout had deliberately determined to lay aside all forms of law and inaugurate an entirely new form of punishment for the murder. They absolutely refused to make any inquiry as to the sanity or insanity of their prisoner, but set the day and hour when in the presence of assembled thousands they put their helpless victim to the stake, tortured him, and then burned him to death for the delectation and satisfaction of Christian people.

Lest it might be charged that any description of the deeds of that day are exaggerated, a white man's description which was published in the white journals of this country is used. The New York Sun of February 2d, 1893, contains an account, from which we make the following excerpt:

> PARIS, Tex., Feb. 1, 1893—Henry Smith, the negro ravisher of 4-year-old Myrtle Vance, has expiated in part his awful crime by death at the stake. Ever since the perpetration of his awful crime this city and the entire surrounding country has been in a wild frenzy of excitement. When the news came last night that he had been captured at Hope, Ark., that he had been identified by B. B. Sturgeon, James T. Hicks, and many other of the Paris searching party, the city was wild with joy over the apprehension of the brute. Hundreds of people poured into the city from the adjoining country and the word passed from lip to lip that the punishment of the fiend should fit the crime—that death by fire was the penalty Smith should pay for the most atrocious murder and terrible outrage in Texas history. Curious and sympathizing alike, they came on train and wagons, on horse, and on foot to see if the frail mind of a man could think of a way to sufficiently punish the perpetrator of so terrible a crime. Whisky shops were closed, unruly mobs were dispersed, schools were dismissed by a proclamation from the mayor, and everything was done in a business-like manner.

> ### MEETING OF CITIZENS

> About 2 o'clock Friday a mass meeting was called at the courthouse and captains appointed to search for the child. She was found mangled beyond recognition, covered with leaves and brush as above mentioned. As soon as it was learned upon the recovery of the body that the crime was so atrocious

the whole town turned out in the chase. The railroads put up
bulletins offering free transportation to all who would join in
the search. Posses went in every direction, and not a stone
was left unturned. Smith was tracked to Detroit on foot,
where he jumped on a freight train and left for his old home
in Hempstead county, Arkansas. To this county he was
tracked and yesterday captured at Clow, a flag station on the
Arkansas & Louisiana railway about twenty miles north of
Hope. Upon being questioned the fiend denied everything,
but upon being stripped for examination his undergarments
were seen to be spattered with blood and a part of his shirt
was torn off. He was kept under heavy guard at Hope last
night, and later on confessed the crime.

This morning he was brought through Texarkana, where
5,000 people awaited the train, anxious to see a man who had
received the fate of Ed. Coy. At that place speeches were
made by prominent Paris citizens, who asked that the prisoner
be not molested by Texarkana people, but that the guard be
allowed to deliver him up to the outraged and indignant
citizens of Paris. Along the road the train gathered strength
from the various towns, the people crowded upon the plat-
forms and tops of coaches anxious to see the lynching and the
negro who was soon to be delivered to an infuriated mob.

BURNED AT THE STAKE

Arriving here at 12 o'clock the train was met by a surging
mass of humanity 10,000 strong. The negro was placed upon
a carnival float in mockery of a king upon his throne, and,
followed by an immense crowd, was escorted through the city
so that all might see the most inhuman monster known in
current history. The line of march was up Main street to the
square, around the square down Clarksville street to Church
street, thence to the open prairies about 300 yards from the
Texas & Pacific depot. Here Smith was placed upon a
scaffold, six feet square and ten feet high, securely bound,
within the view of all beholders. Here the victim was tortured

for fifty minutes by red-hot iron brands thrust against his
quivering body. Commencing at the feet the brands were
placed against him inch by inch until they were thrust against
the face. Then, being apparently dead, kerosene was poured
upon him, cottonseed hulls placed beneath him and set on
fire. In less time than it takes to relate it, the tortured man
was wafted beyond the grave to another fire, hotter and more
terrible than the one just experienced.

Curiosity seekers have carried away already all that was
left of the memorable event, even to pieces of charcoal. The
cause of the crime was that Henry Vance when a deputy
policemen, in the course of his duty was called to arrest
Henry Smith for being drunk and disorderly. The Negro
was unruly, and Vance was forced to use his club. The Negro
swore vengeance, and several times assaulted Vance. In his
greed for revenge, last Thursday, he grabbed up the little
girl and committed the crime. The father is prostrated with
grief and the mother now lies at death's door, but she has
lived to see the slayer of her innocent babe suffer the most
horrible death that could be conceived.

TORTURE BEYOND DESCRIPTION

Words to describe the awful torture inflicted upon Smith
cannot be found. The Negro, for a long time after starting
on the journey to Paris, did not realize his plight. At last
when he was told that he must die by slow torture he begged
for protection. His agony was awful. He pleaded and writhed
in bodily and mental pain. Scarcely had the train reached
Paris than this torture commenced. His clothes were torn off
piecemeal and scattered in the crowd, people catching the
shreds and putting them away as mementoes. The child's
father, her brother, and two uncles then gathered about the
Negro as he lay fastened to the torture platform and thrust
hot irons into his quivering flesh. It was horrible—the man
dying by slow torture in the midst of smoke from his own
burning flesh. Every groan from the fiend, every contortion

of his body was cheered by the thickly packed crowd of 10,000 persons. The mass of beings 600 yards in diameter, the scaffold being the center. After burning the feet and legs, the hot irons—plenty of fresh ones being at hand—were rolled up and down Smith's stomach, back, and arms. Then the eyes were burned out and irons were thrust down his throat.

The men of the Vance family having wreaked vengeance, the crowd piled all kinds of combustible stuff around the scaffold, poured oil on it and set it afire. The Negro rolled and tossed out of the mass, only to be pushed back by the people nearest him. He tossed out again, and was roped and pulled back. Hundreds of people turned away, but the vast crowd still looked calmly on. People were here from every part of this section. They came from Dallas, Fort Worth, Sherman, Denison, Bonham, Texarkana, Fort Smith, Ark., and a party of fifteen came from Hempstead county, Arkansas, where he was captured. Every train that came in was loaded to its utmost capacity, and there were demands at many points for special trains to bring the people here to see the unparalleled punishment for an unparalleled crime. When the news of the burning went over the country like wildfire, at every country town anvils boomed forth the announcement.

SHOULD HAVE BEEN IN AN ASYLUM

It may not be amiss in connection with this awful affair, in proof of our assertion that Smith was an imbecile, to give the testimony of a well known colored minister, who lived at Paris, Texas, at the time of the lynching. He was a witness of the awful scenes there enacted, and attempted, in the name of God and humanity, to interfere in the programme. He barely escaped with his life, was driven out of the city and became an exile because of his actions. Reverend King was in New York about the middle of February, and he was there interviewed for a daily paper for that city, and we quote his account as an eye witness of the affair. Said he:

"I was ridden out of Paris on a rail because I was the only man in Lamar county to raise my voice against the lynching of Smith. I opposed the illegal measures before the arrival of Henry Smith as a prisoner, and I was warned that I might meet his fate if I was not careful; but the sense of justice made me bold, and when I saw the poor wretch trembling with fear, and got so near him that I could hear his teeth chatter, I determined to stand by him to the last.

"I hated him for his crime, but two crimes do not make a virtue; and in the brief conversation I had with Smith I was more firmly convinced than ever that he was irresponsible.

"I had known Smith for years, and there were times when Smith was out of his head for weeks. Two years ago I made an effort to have him put in an asylum, but the white people were trying to fasten the murder of a young colored girl upon him, and would not listen. For days before the murder of the little Vance girl, Smith was out of his head and dangerous. He had just undergone an attack of delirium tremens and was in no condition to be allowed at large. He realized his condition, for I spoke with him not three weeks ago, and in answer to my exhortations, he promised to reform. The next time I saw him was on the day of his execution.

" 'Drink did it! drink did it;' he sobbed. Then bowing his face in his hands, he asked: 'Is it true, did I kill her? Oh, my God, my God!' for a moment he seemed to forget the awful fate that awaited him, and his body swayed to and fro with grief. Some one seized me by the shoulder and hurled me back, and Smith fell writhing to the ground in terror as four men seized his arms to drag him to the float on which he was to be exhibited before he was finally burned at the stake.

"I followed the procession and wept aloud as I saw little children of my own race follow the unfortunate man and taunt him with jeers. Even at the stake, children of both sexes and colors gathered in groups, and when the father of the murdered child raised the hissing iron with which he was about to torture the helpless victim, the children became as frantic as the grown people and struggled forward to obtain places of advantage.

"It was terrible. One little tot scarcely older than little Myrtle Vance clapped her baby hands as her father held her on his shoulders above the heads of the people.

" 'For God's sake,' I shouted, 'send the children home.'

" 'No, no.' shouted a hundred maddened voices; 'let them learn a lesson.'

"I love children, but as I looked about the little faces distorted with passion and the bloodshot eyes of the cruel parents who held them high in their arms, I thanked God that I have none of my own.

"As the hot iron sank deep into poor Henry's flesh a hideous yell rent the air, and, with a sound as terrible as the cry of lost souls on judgment day, 20,000 maddened people took up the victim's cry of agony and a prolonged howl of maddened glee rent the air.

"No one was himself now. Every man, woman and child in that awful crowd was worked up to a greater frenzy than that which actuated Smith's horrible crime. The people were capable of any new atrocity now, and as Smith's yells became more and more frequent, it was difficult to hold the crowd back, so anxious were the savages to participate in the sickening tortures.

"For half an hour I tried to pray as the beads of agony rolled down my forehead and bathed my face.

"For an instant a hush spread over the people. I could stand no more, and with a superhuman effort dashed through the compact mass of humanity and stood at the foot of the burning scaffold.

" 'In the name of God,' I cried, 'I command you to cease this torture.'

"The heavy butt of a Winchester rifle descended on my head and I fell to the ground. Rough hands seized me and angry men bore me away, and I was thankful.

"At the outskirts of the crowd I was attacked again, and then several men, no doubt glad to get away from the fearful place, escorted me to my home, where I was allowed to take a small amount of clothing. A jeering crowd gathered without, and when I appeared at the door ready hands seized me and I was placed upon a rail, and, with curses and oaths, taken to the railway station and placed upon a train. As the train moved out some one thrust a roll of bills into my hand and said, 'God bless you, but it was no use.' "

When asked if he should ever return to Paris, Mr. King said: "I shall never go south again. The impressions of that awful day will stay with me forever."

CHAPTER IV
LYNCHING OF INNOCENT MEN

(LYNCHED ON ACCOUNT OF RELATIONSHIP)

If no other reason appealed to the sober sense of the American people to check the growth of Lynch Law, the absolute unreliability and recklessness of the mob in inflicting punishment for crimes done, should do so. Several instances of this spirit have occurred in the year past. In Louisiana, near New Orleans, in July, 1893, Roselius Julian, a colored man, shot and killed a white judge, named Victor Estopinal. The cause of the shooting has never been definitely ascertained. It is claimed that the Negro resented an insult to his wife, and the killing of the white man was an act of a Negro (who dared) to defend his home. The judge was killed in the court house, and Julian, heavily armed, made his escape to the swamps near the city. He has never been apprehended, nor has any information ever been gleaned as to his whereabouts. A mob determined to secure the fugitive murderer and burn him alive. The swamps were hunted through and through in vain, when, being unable to wreak their revenge upon the murderer, the mob turned its attention to his unfortunate relatives. Dispatches from New Orleans, dated September 19, 1893, described the affair as follows:

"Posses were immediately organized and the surrounding country was scoured, but the search was fruitless so far as the real criminal was concerned. The mother, three brothers and two sisters of the Negro were arrested yesterday at the Black Ridge in the rear of the city by the police and taken to the little jail on Judge Estopinal's place about Southport, because of the belief that they were succoring the fugitive.

"About 11 o'clock twenty-five men, some armed with rifles and shotguns, came up to the jail. They unlocked the door and held a conference among themselves as to what they should do. Some were in favor of hanging the five, while others insisted that only two of the brothers should be strung up. This was finally agreed to, and the two doomed negroes were hurried to a pasture one hundred yards distant, and there asked to take their last chance of saving their lives by making a confession, but the Negroes made no reply. They were then told to kneel down and pray. One did so, the other remained standing, but both prayed fervently. The taller Negro was hoisted up. The shorter Negro stood gazing at the horrible death of his brother without flinching. Five minutes later he was also hanged. The mob decided to take the remaining brother out to Camp Parapet and hang him there. The other two were to be taken out and flogged, with an order to get out of the parish in less than half an hour. The third brother, Paul, was taken out to the camp, which is about a mile distant in the interior, and there he was hanged to a tree."

Another young man, who was in no way related to Julian, who perhaps did not even know the man and who was entirely innocent of any offense in connection therewith, was murdered by the same mob. The same paper says:

"During the search for Julian on Saturday one branch of the posse visited the house of a Negro family in the neighborhood of Camp Parapet, and failing to find the object of their search, tried to induce John Willis, a young Negro, to disclose the whereabouts of Julian. He refused to do so, or could not do so, and was kicked to death by the gang."

AN INDIANA CASE

Almost equal to the ferocity of the mob which killed the three brothers, Julian and the unoffending, John Willis, because of the murder of Judge Estopinal, was the action of a mob near Vincennes, Ind. In this case a wealthy colored man, named Allen Butler, who was well known in the community, and enjoyed the confidence and respect of the entire country, was made the victim of a mob and hung because his son had become unduly intimate with a white girl who was a servant around his house. There was no pretense that the facts were otherwise than as here stated. The woman lived at Butler's house as a servant, and she and Butler's son fell in love with each other, and later it was found that the girl was in a delicate condition. It was claimed, but with how much truth no one has ever been able to tell, that the father had procured an abortion, or himself had operated on the girl, and that she had left the house to go back to her home. It was never claimed that the father was in any way responsible for the action of his son, but the authorities procured the arrest of both father and son, and at the preliminary examination the father gave bail to appear before the Grand Jury when it should convene. On the same night, however, the mob took the matter in hand and with the intention of hanging the son. It assembled near Sumner, while the boy, who had been unable to give bail, was lodged in jail at Lawrenceville. As it was impossible to reach Lawrenceville and hang the son, the leaders of the mob concluded they would go to Butler's house and hang him. Butler was found at his home, taken out by the mob and hung to a tree. This was in the law-abiding state of Indiana, which furnished the United States its last president and which claims all the honor, pride and glory of northern civilization. None of the leaders of the mob were apprehended, and no steps whatever were taken to bring the murderers to justice.

KILLED FOR HIS STEPFATHER'S CRIME

An account has been given of the cremation of Henry Smith, at Paris, Texas, for the murder of the infant child of a man named Vance. It would appear that human ferocity was not sated when it vented itself upon a human being by burning his eyes out, by thrusting a red hot iron down his throat, and then by burning his body to ashes. Henry Smith, the victim of these savage orgies, was beyond all the power of torture, but a few miles outside of Paris, some members of the community concluded that it would be proper to kill a stepson named William Butler as a partial penalty for the original crime. This young man, against whom no word has ever been said, and who was in fact an orderly, peaceable boy, had been watched with the severest scrutiny by members of the mob who believed he knew something of the whereabouts of Smith. He declared from the very first that he did not know where his stepfather was, which statement was well proven to be a fact after the discovery of Smith in Arkansas, whence he had fled through swamps and woods and unfrequented places. Yet Butler was apprehended, placed under arrest, and on the night of February 6th, taken out on Hickory Creek, five miles southeast of Paris, and hung for his stepfather's crime. After his body was suspended in the air, the mob filled it with bullets.

LYNCHED BECAUSE THE JURY ACQUITTED HIM

The entire system of the judiciary of this country is in the hands of white people. To this add the fact of the inherent prejudice against colored people, and it will be clearly seen that a white jury is certain to find a Negro prisoner guilty if there is the least evidence to warrant such a finding.

Meredith Lewis was arrested in Roseland, La., in July of last year. A white jury found him not guilty of the crime of murder wherewith he stood charged. This did not suit the mob. A few nights after the verdict was rendered, and he declared to be innocent, a mob gathered in his vicinity and went to his house. He was called, and suspecting nothing, went outside. He was seized and hurried off to a convenient spot and hanged by the neck until he was dead for the murder of a woman of which the jury had said he was innocent.

LYNCHED AS A SCAPEGOAT

Wednesday, July 5th, about 10 o'clock in the morning, a terrible crime was committed within four miles of Wickliffe, Ky. Two girls, Mary and Ruby Ray, were found murdered a short distance from their home. The news of this terrible cowardly murder of two helpless young girls spread like wild fire, and searching parties scoured the territory surrounding Wickliffe and Bardwell. Two of the searching party, the

Clark brothers, saw a man enter the Dupoyster cornfield; they got their guns and fired at the fleeing figure, but without effect; he got away, but they said he was a white man or nearly so. The search continued all day without effect, save the arrest of two or three strange Negroes. A bloodhound was brought from the penitentiary and put on the trail which he followed from the scene of the murder to the river and into the boat of a fisherman named Gordon. Gordon stated that he had ferried one man and only one across the river about half past six the evening of July 5th; that his passenger sat in front of him, and he was a white man or a very bright mulatto, who could not be told from a white man. The bloodhound was put across the river in the boat, and he struck a trail again at Bird's Point on the Missouri side, ran about three hundred yards to the cottage of a white farmer named Grant and there lay down refusing to go further.

Thursday morning a brakesman on a freight train going out of Sikeston, Mo., discovered a Negro stealing a ride; he ordered him off and had hot words which terminated in a fight. The brakesman had the Negro arrested. When arrested, between 11 and 12 o'clock, he had on a dark woolen shirt, light pants and coat, and no vest. He had twelve dollars in paper, two silver dollars and ninety-five cents in change; he had also four rings in his pockets, a knife and a razor which were rusted and stained. The Sikeston authorities immediately jumped to the conclusion that this man was the murderer for whom the Kentuckians across the river were searching. They telegraphed to Bardwell that their prisoner had on no coat, but wore a blue vest and pants which would perhaps correspond with the coat found at the scene of the murder, and that the names of the murdered girls were in the rings found in his possession.

As soon as this news was received, the sheriffs of Ballard and Carlisle counties and a posse (?) of thirty well armed and determined Kentuckians, who had pledged their word the prisoner should be taken back to the scene of the supposed crime, to be executed there if proved to be the guilty man, chartered a train and at nine o'clock Thursday night started for Sikeston. Arriving there two hours later, the sheriff at Sikeston, who had no warrant for the prisoner's arrest and detention, delivered him into the hands of the mob without authority for so doing, and accompanied them to Bird's Point. The prisoner gave his name as Miller, his home at Springfield, and said he had never been in Kentucky in his life, but the sheriff turned him over to the mob to be taken to Wickliffe, that Frank Gordon, the fisherman, who had put a man across the river might identify him.

In other words, the protection of the law was withdrawn from C. J. Miller, and he was given to a mob by this sheriff at Sikeston, who knew that the prisoner's life depended on one man's word. After an altercation with the train men, who wanted another $50 for taking the train back to Bird's Point, the crowd arrived there at three o'clock, Friday morning. Here was anchored "The Three States," a ferry boat plying between Wickliffe, Ky., Cairo, Ill., and Bird's Point, Mo. This boat left Cairo at twelve o'clock, Thursday, with nearly three hundred of Cairo's best (?) citizens and thirty kegs of beer on board. This was consumed while the crowd and the bloodhound waited for the prisoner.

When the prisoner was on board "The Three States" the dog was turned loose, and after moving aimlessly around followed the crowd to where Miller sat handcuffed and there stopped. The crowd closed in on the pair and insisted that the brute had identified him because of that action. When the boat reached Wickliffe, Gordon, the fisherman, was called on to say whether the prisoner was the man he ferried over the river the day of the murder.

The sheriff of Ballard county informed him, sternly that if the prisoner was not the man, he (the fisherman) would be held responsible as knowing who the guilty man was. Gordon stated before, that the man he ferried across was a white man or a bright colored man; Miller was a dark brown skinned man, with kinky hair, "neither yellow nor black," says the Cairo Evening Telegram of Friday, July 7th. The fisherman went up to Miller from behind, looked at him without speaking for fully five minutes, then slowly said, "Yes, that's the man I crossed over." This was about six o'clock, Friday morning, and the crowd wished to hang Miller then and there. But Mr. Ray, the father of the girls, insisted that he be taken to Bardwell, the county seat of Ballard, and twelve miles inland. He said he thought a white man committed the crime, and that he was not satisfied that was the man. They took him to Bardwell and at ten o'clock, this same excited, unauthorized mob undertook to determine Miller's guilt. One of the Clark brothers who shot at a fleeing man in the Dupoyster cornfield, said the prisoner was the same man; the other said he was not, but the testimony of the first was accepted. A colored woman who had said she gave breakfast to a colored man clad in a blue flannel suit the morning of the murder, said positively that she had never seen Miller before. The gold rings found in his possession had no names in them, as had been asserted, and Mr. Ray said they did not belong to his daughters. Meantime a funeral pyre for the purpose of burning Miller to death had been erected in the center of the village. While the crowd swayed by passion was clamoring that he be burnt, Miller stepped forward and made the following statement: "My name is C. J. Miller. I am

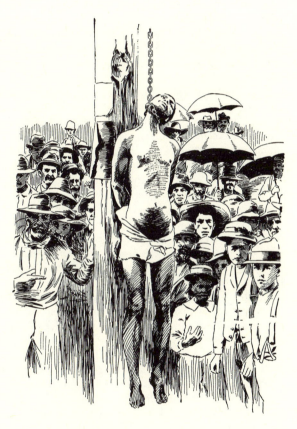

Lynching of C. J. Miller, at Bardwell, Kentucky,
July 7th, 1893.

from Springfield, Ill.; my wife lives at 716 N. 2d street. I am here among you today, looked upon as one of the most brutal men before the people. I stand here surrounded by men who are excited, men who are not willing to let the law take its course, and as far as the crime is concerned, I have committed no crime, and certainly no crime gross enough to deprive me of my life and liberty to walk upon the green earth."

A telegram was sent to the chief of the police at Springfield, Ill., asking if one C. J. Miller lived there. An answer in the negative was returned. A few hours after, it was ascertained that a man named Miller, and his wife, did live at the number the prisoner gave in his speech, but the information came to Bardwell too late to do the prisoner any good. Miller was taken to jail, every stitch of clothing literally torn from his body and examined again. On the lower left side of the bosom of his shirt was found a dark reddish spot about the size of a dime. Miller said it was paint which he had gotten on him at Jefferson Barracks. This spot was only on the right side, and could not be seen from the underside at all, thus showing it had not gone through the cloth as blood or any liquid substance would do.

Chief-of-Police Mahaney, of Cairo, Ill., was with the prisoner, and he took his knife and scraped at the spot, particles of which came off in his hand. Miller told them to take his clothes to any expert, and if the spot was shown to be blood, they might do anything they wished with him. They took his clothes away and were gone some time. After a while they were brought back and thrown into the cell without a word. It is needless to say that if the spot had been found to be blood, that fact would have been announced, and the shirt retained as evidence. Meanwhile numbers of rough, drunken men crowded into the cell and tried to force a confession of the deed from the prisoner's lips. He refused to talk save to reiterate his innocence. To Mr. Mahaney, who talked seriously and kindly to him, telling him the mob meant to burn and torture him at three o'clock, Miller said: "Burning and torture here lasts but a little while, but if I die with a lie on my soul, I shall be tortured forever. I am innocent." For more than three hours, all sorts of pressure in the way of threats, abuse and urging, was brought to bear to force him to confess to the murder and thus justify the mob in its deed of murder. Miller remained firm; but as the hour drew near, and the crowd became more impatient, he asked for a priest. As none could be procured, he then asked for a Methodist minister, who came, prayed with the doomed man, baptized him and exhorted Miller to confess. To keep up the flagging spirits of the dense crowd around the jail, the rumor went out more than once, that Miller had confessed. But the solemn assurance of the minister, chief-of-police, and leading editor—who were with Miller all along—is that this rumor is absolutely false.

At three o'clock the mob rushed to the jail to secure the prisoner. Mr. Ray had changed his mind about the promised burning; he was still in doubt as to the prisoner's guilt. He again addressed the crowd to that effect, urging them not to burn Miller, and the mob heeded him so far, that they compromised on hanging instead of burning, which was agreed to by Mr. Ray. There was a loud yell, and a rush was made for the prisoner. He was stripped naked, his clothing literally torn from his body, and his shirt was tied around his loins. Some one declared the rope was a "white man's death," and a log-chain, nearly a hundred feet in length, weighing over one hundred pounds, was placed round Miller's neck and body, and he was led and dragged through the streets of the village in that condition followed by thousands of people. He fainted from exhaustion several times, but was supported to the platform where they first intended burning him.

The chain was hooked around his neck, a man climbed the telegraph pole and the other end of the chain was passed up to him and made fast to the cross-arm. Others brought a long forked stick which Miller was made to straddle. By this means he was raised several feet from the ground and then let fall. The first fall broke his neck, but he was raised in this way and let fall a second time. Numberless shots were fired into the dangling body, for most of that crowd were heavily armed, and had been drinking all day.

Miller's body hung thus exposed from three to five o'clock, during which time, several photographs of him as he hung dangling at the end of the chain were taken, and his toes and fingers were cut off. His body was taken down, placed on the platform, the torch applied, and in a few moments there was nothing left of C. J. Miller save a few bones and ashes. Thus perished another of the many victims of Lynch Law, but it is the honest and sober belief of many who witnessed the scene that an innocent man has been barbarously and shockingly put to death in the glare of the 19th century civilization, by those who profess to believe in Christianity, law and order.

CHAPTER V
LYNCHED FOR ANYTHING OR NOTHING

(LYNCHED FOR WIFE BEATING)

In nearly all communities wife beating is punishable with a fine, and in no community is it made a felony. Dave Jackson, of Abita, La., was a colored man who had beaten his wife. He had not killed her, nor seriously wounded her, but as Louisiana lynchers had not filled out their quota of crimes, his case was deemed of sufficient importance to apply the method of that barbarous people. He was in the custody of the officials, but the mob went to the jail and took him out in front of the prison and hanged him by the neck until he was dead. This was in Nov. 1893.

HANGED FOR STEALING HOGS

Details are very meagre of a lynching which occurred near Knox Point, La., on the 24th of October, 1893. Upon one point, however, there was no uncertainty, and that is, that the persons lynched were Negroes. It was claimed that they had been stealing hogs, but even this claim had not been subjected to the investigation of a court. That matter was not considered necessary. A few of the neighbors who had lost hogs suspected these men were responsible for their loss, and made up their minds to furnish an example for others to be warned by. The two men were secured by a mob and hanged.

LYNCHED FOR NO OFFENSE

Perhaps the most characteristic feature of this record of lynch law for the year 1893, is the remarkable fact that five human beings were lynched and that the matter was considered of so little importance that the powerful press bureaus of the country did not consider the matter of enough importance to ascertain the causes for which they were hanged. It tells the world, with perhaps greater emphasis than any other feature of the record, that Lynch Law has become so common in the United States that the finding of the dead body of a Negro, suspended between heaven and earth to the limb of a tree, is of so slight importance that neither the civil authorities nor press agencies consider the matter worth investigating. July 21st, in Shelby county, Tenn., a colored man by the name of Charles Martin was lynched. July 30th, at Paris, Mo., a colored man named William Steen shared the same fate. December 28th, Mack Segars was announced to have been lynched at Brantley, Alabama. August 31st, at Yarborough, Texas, and on September 19th, at Houston, a colored man was found lynched, but so little attention was paid to the matter that not only was no record made as to why these last two men were lynched, but even their names were not given. The dispatches simply stated that an unknown Negro was found lynched in each case.

There are friends of humanity who feel their souls shrink from any compromise with murder, but whose deep and abiding reverence for womanhood causes them to hesitate in giving their support to this crusade against Lynch Law, out of fear that they may encourage the miscreants whose deeds are worse than murder. But to these friends it must appear certain that these five men could not have been guilty of any terrible crime. They were simply lynched by parties of men who had it in their power to kill them, and who chose to avenge some fancied wrong by murder, rather than submit their grievances to court.

LYNCHED BECAUSE THEY WERE SAUCY

At Moberly, Mo., February 18th and at Fort Madison, S.C., June 2d, both in 1892, a record was made in the line of lynching which should certainly appeal to every humanitarian who has any regard for the sacredness of human life. John Hughes, of Moberly, and Isaac Lincoln, of Fort Madison, and Will Lewis in Tullahoma, Tenn., suffered death for no more serious charge than that they "were saucy to white people." In the days of slavery it was held to be a very serious matter for a colored person to fail to yield the sidewalk at the demand of a white person, and it will not be surprising to find some evidence of this intolerance existing in the days of freedom. But the most that could be expected as a penalty for acting or speaking saucily to a white person would be a slight physical chastisement to make the Negro "know his place" or an arrest and fine. But Missouri, Tennessee and South Carolina chose to make precedents in their cases and as a result both men, after being charged with their offense and apprehended, were taken by a mob and lynched. The civil authorities, who in either case would have been very quick to satisfy the aggrieved white people had they complained and brought the prisoners to court, by imposing proper penalty upon them, did not feel it their duty to make any investigation after the Negroes were killed. They were dead and out of the way and as no one would be called upon to render an account for their taking off, the matter was dismissed from the public mind.

LYNCHED FOR A QUARREL

One of the most notable instances of lynching for the year 1893, occurred about the 20th of September. It was notable for the fact that the mayor of the city exerted every available power to protect the victim of the lynching from the mob. In his splendid endeavor to uphold the law, the mayor called out the troops, and the result was a deadly fight between the militia and mob, nine of the mob being killed.

The trouble occurred at Roanoke, Va. It is frequently claimed that lynchings occur only in sparsely settled districts, and, in fact, it is a favorite plea of governors and reverend apologists to couple two arrant falsehoods, stating that lynchings occur only because of assaults upon white women, and that these assaults occur and the lynchings follow in thinly inhabited districts where the power of the law is entirely inadequate to meet the emergency. This Roanoke case is a double refutation, for it not only disproves the alleged charge that the Negro assaulted a white woman, as was telegraphed all over the country at the time, but it also shows conclusively that even in one of the largest cities of the old state of Virginia, one of the original thirteen colonies, which prides itself of being the mother of presidents, it was possible for a lynching to occur in broad daylight under circumstances of revolting savagery.

When the news first came from Roanoke of the contemplated lynching, it was stated that a big burly Negro had assaulted a white woman, that he had been apprehended and that the citizens were determined to summarily dispose of his case. Mayor Trout was a man who believed in maintaining the majesty of the law, and who at once gave notice that no lynching would be permitted in Roanoke, and that the Negro, whose name was Smith, being in the custody of the law, should be dealt with according to law; but the mob did not pay any attention to the brave words of the mayor. It evidently thought that it was only another case of swagger, such as frequently characterizes lynching episodes. Mayor Trout, finding immense crowds gathering about the city, and fearing an attempt to lynch Smith, called out the militia and stationed them at the jail.

It was known that the woman refused to accuse Smith of assaulting her, and that his offense consisted in quarreling with her about the change of money in a transaction in which he bought something from her market booth. Both parties lost their temper, and the result was a row from which Smith had to make his escape. At once the old cry was sounded that the woman had been assaulted, and in a few hours all the town was wild with people thirsting for the assailant's blood.

The further incidents of that day may well be told by a dispatch from Roanoke under date of the 21st of September and published in the Chicago Record. It says:

"It is claimed by members of the military company that they frequently warned the mob to keep away from the jail, under penalty of being shot. Capt. Bird told them he was under orders to protect the prisoner whose life the mob so eagerly sought, and come what may he would not allow him to be taken by the mob. To this the crowd replied with hoots and derisive jeers. The rioters appeared to become frenzied at the determined stand taken by the men and Captain Bird, and finally a crowd of excited men made a rush for the side door of the jail. The captain directed his men to drive the would-be lynchers back.

"At this moment the mob opened fire on the soldiers. This appeared for a moment to startle the captain and his men. But it was only for a moment. Then he cooly gave the command: 'Ready! aim! fire!' The company obeyed to the instant, and poured a volley of bullets into that part of the mob which was trying to batter down the side door of the jail.

"The rioters fell back before the fire of the militia, leaving one man writhing in the agonies of death at the doorstep. There was a lull for a moment. Then the word was quickly passed through the throng in front of the jail and down the street that a man was killed. Then there was an awful rush toward the little band of soldiers. Excited men were yelling like demons.

"The fight became general, and ere it was ended nine men were dead and more than forty wounded."

This stubborn stand on behalf of law and order disconcerted the crowd and it fell back in disorder. It did not long remain inactive but assembled again for a second assault. Having only a small band of militia, and knowing they would be absolutely at the mercy of the thousands who were gathering to wreak vengeance upon them, the mayor ordered them to disperse and go to their homes, and he himself, having been wounded, was quietly conveyed out of the city.

The next day the mob grew in numbers and its rage increased in its intensity. There was no longer any doubt that Smith, innocent as he was of any crime, would be killed, for with the mayor out of the city and the governor of the state using no effort to control the mob, it was only a question of a few hours when the assault would be repeated and its victim put to death. All this happened as per programme. The description of that morning's carnival appeared in the paper above quoted and reads as follows:

"A squad of twenty men took the negro Smith from three policemen just before five o'clock this morning and hanged him to a hickory limb on Ninth avenue, in the residence section of the city. They riddled his body with bullets and put a placard on it saying: 'This is Mayor Trout's friend.' A coroner's jury of Bismel was summoned and viewed the body and rendered a verdict of death at the hands of unknown men. Thousands of persons visited the scene of the lynching between daylight and eight o'clock when the body was cut down. After the jury had completed its work the body was placed in the hands of officers, who were unable to keep back the mob. Three hundred men tried to drag the body through the streets of the town, but the Rev. Dr. Campbell of the First Presbyterian church and Capt. R. B. Moorman, with pleas and by force prevented them.

"Capt. Moorman hired a wagon and the body was put in it. It was then conveyed to the bank of the Roanoke, about two miles from the scene of the lynching. Here the body was dragged from the wagon by ropes for about 200 yards and burned. Piles of dry brushwood were brought, and the body was placed upon it, and more brushwood piled on the body, leaving only the head bare. The whole pile was then saturated with coal oil and a match was applied. The body was consumed within an hour. The cremation was witnessed by several thousand people. At one time the mob threatened to burn the Negro in Mayor Trout's yard."

Thus did the people of Roanoke, Va., add this measure of proof to maintain our contention that it is only necessary to charge a Negro with a crime in order to secure his certain death. It was well known in the city before he was killed that he had not assaulted the woman with whom he had the trouble, but he dared to have an altercation with a white woman, and he must pay the penalty. For an offense which would not in any civilized community have brought upon him a punishment greater than a fine of a few dollars, this unfortunate Negro was hung, shot and burned.

SUSPECTED, INNOCENT AND LYNCHED

Five persons, Benjamin Jackson, his wife, Mahala Jackson, his mother-in-law, Lou Carter, Rufus Bigley, were lynched near Quincy, Miss., the charge against them being suspicion of well poisoning. It appears from the newspaper dispatches at that time that a family by the name of Woodruff was taken ill in September of 1892. As a result of their illness one or more of the family are said to have died, though that matter is not stated definitely. It was suspected that the cause of their illness was the existence of poison in the water, some miscreant having placed poison in the well. Suspicion pointed to a colored man named Benjamin Jackson who was at once arrested. With him also were arrested his wife and mother-in-law and all were held on the same charge.

The matter came up for judicial investigation, but as might

have been expected, the white people concluded it was un-
necessary to wait the result of the investigation—that it was
preferable to hang the accused first and try him afterward.
By this method of procedure, the desired result was always
obtained—the accused was hanged. Accordingly Benjamin
Jackson was taken from the officers by a crowd of about two
hundred people, while the inquest was being held, and
hanged. After the killing of Jackson, the inquest was continued to ascertain the possible connection of the other persons
charged with the crime. Against the wife and mother-in-law
of the unfortunate man there was not the slightest evidence
and the coroner's jury was fair enough to give them their
liberty. They were declared innocent and returned to their
homes. But this did not protect the women from the demands
of the Christian white people of that section of the country.
In any other land and with any other people, the fact that
these two accused persons were women would have pleaded
in their favor for protection and fair play, but that had no
weight with the Mississippi Christians nor the further fact
that a jury of white men had declared them innocent. The
hanging of one victim on an unproven charge did not begin
to satisfy the mob in its bloodthirsty demands and the result
was that even after the women had been discharged, they
were at once taken in charge by a mob, which hung them by
the neck until they were dead.

Still the mob was not satisfied. During the coroner's investigation the name of a fourth person, Rufus Bigley, was
mentioned. He was acquainted with the Jacksons and that
fact, together with some testimony adduced at the inquest,
prompted the mob to decide that he should die also. Search
was at once made for him and the next day he was apprehended. He was not given over into the hands of the civil
authorities for trial nor did the coroner's inquest find that he

was guilty, but the mob was quite sufficient in itself. After finding Bigley, he was strung up to a tree and his body left hanging, where it was found the next day. It may be remarked here in passing that this instance of the moral degradation of the people of Mississippi did not excite any interest in the public at large. American Christianity heard of this awful affair and read of its details and neither press nor pulpit gave the matter more than a passing comment. Had it occurred in the wilds of interior Africa, there would have been an outcry from the humane people of this country against the savagery which would so mercilessly put men and women to death. But it was an evidence of American civilization to be passed by unnoticed, to be denied or condoned as the requirements of any future emergency might determine.

LYNCHED FOR AN ATTEMPTED ASSAULT

With only a little more aggravation than that of Smith who quarreled at Roanoke with the market woman, was the assault which operated as the incentive to a most brutal lynching in Memphis, Tenn. Memphis is one of the queen cities of the south, with a population of about seventy thousand souls— easily one of the twenty largest, most progressive and wealthiest cities of the United States. And yet in its streets there occurred a scene of shocking savagery which would have disgraced the Congo. No woman was harmed, no serious indignity suffered. Two women driving to town in a wagon, were suddenly accosted by Lee Walker. He claimed that he demanded something to eat. The women claimed that he attempted to assault them. They gave such an alarm that he ran away. At once the dispatches spread over the entire country that a big, burly Negro had brutally assaulted two women. Crowds began to search for the alleged fiend. While hunting him they shot another Negro dead in his tracks for refusing to stop when ordered to do so. After a few days Lee Walker was found, and put in jail in Memphis until the mob there was ready for him.

The Memphis Commercial of Sunday, July 23, contains a full account of the tragedy from which the following extracts are made:

> At 12 o'clock last night, Lee Walker, who attempted to outrage Miss Mollie McCadden, last Tuesday morning, was taken from the county jail and hanged to a telegraph pole just north of the prison. All day rumors were afloat that with nightfall an attack would be made upon the jail, and as everyone anticipated that a vigorous resistance would be made, a conflict between the mob and the authorities was feared.
>
> At 10 o'clock Capt. O'Haver, Sergt. Horan and several patrolmen were on hand, but they could do nothing with the crowd. An attack by the mob was made on the door in the south wall, and it yielded. Sheriff McLendon and several of his men threw themselves into the breach, but two or three of the storming party shoved by. They were seized by the police, but were not subdued, the officers refraining from using their clubs. The entire mob might at first have been dispersed by ten policemen who would use their clubs, but the sheriff insisted that no violence be done.
>
> The mob got an iron rail and used it as a battering ram against the lobby doors. Sheriff McLendon tried to stop them, and some one of the mob knocked him down with a chair. Still he counseled moderation and would not order his deputies and the police to disperse the crowd by force. The pacific policy of the sheriff impressed the mob with the idea that the officers were afraid, or at least would do them no harm, and they redoubled their efforts, urged on by a big switchman. At 12 o'clock the door of the prison was broken in with a rail.
>
> As soon as the rapist was brought out of the door calls were heard for a rope; then some one shouted, "Burn him!"

But there was no time to make a fire. When Walker got into the lobby a dozen of the men began beating and stabbing him. He was half dragged, half carried to the corner of Front street and the alley between Sycamore and Mill, and hung to a telegraph pole.

Walker made a desperate resistance. Two men entered his cell first and ordered him to come forth. He refused, and they failing to drag him out, others entered. He scratched and bit his assailants, wounding several of them severely with his teeth. The mob retaliated by striking and cutting him with fists and knives. When he reached the steps leading down to the door he made another stand and was stabbed again and again. By the time he reached the lobby his power to resist was gone, and he was shoved along through the mob of yelling, cursing men and boys, who beat, spat upon and slashed the wretch-like demon. One of the leaders of the mob fell, and the crowd walked ruthlessly over him. He was badly hurt—a jawbone fractured and internal injuries inflicted. After the lynching friends took charge of him.

The mob proceeded north on Front street with the victim, stopping at Sycamore street to get a rope from a grocery. "Take him to the iron bridge on Main street," yelled several men. The men who had hold of the Negro were in a hurry to finish the job, however, and when they reached the telephone pole at the corner of Front street and the first alley north of Sycamore they stopped. A hastily improvised noose was slipped over the Negro's head, and several young men mounted a pile of lumber near the pole and threw the rope over one of the iron stepping pins. The Negro was lifted up until his feet were three feet above the ground, the rope was made taut, and a corpse dangled in midair. A big fellow who helped lead the mob pulled the Negro's legs until his neck cracked. The wretch's clothes had been torn off, and, as he swung, the man who pulled his legs mutilated the corpse.

One or two knife cuts, more or less, made little difference in the appearance of the dead rapist, however, for before the rope was around his neck his skin was cut almost to ribbons. One pistol shot was fired while the corpse was hanging. A dozen voices protested against the use of firearms, and there was no more shooting. The body was permitted to hang for half an hour, then it was cut down and the rope divided among those who lingered around the scene of the tragedy. Then it was suggested that the corpse be burned, and it was done. The entire performance, from the assault on the jail to the burning of the dead Negro was witnessed by a score or so of policemen and as many deputy sheriffs, but not a hand was lifted to stop the proceedings after the jail door yielded.

As the body hung to the telegraph pole, blood streaming down from the knife wounds in his neck, his hips and lower part of his legs also slashed with knives, the crowd hurled expletives at him, swung the body so that it was dashed against the pole, and, so far from the ghastly sight proving trying to the nerves, the crowd looked on with complaisance, if not with real pleasure. The Negro died hard. The neck was not broken, as the body was drawn up without being given a fall, and death came by strangulation. For fully ten minutes after he was strung up the chest heaved occasionally, and there were convulsive movements of the limbs. Finally he was pronounced dead, and a few minutes later Detective Richardson climbed on a pile of staves and cut the rope. The body fell in a ghastly heap, and the crowd laughed at the sound and crowded around the prostrate body, a few kicking the inanimate carcass.

Detective Richardson, who is also a deputy coroner, then proceeded to impanel the following jury of inquest: J. S. Moody, A. C. Waldran, B. J. Childs, J. N. House, Nelson Bills, T. L. Smith, and A. Newhouse. After viewing the body the inquest was adjourned without any testimony being taken until 9 o'clock this morning. The jury will meet at the coroner's office, 51 Beale street, up stairs, and decide on a verdict. If no witnesses are forthcoming, the jury will be able to arrive at a verdict just the same, as all members of it saw the lynching. Then some one raised the cry of "Burn him!" It was quickly taken up and soon resounded from a hundred throats. Detective Richardson, for a long time, single-handed, stood the crowd off. He talked and begged the men not to bring disgrace on the city by burning the body, arguing that all the vengeance possible had been wrought.

While this was going on a small crowd was busy starting a fire in the middle of the street. The material was handy. Some bundles of staves were taken from the adjoining lumber yard for kindling. Heavier wood was obtained from the same source, and coal oil from a neighboring grocery. Then the cries of "Burn him! Burn him!" were redoubled.

Half a dozen men seized the naked body. The crowd cheered. They marched to the fire, and giving the body a swing, it was landed in the middle of the fire. There was a cry for more wood, as the fire had begun to die owing to the long delay. Willing hands procured the wood, and it was piled up on the Negro, almost, for a time, obscuring him from view. The head was in plain view, as also were the limbs, and one arm which stood out high above the body, the elbow crooked, held in that position by a stick of wood. In a few moments the hands began to swell, then came great blisters over all the exposed parts of the body; then in places the flesh was burned away and the bones began to show through. It was a horrible sight, one which, perhaps, none there had ever witnessed before. It proved too much for a large part of the crowd and the majority of the mob left very shortly after the burning began.

But a large number stayed, and were not a bit set back by the sight of a human body being burned to ashes. Two or three white women, accompanied by their escorts, pushed to the front to obtain an unobstructed view, and looked on with astonishing coolness and nonchalance. One man and woman brought a little girl, not over 12 years old, apparently their daughter, to view a scene which was calculated to drive sleep from the child's eyes for many nights, if not to produce a permanent injury to her nervous system. The comments of the crowd were varied. Some remarked on the efficacy of this style of cure for rapists, others rejoiced that men's wives and daughters were now safe from this wretch. Some laughed as the flesh cracked and blistered, and while a large number pronounced the burning of a dead body as a useless episode, not in all that throng was a word of sympathy heard for the wretch himself.

The rope that was used to hang the Negro, and also that which was used to lead him from the jail, were eagerly sought by relic hunters. They almost fought for a chance to cut off a piece of rope, and in an incredibly short time both ropes had disappeared and were scattered in the pockets of the crowd in sections of from an inch to six inches long. Others of the relic hunters remained until the ashes cooled to obtain such ghastly relics as the teeth, nails, and bits of charred skin of the immolated victim of his own lust. After burning the body the mob tied a rope around the charred trunk and dragged it down Main street to the court house, where it was hanged to a center pole. The rope broke and the corpse dropped with a thud, but it was again hoisted, the charred legs barely touching the ground. The teeth were knocked out and the finger nails cut off as souvenirs. The crowd made so much noise that the police interfered. Undertaker Walsh was telephoned for, who took charge of the body and carried it to his establishment, where it will be prepared for burial in the potter's field today.

A prelude to this exhibition of 19th century barbarism was the following telegram received by the Chicago Inter Ocean, at 2 o'clock, Saturday afternoon—ten hours before the lynching:

"MEMPHIS, TENN., July 22, To Inter-Ocean, Chicago.

"Lee Walker, colored man, accused of raping white women, in jail here, will be taken out and burned by whites to-night.

Can you send Miss Ida Wells to write it up? Answer. R. M. Martin, with Public Ledger."

The Public Ledger is one of the oldest evening daily papers in Memphis, and this telegram shows that the intentions of the mob were well known long before they were executed. The Personnel of the mob is given by the Memphis Appeal-Avalanche. It says, "At first it seemed as if a crowd of roughs were the principals, but as it increased in size, men in all walks of life figured as leaders, although the majority were young men."

This was the punishment meted out to a Negro, charged, not with rape, but attempted assault, and without any proof as to his guilt, for the women were not given a chance to identify him. It was only a little less horrible than the burning alive of Henry Smith, at Paris, Texas, February 1st, 1893, or that of Edward Coy, in Texarkana, Texas, February 20, 1892. Both were charged with assault on white women, and both were tied to the stake and burned while yet alive, in the presence of ten thousand persons. In the case of Coy, the white woman in the case, applied the match, even while the victim protested his innocence.

The cut which is here given is the exact reproduction of the photograph taken at the scene of the lynching at Clanton, Alabama, August, 1891. The cause for which the man was hanged is given in the words of the mob which were written on the back of the photograph, and they are also given. This photograph was sent to Judge A. W. Tourgee, of Mayville, N. Y.

In some of these cases the mob affects to believe in the Negro's guilt. The world is told that the white woman in the case identifies him, or the prisoner "confesses." But in the lynching which took place in Barnwell County, South Carolina, April 24, 1893, the mob's victim, John Peterson,

Scene of Lynching at Clanton, Alabama, Aug. 1891.

This S — O — B was hung at Clanton Ala. Friday Aug 21st/91 for murdering a little boy in cold blood ... 35 ... cash He is a good specimen of "your" Black ... Chr ... can ... ... by "White Heathens" ... ... of "The Committee"

W. R. MARTIN,
Traveling Photographer.

Facsimile of back of photograph.

escaped and placed himself under Governor Tillman's protection; not only did he declare his innocence, but offered to
prove an alibi, by white witnesses. Before his witnesses could
be brought, the mob arrived at the Governor's mansion and
demanded the prisoner. He was given up, and although the
white woman in the case said he was not the man, he was
hanged 24 hours after, and over a thousand bullets fired into
his body, on the declaration that "a crime had been committed
and some one had to hang for it."

CHAPTER VI
HISTORY OF SOME CASES OF RAPE

It has been claimed that the Southern white women have been
slandered because, in defending the Negro race from the
charge that all colored men, who are lynched, only pay penalty
for assaulting women. It is certain that lynching mobs have
not only refused to give the Negro a chance to defend himself,
but have killed their victim with a full knowledge that the
relationship of the alleged assailant with the woman who
accused him, was voluntary and clandestine. As a matter of
fact, one of the prime causes of the Lynch Law agitation has
been a necessity for defending the Negro from this awful
charge against him. The defense has been necessary because
the apologists for outlawry insist that in no case has the
accusing woman been a willing consort of her paramour, who
is lynched because overtaken in wrong. It is well known,
however, that such is the case. In July of this year, 1894,
John Paul Bocock, a Southern white man living in New
York, and assistant editor of the New York Tribune, took
occasion to defy the publication of any instance where the
lynched Negro was the victim of a white woman's falsehood.

Such cases are not rare, but the press and people conversant with the facts, almost invariably suppress them.

The New York Sun of July 30th, 1894, contained a synopsis of interviews with leading congressmen and editors of the South. Speaker Crisp, of the House of Representatives, who was recently a Judge of the Supreme Court of Georgia, led in declaring that lynching seldom or never took place, save for vile crime against women and children. Dr. Hoss, editor of the leading organ of the Methodist Church South, published in its columns that it was his belief that more than three hundred women had been assaulted by Negro men within three months. When asked to prove his charges, or give a single case upon which his "belief" was founded, he said that he could do so, but the details were unfit for publication. No other evidence but his "belief" could be adduced to substantiate this grave charge, yet Bishop Haygood, in the Forum of October, 1893, quotes this "belief" in apology for lynching, and voluntarily adds: "It is my opinion that this is an underestimate." The "opinion" of this man, based upon a "belief," had greater weight coming from a man who has posed as a friend to "Our Brother in Black," and was accepted as authority. An interview of Miss Frances E. Willard, the great apostle of temperance, the daughter of abolitionists and a personal friend and helper of many individual colored people, has been quoted in support of the utterance of this calumny against a weak and defenseless race. In the New York Voice of October 23, 1890, after a tour in the South, where she was told all these things by the "best white people," she said: "The grogshop is the Negro's center of power. Better whisky and more of it is the rallying cry of great, dark-faced mobs. The colored race multiplies like the locusts of Egypt. The grogshop is its center of power. The safety of woman, of childhood, the home, is menaced in a thousand localities at this moment, so that men dare not go beyond the sight of their own roof-tree."

These charges so often reiterated, have had the effect of fastening the odium upon the race of a peculiar propensity for this foul crime. The Negro is thus forced to a defense of his good name, and this chapter will be devoted to the history of some of the cases where assault upon white women by Negroes is charged. He is not the aggressor in this fight, but the situation demands that the facts be given, and they will speak for themselves. Of the 1,115 Negro men, women and children hanged, shot and roasted alive from January 1st, 1882, to January 1st, 1894, inclusive, only 348 of that number were charged with rape. Nearly 700 of these persons were lynched for any other reason which could be manufactured by a mob wishing to indulge in a lynching bee.

A WHITE WOMAN'S FALSEHOOD

The Cleveland, Ohio, Gazette, January 16, 1892, gives an account of one of these cases of "rape."

Mrs. J. C. Underwood, the wife of a minister of Elyria, Ohio, accused an Afro-American of rape. She told her husband that during his absence in 1888, stumping the state for the Prohibition Party, the man came to the kitchen door, forced his way in the house and insulted her. She tried to drive him out with a heavy poker, but he overpowered and chloroformed her, and when she revived her clothing was torn and she was in a horrible condition. She did not know the man, but could identify him. She subsequently pointed out William Offett, a married man, who was arrested, and, being in Ohio, was granted a trial.

The prisoner vehemently denied the charge of rape, but confessed he went to Mrs. Underwood's residence at her invitation and was criminally intimate with her at her request.

This availed him nothing against the sworn testimony of a minister's wife, a lady of the highest respectability. He was found guilty, and entered the penitentiary, December 14, 1888, for fifteen years. Sometime afterwards the woman's remorse led her to confess to her husband that the man was innocent. These are her words: "I met Offett at the postoffice. It was raining. He was polite to me, and as I had several bundles in my arms he offered to carry them home for me, which he did. He had a strange fascination for me, and I invited him to call on me. He called, bringing chestnuts and candy for the children. By this means we got them to leave us alone in the room. Then I sat on his lap. He made a proposal to me and I readily consented. Why I did so I do not know, but that I did is true. He visited me several times after that and each time I was indiscreet. I did not care after the first time. In fact I could not have resisted, and had no desire to resist."

When asked by her husband why she told him she had been outraged, she said: "I had several reasons for telling you. One was the neighbors saw the fellow here, another was, I was afraid I had contracted a loathsome disease, and still another was that I feared I might give birth to a Negro baby. I hoped to save my reputation by telling you a deliberate lie." Her husband, horrified by the confession, had Offett, who had already served four years, released and secured a divorce.

There have been many such cases throughout the South, with the difference that the Southern white men in insensate fury wreak their vengeance without intervention of law upon the Negro who consorts with their women.

TRIED TO MANUFACTURE AN OUTRAGE

The Memphis (Tenn.) Ledger, of June 8, 1892, has the following: "If Lillie Bailey, a rather pretty white girl, seventeen years of age, who is now at the city hospital, would be somewhat less reserved about her disgrace there would be some very nauseating details in the story of her life. She is the mother of a little coon. The truth might reveal fearful depravity or the evidence of a rank outrage. She will not divulge the name of the man who has left such black evidence of her disgrace, and in fact says it is a matter in which there can be no interest to the outside world. She came to Memphis nearly three months ago, and was taken in at the Woman's Refuge in the southern part of the city. She remained there until a few weeks ago when the child was born. The ladies in charge of the Refuge were horrified. The girl was at once sent to the city hospital, where she has been since May 30th. She is a country girl. She came to Memphis from her father's farm, a short distance from Hernando, Miss. Just when she left there she would not say. In fact she says she came to Memphis from Arkansas, and says her home is in that state. She is rather good looking, has blue eyes, a low forehead and dark red hair. The ladies at the Woman's Refuge do not know anything about the girl further than what they learned when she was an inmate of the institution; and she would not tell much. When the child was born an attempt was made to get the girl to reveal the name of the Negro who had disgraced her, she obstinately refused and it was impossible to elicit any information from her on the subject."

Note the wording: "The truth might reveal fearful depravity or rank outrage." If it had been a white child or if Little Bailey had told a pitiful story of Negro outrage, it would have been a case of woman's weakness or assault and she could have remained at the Woman's Refuge. But a Negro child and to withhold its father's name and thus prevent the killing of another Negro "rapist" was a case of "fearful depravity." Had she revealed the father's name, he would have been lynched and his taking off charged to an assault upon a white woman.

BURNED ALIVE FOR ADULTERY

In Texarkana, Arkansas, Edward Coy was accused of assaulting a white woman. The press dispatches of February 18, 1892, told in detail how he was tied to a tree, the flesh cut from his body by men and boys, and after coal oil was poured over him, the woman he had assaulted gladly set fire to him, and 15,000 persons saw him burn to death. October 1st, the Chicago Inter Ocean contained the following account of that horror from the pen of the "Bystander"—Judge Albion W. Tourgee—as the result of his investigations:

"1. The woman who was paraded as victim of violence was of bad character; her husband was a drunkard and a gambler.

"2. She was publicly reported and generally known to have been criminally intimate with Coy for more than a year previous.

"3. She was compelled by threats, if not by violence, to make the charge against the victim.

"4. When she came to apply the match Coy asked her if she would burn him after they had 'been sweethearting' so long.

"5. A large majority of the 'superior' white men prominent in the affair are the reputed fathers of mulatto·children.

"These are not pleasant facts, but they are illustrative of the vital phase of the so-called 'race question,' which should properly be designated an earnest inquiry as to the best methods by which religion, science, law and political power may be employed to excuse injustice, barbarity and crime done to a people because of race and color. There can be no possible belief that these people were inspired by any consum-

ing zeal to vindicate God's law against miscegenationists of
the most practical sort. The woman was a willing partner in
the victim's guilt, and being of the 'superior' race must
naturally have been more guilty."

NOT IDENTIFIED BUT LYNCHED

February 11th, 1893, there occurred in Shelby county, Tennessee, the fourth Negro lynching within fifteen months. The
three first were lynched in the city of Memphis for firing on
white men in self-defense. This Negro, Richard Neal, was
lynched a few miles from the city limits, and the following
is taken from the Memphis (Tenn.) Scimitar:

"As the Scimitar stated on Saturday the Negro, Richard
Neal, who raped Mrs. Jack White near Forest Hill, in this
county, was lynched by a mob of about 200 white citizens of
the neighborhood. Sheriff McLendon, accompanied by Deputies Perkins, App and Harvey and a Scimitar reporter,
arrived on the scene of the execution about 3:30 in the
afternoon. The body was suspended from the first limb of a
post oak tree by a new quarter inch grass rope. A hangman's
knot, evidently tied by an expert, fitted snugly under the left
ear of the corpse, and a new hame string pinioned the victim's
arms behind him. His legs were not tied. The body was
perfectly limber when the Sheriff's posse cut it down and
retained enough heat to warm the feet of Deputy Perkins,
whose road cart was converted into a hearse. On arriving
with the body at Forest Hill the Sheriff made a bargain with
a stalwart young man with a blonde mustache and deep blue
eyes, who told the Scimitar reporter that he was the leader of
the mob, to haul the body to Germantown for $3.

"When within half-a-mile of Germantown the Sheriff and
posse were overtaken by Squire McDonald of Collierville,
who had come down to hold the inquest. The Squire had his

jury with him, and it was agreed for the convenience of all parties that he should proceed with the corpse to Germantown and conduct the inquiry as to the cause of death. He did so, and a verdict of death from hanging by parties unknown was returned in due form.

"The execution of Neal was done deliberately and by the best people of the Collierville, Germantown and Forest Hill neighborhoods, without passion or exhibition of anger.

"He was arrested on Friday about ten o'clock, by Constable Bob Cash, who carried him before Mrs. White. She said: 'I think he is the man. I am almost certain of it. If he isn't the man he is exactly like him.'

"The Negro's coat was torn also, and there were other circumstances against him. The committee returned and made its report, and the chairman put the question of guilt or innocence to a vote.

"All who thought the proof strong enough to warrant execution were invited to cross over to the other side of the road. Everybody but four or five negroes crossed over.

"The committee then placed Neal on a mule with his arms tied behind him, and proceeded to the scene of the crime, followed by the mob. The rope, with a noose already prepared, was tied to the limb nearest the spot where the unpardonable sin was committed, and the doomed man's mule was brought to a standstill beneath it.

"Then Neal confessed. He said he was the right man, but denied that he used force or threats to accomplish his purposes. It was a matter of purchase, he claimed, and said the price paid was twenty-five cents. He warned the colored men present to beware of white women and resist temptation, for to yield to their blandishments or to the passions of men, meant death.

"While he was speaking, Mrs. White came from her home

and calling Constable Cash to one side, asked if he could not save the Negro's life. The reply was, 'No,' and Mrs. White returned to the house.

"When all was in readiness, the husband of Neal's victim leaped upon the mule's back and adjusted the rope around the Negro's neck. No cap was used, and Neal showed no fear, nor did he beg for mercy. The mule was struck with a whip and bounded out from under Neal, leaving him suspended in the air with his feet about three feet from the ground."

DELIVERED TO THE MOB BY THE GOVERNOR OF THE STATE

John Peterson, near Denmark, S. C., was suspected of rape, but escaped, went to Columbia, and placed himself under Gov. Tillman's protection, declaring he too could prove an alibi by white witnesses. A white reporter hearing his declaration volunteered to find these witnesses, and telegraphed the governor that he would be in Columbia with them on Monday. In the meantime the mob at Denmark, learning Peterson's whereabouts, went to the governor and demanded the prisoner. Gov. Tillman, who had during his canvas for re-election the year before, declared that he would lead a mob to lynch a Negro that assaulted a white woman, gave Peterson to the mob. He was taken back to Denmark, and the white girl in the case as positively declared that he was not the man. But the verdict of the mob was that "the crime had been committed and somebody had to hang for it, and if he, Peterson, was not guilty of that he was of some other crime," and he was hung, and his body riddled with 1,000 bullets.

LYNCHED AS A WARNING

Alabama furnishes a case in point. A colored man named Daniel Edwards, lived near Selma, Alabama, and worked for a family of a farmer near that place. This resulted in an intimacy between the young man and a daughter of the householder, which finally developed in the disgrace of the girl. After the birth of the child, the mother disclosed the fact that Edwards was its father. The relationship had been sustained for more than a year, and yet this colored man was apprehended, thrown into jail from whence he was taken by a mob of one hundred neighbors and hung to a tree and his body riddled with bullets. A dispatch which describes the lynching, ends as follows. "Upon his back was found pinned this morning the following: 'Warning to all Negroes that are too intimate with white girls. This the work of one hundred best citizens of the South Side.' "

There can be no doubt from the announcement made by this "one hundred best citizens" that they understood full well the character of the relationship which existed between Edwards and the girl, but when the dispatches were sent out, describing the affair, it was claimed that Edwards was lynched for rape.

SUPPRESSING THE TRUTH

In a county in Mississippi during the month of July the Associated Press dispatches sent out a report that the sheriff's eight year old daughter had been assaulted by a big, black, burly brute who had been promptly lynched. The facts which have since been investigated show that the girl was more than eighteen years old and that she was discovered by her father in this young man's room who was a servant on the place. But these facts the Associated Press has not given to the world, nor did the same agency acquaint the world with the fact that a Negro youth who was lynched in Tuscumbia, Ala., the same year on the same charge told the white girl who accused him before the mob, that he had met her in the woods often by appointment. There is a young mulatto in one of the

State prisons of the South to-day who is there by charge of a young white woman to screen herself. He is a college graduate and had been corresponding with, and clandestinely visiting her until he was surprised and run out of her room en deshabille by her father. He was put in prison in another town to save his life from the mob and his lawyer advised that it were better to save his life by pleading guilty to charges made and being sentenced for years, than to attempt a defense by exhibiting the letters written him by this girl. In the latter event, the mob would surely murder him, while there was a chance for his life by adopting the former course. Names, places and dates are not given for the same reason.

The excuse has come to be so safe, it is not surprising that a Philadelphia girl, beautiful and well educated, and of good family, should make a confession published in all the daily papers of that city October, 1894, that she had been stealing for some time, and that to cover one of her thefts, she had said she had been bound and gagged in her father's house by a colored man, and money stolen therefrom by him. Had this been done in many localities, it would only have been necessary for her to "identify" the first Negro in that vicinity, to have brought about another lynching bee.

A VILE SLANDER WITH SCANT RETRACTION

The following published in the Cleveland (Ohio) Leader of Oct. 23d, 1894, only emphasizes our demand that a fair trial shall be given those accused of crime, and the protection of the law be extended until time for a defense be granted.

"The sensational story sent out last night from Hicksville that a Negro had outraged a little four-year-old girl proves to be a base canard. The correspondents who went into the details should have taken the pains to investigate, and the officials should have known more of the matter before they gave out such grossly exaggerated information.

"The Negro, Charles O'Neil, had been working for a couple of women and, it seems, had worked all winter without being remunerated. There is a little girl, and the girl's mother and grandmother evidently started the story with idea of frightening the Negro out of the country and thus balancing accounts. The town was considerably wrought up and for a time things looked serious. The accused had a preliminary hearing to-day and not an iota of evidence was produced to indicate that such a crime had been committed, or that he had even attempted such an outrage. The village marshal was frightened nearly out of his wits and did little to quiet the excitement last night.

"The affair was an outrage on the Negro, at the expense of innocent childhood, a brainless fabrication from start to finish."

The original story was sent throughout this country and England, but the Cleveland Leader, so far as known, is the only journal which has published these facts in refutation of the slander so often published against the race.

Not only is it true that many of the alleged cases of rape against the Negro, are like the foregoing, but the same crime committed by white men against Negro women and girls, is never punished by mob or the law. A leading journal in South Carolina openly said some months ago that "it is not the same thing for a white man to assault a colored woman as for a colored man to assault a white woman, because the colored woman had no finer feelings nor virtue to be outraged!" Yet colored women have always had far more reason to complain of white men in this respect than ever white women have had of Negroes.

ILLINOIS HAS A LYNCHING

In the month of June, 1893, the proud commonwealth of Illinois joined the ranks of Lynching States. Illinois, which gave to the world the immortal heroes, Lincoln, Grant and Logan, trailed its banner of justice in the dust—dyed its hands red in the blood of a man not proven guilty of crime.

June 3, 1893, the country about Decatur, one of the largest cities of the state was startled with the cry that a white woman had been assaulted by a colored tramp. Three days later a colored man named Samuel Bush was arrested and put in jail. A white man testified that Bush, on the day of the assault, asked him where he could get a drink and he pointed to the house where the farmer's wife was subsequently said to have been assaulted. Bush said he went to the well but did not go near the house, and did not assault the woman. After he was arrested the alleged victim did not see him to identify him— he was presumed to be guilty.

The citizens determined to kill him. The mob gathered, went to the jail, met with no resistance, took the suspected man, dragged him out tearing every stitch of clothing from his body, then hanged him to a telegraph pole. The grand jury refused to indict the lynchers though the names of over twenty persons who were leaders in the mob were well known. In fact twenty-two persons were indicted, but the grand jurors and the prosecuting attorney disagreed as to the form of the indictments, which caused the jurors to change their minds. All indictments were reconsidered and the matter was dropped. Not one of the dozens of men prominent in that murder have suffered a whit more inconvenience for the butchery of that man, than they would have suffered for shooting a dog.

COLOR LINE JUSTICE

In Baltimore, Maryland, a gang of white ruffians assaulted a respectable colored girl who was out walking with a young

man of her own race. They held her escort and outraged the
girl. It was a deed dastardly enough to arouse Southern blood,
which gives its horror of rape as excuse for lawlessness, but
she was a colored woman. The case went to the courts and
they were acquitted.

In Nashville, Tennessee, there was a white man, Pat
Hanifin, who outraged a little colored girl, and from the
physical injuries received she was ruined for life. He was
jailed for six months, discharged, and is now a detective in
that city. In the same city, last May, a white man outraged a
colored girl in a drug store. He was arrested and released on
bail at the trial. It was rumored that five hundred colored
men had organized to lynch him. Two hundred and fifty
white citizens armed themselves with Winchesters and guarded
him. A cannon was placed in front of his home, and the
Buchanan Rifles (State Militia) ordered to the scene for his
protection. The colored mob did not show up. Only two
weeks before, Eph. Grizzard, who had only been charged
with rape upon a white woman, had been taken from the jail,
with Governor Buchanan and the police and militia standing
by, dragged through the streets in broad daylight, knives
plunged into him at every step, and with every fiendish
cruelty that a frenzied mob could devise, he was at last swung
out on the bridge with hands cut to pieces as he tried to climb
up the stanchions. A naked, bloody example of the blood-
thirstiness of the nineteenth century civilization of the Athens
of the South! No cannon nor military were called out in his
defense. He dared to visit a white woman.

At the very moment when these civilized whites were
announcing their determination "to protect their wives and
daughters," by murdering Grizzard, a white man was in the
same jail for raping eight-year-old Maggie Reese, a colored
girl. He was not harmed. The "honor" of grown women

who were glad enough to be supported by the Grizzard boys and Ed Coy, as long as the liaison was not known, needed protection; they were white. The outrage upon helpless childhood needed no avenging in this case; she was black.

A white man in Guthrie, Oklahoma Territory, two months after inflicted such injuries upon another colored girl that she died. He was not punished, but an attempt was made in the same town in the month of June to lynch a colored man who visited a white woman.

In Memphis, Tennessee, in the month of June, Ellerton L. Dorr, who is the husband of Russell Hancock's widow, was arrested for attempted rape on Mattie Cole, a neighbor's cook; he was only prevented from accomplishing his purpose by the appearance of Mattie's employer. Dorr's friends say he was drunk and not responsible for his actions. The grand jury refused to indict him and he was discharged.

In Tallahassee, Florida, a colored girl, Charlotte Gilliam, was assaulted by white men. Her father went to have a warrant for their arrest issued, but the judge refused to issue it.

In Bowling Green, Virginia, Moses Christopher, a colored lad, was charged with assault, September 10. He was indicted, tried, convicted and sentenced to death in one day. In the same state at Danville, two weeks before—August 29, Thomas J. Penn, a white man, committed a criminal assault upon Linda Hanna, a twelve-year-old colored girl, but he has not been tried, certainly not killed either by the law or the mob.

In Surrey county, Virginia, C. L. Brock, a white man, criminally assaulted a ten-year-old colored girl, and threatened to kill her if she told. Notwithstanding, she confessed to her aunt, Mrs. Alice Bates, and the white brute added further crime by killing Mrs. Bates when she upbraided him about his crime upon her niece. He emptied the contents of his revolver into her body as she lay. Brock has never been apprehended, and no effort has been made to do so by the legal authorities.

But even when punishment is meted out by law to white villains for this horrible crime, it is seldom or never that capital punishment is invoked. Two cases just clipped from the daily papers will suffice to show how this crime is punished when committed by white offenders and black.

LOUISVILLE, KY., October 19.—Smith Young, colored, was to-day sentenced to be hanged. Young criminally assaulted a six-year-old child about six months ago.

Jacques Blucher, the Pontiac Frenchman who was arrested at that place for a criminal assault on his daughter Fanny on July 29 last, pleaded nolo contendere when placed on trial at East Greenwich, near Providence, R.I., Tuesday, and was sentenced to five years in State Prison.

Charles Wilson was convicted of assault upon seven-year-old Mamie Keys in Philadelphia, in October, and sentenced to ten years in prison. He was white. Indianapolis courts sentenced a white man in September to eight years in prison for assault upon a twelve-year-old white girl.

April 24, 1893, a lynching was set for Denmark, S. C., on the charge of rape. A white girl accused a Negro of assault, and the mob was about to lynch him. A few hours before the lynching three reputable white men rode into the town and solemnly testified that the accused Negro was at work with them 25 miles away on the day and at the hour the crime had been committed. He was accordingly set free. A white person's word is taken as absolutely for as against a Negro.

CHAPTER VII
THE CRUSADE JUSTIFIED

(APPEAL FROM AMERICA TO THE WORLD)

It has been urged in criticism of the movement appealing to the English people for sympathy and support in our crusade against Lynch Law that our action was unpatriotic, vindictive and useless. It is not a part of the plan of this pamphlet to make any defense for that crusade nor to indict any apology for the motives which led to the presentation of the facts of American lynchings to the world at large. To those who are not willfully blind and unjustly critical, the record of more than a thousand lynchings in ten years is enough to justify any peaceable movement tending to ameliorate the conditions which led to this unprecedented slaughter of human beings.

If America would not hear the cry of men, women and children whose dying groans ascended to heaven praying for relief, but not only for them but for others who might soon be treated as they, then certainly no fair-minded person can charge disloyalty to those who make an appeal to the civilization of the world for such sympathy and help as it is possible to extend. If stating the facts of these lynchings, as they appeared from time to time in the white newspapers of America—the news gathered by white correspondents, compiled by white press bureaus and disseminated among white people—shows any vindictiveness, then the mind which so charges is not amenable to argument.

But it is the desire of this pamphlet to urge that the crusade started and thus far continued has not been useless, but has been blessed with the most salutary results. The many evidences of the good results can not here be mentioned, but the thoughtful student of the situation can himself find ample proof. There need not here be mentioned the fact that for the first time since lynching began, has there been any occasion for the governors of the several states to speak out in reference to these crimes against law and order.

No matter how heinous the act of the lynchers may have been, it was discussed only for a day or so and then dismissed from the attention of the public. In one or two instances the governor has called attention to the crime, but the civil processes entirely failed to bring the murderers to justice. Since the crusade against lynching was started, however, governors of states, newspapers, senators and representatives and bishops of churches have all been compelled to take cognizance of the prevalence of this crime and to speak in one way or another in the defense of the charge against this barbarism in the United States. This has not been because there was any latent spirit of justice voluntarily asserting itself, especially in those who do the lynching, but because the entire American people now feel, both North and South, that they are objects in the gaze of the civilized world and that for every lynching humanity asks that America render its account to civilization and itself.

AWFUL BARBARISM IGNORED

Much has been said during the months of September and October of 1894 about the lynching of six colored men who on suspicion of incendiarism were made the victims of a most barbarous massacre. They were arrested, one by one, by officers of the law; they were handcuffed and chained together and by the officers of the law loaded in a wagon and deliberately driven into an ambush where a mob of lynchers awaited them. At the time and upon the chosen spot, in the darkness of the night and far removed from the habitation of any human soul, the wagon was halted and the mob fired upon the six manacled men, shooting them to death as no humane person would have shot dogs. Chained together as they were, in their awful struggles after the first volley, the victims tumbled out of the wagon upon the ground and there in the mud, struggling in their death throes, the victims were made the target of the murderous shotguns, which fired into the writhing, struggling, dying mass of humanity, until every spark of life was gone. Then the officers of the law who had them in charge, drove away to give the alarm and to tell the world that they had been waylaid and their prisoners forcibly taken from them and killed.

It has been claimed that the prompt, vigorous and highly commendable steps of the governor of the State of Tennessee and the judge having jurisdiction over the crime, and of the citizens of Memphis generally, was the natural revolt of the humane conscience in that section of the country, and the determination of honest and honorable men to rid the community of such men as those who were guilty of this terrible massacre. It has further been claimed that this vigorous uprising of the people and this most commendably prompt action of the civil authorities, is ample proof that the American people will not tolerate the lynching of innocent men, and that in cases where brutal lynchings have not been promptly dealt with, the crimes on the part of the victims were such as to put them outside the pale of humanity and that the world considered their death a necessary sacrifice for the good of all.

But this line of argument can in no possible way be truthfully sustained. The lynching of the six men in 1894, barbarous as it was, was in no way more barbarous than took nothing more than a passing notice. It was only the other lynchings which preceded it, and of which the public fact that the attention of the civilized world has been called to lynching in America which made the people of Tennessee feel the absolute necessity for a prompt, vigorous and just arraignment of all the murderers connected with that crime. Lynching is no longer "Our Problem," it is the problem of the civilized world, and Tennessee could not afford to refuse the legal measures which Christianity demands shall be used for the punishment of crime.

MEMPHIS THEN AND NOW

Only two years prior to the massacre of the six men near Memphis, that same city took part in a massacre in every way as bloody and brutal as that of September last. It was the murder of three young colored men and who were known to be among the most honorable, reliable, worthy and peaceable colored citizens of the community. All of them were engaged in the mercantile business, being members of a corporation which conducted a large grocery store, and one of the three being a letter carrier in the employ of the government. These three men were arrested for resisting an attack of a mob upon their store, in which melee none of the assailants, who had armed themselves for their devilish deeds by securing court processes, were killed or even seriously injured. But these three men were put in jail, and on three or four nights after their incarceration a mob of less than a dozen men, by collusion with the civil authorities, entered the jail, took the three men from the custody of the law and shot them to death. Memphis knew of this awful crime, knew then and knows today who the men were who committed it, and yet not the first step was ever taken to apprehend the guilty wretches who walk the streets today with the brand of murder upon their foreheads, but as safe from harm as the most upright citizen of that community. Memphis would have been just as calm and complacent and self-satisfied over the murder of the six colored men in 1894 as it was over these three colored men in 1892, had it not recognized the fact that to escape the brand of barbarism it had not only to speak its denunciation but to act vigorously in vindication of its name.

AN ALABAMA HORROR IGNORED

A further instance of this absolute disregard of every principle of justice and the indifference to the barbarism of Lynch Law may be cited here, and is furnished by white residents in the city of Carrolton, Alabama. Several cases of arson had been discovered, and in their search for the guilty parties, suspicion was found to rest upon three men and a woman. The four suspects were Paul Hill, Paul Archer, William Archer, his brother, and a woman named Emma Fair. The prisoners were apprehended, earnestly asserted their innocence, but went to jail without making any resistance. They claimed that they could easily prove their innocence upon trial.

One would suspect that the civilization which defends itself against the barbarisms of Lynch Law by stating that it lynches human beings only when they are guilty of awful attacks upon women and children, would have been very careful to have given these four prisoners, who were simply charged with arson, a fair trial, to which they were entitled upon every principle of law and humanity. Especially would this seem to be the case when it is considered that one of the prisoners charged was a woman, and if the Nineteenth Century has shown any advancement upon any lines of human action, it is pre-eminently shown in its reverence, respect and protection of its womanhood. But the people of Alabama failed to have any regard for womanhood whatever.

The three men and the woman were put in jail to await trial. A few days later it was rumored that they were to be subjects of Lynch Law, and, sure enough, at night a mob of lynchers went to the jail, not to avenge any awful crime against womanhood, but to kill four people who had been suspected of setting a house on fire. They were caged in their cells, helpless and defenseless; they were at the mercy of civilized white Americans, who, armed with shotguns, were there to maintain the majesty of American law. And most effectively was their duty done by these splendid representatives of Governor Fishback's brave and honorable white southerners, who resent "outside interference." They lined themselves up in the most effective manner and poured volley after volley into the bodies of their helpless, pleading victims, who in their bolted prison cells could no nothing but suffer and die. Then these lynchers went quietly away and the bodies of the woman and three men were taken out and buried with as little ceremony as men would bury hogs.

No one will say that the massacre near Memphis in 1894 was any worse than this bloody crime of Alabama in 1892. The details of this shocking affair were given to the public by the press, but public sentiment was not moved to action in the least; it was only a matter of a day's notice and then went to swell the list of murders which stand charged against the noble, Christian people of Alabama.

AMERICA AWAKENED

But there is now an awakened conscience throughout the land, and Lynch Law can not flourish in the future as it has in the past. The close of the year 1894 witnessed an aroused interest, an assertative humane principle which must tend to the extirpation of that crime. The awful butchery last mentioned failed to excite more than a passing comment in 1894 [1892], but far different is it today. Gov. Jones, of Alabama, in 1893 dared to speak out against the rule of the mob in no uncertain terms. His address indicated a most helpful result of the present agitation. In face of the many denials of the outrages on the one hand and apologies for lynchers on the other, Gov. Jones admits the awful lawlessness charged and refuses to join in the infamous plea made to condone the crime. No stronger nor more effective words have been said than those following from Gov. Jones.

"While the ability of the state to deal with open revolts against the supremacy of its laws has been ably demonstrated, I regret that deplorable acts of violence have been perpetrated, in at least four instances, within the past two years by mobs, whose sudden work and quick dispersions rendered it impossible to protect their victims. Within the past two years nine prisoners, who were either in jail or in the custody of the officers, have been taken from them without resistance and put to death. There was doubt of the guilt of the defendants in most of these cases, and few of them were charged with capital offenses. None of them involved the crime of rape. The largest rewards allowed by law were offered for the apprehension of the offenders, and officers were charged to a vigilant performance of their duties, and aided in some instances by the services of skilled detectives; but not a single arrest has been made and the grand juries in these counties have returned no bills of indictment. This would indicate either that local public sentiment approved these acts of violence or was too weak to punish them, or that the officers charged with that duty were in some way lacking in their performance. The evil cannot be cured or remedied by silence as to its existence. Unchecked, it will continue until it becomes a reproach to our good name, and a menace to our prosperity and peace; and it behooves you to exhaust all remedies within your power to find better preventives for such crimes."

A FRIENDLY WARNING

From England comes a friendly voice which must give to every patriotic citizen food for earnest thought. Writing from London, to the Chicago Inter Ocean, Nov. 25, 1894, the distinguished compiler of our last census, Hon. Robert F. Porter, gives the American people a most interesting review of the anti-lynching crusade in England, submitting editorial opinions from all sections of England and Scotland, showing the consensus of British opinion on this subject. It hardly need be said, that without exception, the current of English thought deprecates the rule of mob law, and the conscience of England is shocked by the revelation made during the present crusade. In his letter Mr. Porter says:

"While some English journals have joined certain American journals in ridiculing the well-meaning people who have formed the anti-lynching committee, there is a deep under current on this subject which is injuring the Southern States far more than those who have not been drawn into the question of English investment for the South as I have can surmise. This feeling is by no means all sentiment. An Englishman whose word and active co-operation could send a million sterling to any legitimate Southern enterprise said the other day: 'I will not invest a farthing in States where these horrors occur. I have no particular sympathy with the anti-lynching committee, but such outrages indicate to my mind that where life is held to be of such little value there is even less assurance that the laws will protect property. As I understand it the States, not the national government, control in such matters, and where those laws are strongest there is the best field for British capital.' "

Probably the most bitter attack on the anti-lynching committee has come from the London Times. Those Southern

Governors who had their bombastic letters published in the Times, with favorable editorial comment, may have had their laugh at the anti-lynchers here too soon. A few days ago, in commenting on an interesting communication from Richard H. Edmonds, editor of the Manufacturer's Record, setting forth the industrial advantages of the Southern States, which was published in its columns, the Times says: "Without in any way countenancing the impertinence of 'anti-lynching' committee, we may say that a state of things in which the killing of Negroes by blood-thirsty mobs is an incident of not unfrequent occurrence is not conducive to success in industry. Its existence, however, is a serious obstacle to the success of the South in industry; for even now Negro labor, which means at best inefficient labor, must be largely relied on there, and its efficiency must be still further diminished by spasmodic terrorism.

"Those interested in the development of the resources of the Southern States, and no one in proportion to his means has shown more faith in the progress of the South than the writer of this article, must take hold of this matter earnestly and intelligently. Sneering at the anti-lynching committee will do no good. Back of them, in fact, if not in form, is the public opinion of Great Britain. Even the Times cannot deny this. It may not be generally known in the United States, but while the Southern and some of the Northern newspapers are making a target of Miss Wells, the young colored woman who started this English movement, and cracking their jokes at the expense of Miss Florence Balgarnie, who, as honorable secretary, conducts the committee's correspondence, the strongest sort of sentiment is really at the back of the movement. Here we have crystallized every phase of political opinion. Extreme Unionists like the Duke of Argyll and advanced home rulers such as Justin McCarthy; Thomas Burt, the labor leader;

Herbert Burrows, the Socialist, and Tom Mann, representing all phases of the Labor party, are co-operating with conservatives like Sir T. Eldon Gorst. But the real strength of this committee is not visible to the casual observer. As a matter of fact it represents many of the leading and most powerful British journals. A. E. Fletcher is editor of the London Daily Chronicle; P. W. Clayden is prominent in the counsels of the London Daily News; Professor James Stuart is Gladstone's great friend and editor of the London Star; William Byles is editor and proprietor of the Bradford Observer; Sir Hugh Gilzen Reid is a leading Birmingham editor; in short, this committee has secured if not the leading editors, certainly important and warm friends, representing the Manchester Guardian, the Leeds Mercury, the Plymouth Western News, Newcastle Leader, the London Daily Graphic, the Westminster Gazette, the London Echo, a host of minor papers all over the kingdom, and practically the entire religious press of the kingdom.

"The greatest victory for the anti-lynchers comes this morning in the publication in the London Times of William Lloyd Garrison's letter. This letter will have immense effect here. It may have been printed in full in the United States, but nevertheless I will quote a paragraph which will strengthen the anti-lynchers greatly in their crusade here:

" 'A year ago the South derided and resented Northern protests; to-day it listens, explains and apologizes for its uncovered cruelties. Surely a great triumph for a little woman to accomplish! It is the power of truth simply and unreservedly spoken, for her language was inadequate to describe the horrors exposed.'

"If the Southern states are wise, and I say this with the earnestness of a friend and one who has built a home in the mountain regions of the South and thrown his lot in with them, they will not only listen, but stop lawlessness of all kinds. If they do, and thus secure the confidence of Englishmen, we may in the next decade realize some of the hopes for the new South we have so fondly cherished."

CHAPTER VIII
MISS WILLARD'S ATTITUDE

No class of American citizens stands in greater need of the humane and thoughtful consideration of all sections of our country than do the colored people, nor does any class exceed us in the measure of grateful regard for acts of kindly interest in our behalf. It is, therefore, to us, a matter of keen regret that a Christian organization so large and influential as the Woman's Christian Temperance Union, should refuse to give its sympathy and support to our oppressed people who ask no further favor than the promotion of public sentiment which shall guarantee to every person accused of crime the safeguard of a fair and impartial trial, and protection from butchery by brutal mobs. Accustomed as we are to the indifference and apathy of Christian people, we would bear this instance of ill fortune in silence, had not Miss Willard gone out of her way to antagonize the cause so dear to our hearts by including in her Annual Address to the W. C. T. U. Convention at Cleveland, November 5, 1894, a studied, unjust and wholly unwarranted attack upon our work.

In her address Miss Willard said:

> The zeal for her race of Miss Ida B. Wells, a bright young colored woman, has, it seems to me, clouded her perception as to who were her friends and well-wishers in all highminded and legitimate efforts to banish the abomination of lynching and torture from the land of the free and the home of the brave. It is my firm belief that in the statements made

by Miss Wells concerning white women having taken the initiative in nameless acts between the races she has put an imputation upon half the white race in this country that is unjust, and, save in the rarest exceptional instances, wholly without foundation. This is the unanimous opinion of the most disinterested and observant leaders of opinion whom I have consulted on the subject, and I do not fear to say that the laudable efforts she is making are greatly handicapped by statements of this kind, nor to urge her as a friend and well-wisher to banish from her vocabulary all such allusions as a source of weakness to the cause she has at heart.

This paragraph, brief as it is, contains two statements which have not the slightest foundation in fact. At no time, nor in any place, have I made statements "concerning white women having taken the initiative in nameless acts between the races." Further, at no time, or place nor under any circumstance, have I directly or inferentially "put an imputation upon half the white race in this country" and I challenge this "friend and well-wisher" to give proof of the truth of her charge. Miss Willard protests against lynching in one paragraph and then, in the next, deliberately misrepresents my position in order that she may criticise a movement, whose only purpose is to protect our oppressed race from vindictive slander and Lynch Law.

What I have said and what I now repeat—in answer to her first charge—is, that colored men have been lynched for assault upon women, when the facts were plain that the relationship between the victim lynched and the alleged victim of his assault was voluntary, clandestine and illicit. For that very reason we maintain, that, in every section of our land, the accused should have a fair, impartial trial, so that a man who is colored shall not be hanged for an offense, which, if he were white, would not be adjudged a crime. Facts cited in another chapter—"History of Some Cases of Rape"—

amply maintain this position. The publication of these facts in defense of the good name of the race casts no "imputation upon half the white race in this country" and no such imputation can be inferred except by persons deliberately determined to be unjust.

But this is not the only injury which this cause has suffered at the hands of our "friend and well-wisher." It has been said that the Women's Christian Temperance Union, the most powerful organization of women in America, was misrepresented by me while I was in England. Miss Willard was in England at the time and knowing that no such misrepresentation came to her notice, she has permitted that impression to become fixed and widespread, when a word from her would have made the facts plain.

I never at any time or place or in any way misrepresented that organization. When asked what concerted action had been taken by churches and great moral agencies in America to put down Lynch Law, I was compelled in truth to say that no such action had occurred, that pulpit, press and moral agencies in the main were silent and for reasons known to themselves, ignored the awful conditions which to the English people appeared so abhorrent. Then the question was asked what the great moral reformers like Miss Frances Willard and Mr. Moody had done to suppress Lynch Law and again I answered—nothing. That Mr. Moody had never said a word against lynching in any of his trips to the South, or in the North either, so far as was known, and that Miss Willard's only public utterance on the situation had condoned lynching and other unjust practices of the South against the Negro. When proof of these statements was demanded, I sent a letter containing a copy of the New York Voice, Oct. 23, 1890, in which appeared Miss Willard's own words of wholesale slander against the colored race and condonation of Southern white people's outrages against us. My letter in part reads as follows:

> But Miss Willard, the great temperance leader, went even further in putting the seal of her approval upon the southerners' method of dealing with the Negro. In October, 1890, the Women's Christian Temperance Union held its national meeting at Atlanta, Georgia. It was the first time in the history of the organization that it had gone south for a national meeting, and met the southerners in their own homes. They were welcomed with open arms. The governor of the state and the legislature gave special audiences in the halls of state legislation to the temperance workers. They set out to capture the northerners to their way of seeing things, and without troubling to hear the Negro side of the question, these temperance people accepted the white man's story of the problem with which he had to deal. State organizers were appointed that year, who had gone through the southern states since then, but in obedience to southern prejudices have confined their work to white persons only. It is only after Negroes are in prison for crimes that efforts of these temperance women are exerted without regard to "race, color, or previous condition." No "ounce of prevention" is used in their case; they are black, and if these women went among the Negroes for this work, the whites would not receive them. Except here and there, are found no temperance workers of the Negro race; "the great dark-faced mobs" are left the easy prey of the saloonkeepers.
>
> There was pending in the National Congress at this time a Federal Election Bill, the object being to give the National Government control of the national elections in the several states. Had this bill become a law, the Negro, whose vote has been systematically suppressed since 1875 in the southern states, would have had the protection of the National Government, and his vote counted. The South would have been no longer "solid"; the Southerners saw that the balance of

power which they unlawfully held in the House of Representatives and the Electoral College, based on the Negro population, would be wrested from them. So they nick-named the pending elections law the "Force Bill"—probably because it would force them to disgorge their ill-gotten political gains—and defeated it. While it was being discussed, the question was submitted to Miss Willard: "What do you think of the race problem and the Force Bill?"

Said Miss Willard: "Now, as to the 'race problem' in its minified, current meaning, I am a true lover of the southern people—have spoken and worked in, perhaps, 200 of their towns and cities; have been taken into their love and confidence at scores of hospitable firesides; have heard them pour out their hearts in the splendid frankness of their impetuous natures. And I have said to them at such times: 'When I go North there will be wafted to you no word from pen or voice that is not loyal to what we are saying here and now.' Going South, a woman, a temperance woman, and a Northern temperance woman—three great barriers to their good will yonder—I was received by them with a confidence that was one of the most delightful surprises of my life. I think we have wronged the South, though we did not mean to do so. The reason was, in part, that we had irreparably wronged ourselves by putting no safeguards on the ballot box at the North that would sift out alien illiterates. They rule our cities today; the saloon is their palace, and the toddy stick their sceptre. It is not fair that they should vote, nor is it fair that a plantation Negro, who can neither read nor write, whose ideas are bounded by the fence of his own field and the price of his own mule, should be entrusted with the ballot. We ought to have put an educational test upon that ballot from the first. The Anglo-Saxon race will never submit to be dominated by the Negro so long as his altitude reaches no higher than the personal liberty of the saloon, and the power of appreciating the amount of liquor that a dollar will buy. New England would no more submit to this than South

Carolina. 'Better whisky and more of it' has been the rallying cry of great dark-faced mobs in the Southern localities where local option was snowed under by the colored vote. Temperance has no enemy like that, for it is unreasoning and unreasonable. Tonight it promises in a great congregation to vote for temperance at the polls tomorrow; but tomorrow twenty-five cents changes that vote in favor of the liquor-seller.

"I pity the southerners, and I believe the great mass of them are as conscientious and kindly-intentioned toward the colored man as an equal number of white church-members of the North. Would-be demagogues lead the colored people to destruction. Half-drunken white roughs murder them at the polls, or intimidate them so that they do not vote. But the better class of people must not be blamed for this, and a more thoroughly American population than the Christian people of the South does not exist. They have the traditions, the kindness, the probity, the courage of our forefathers. The problem on their hands is immeasurable. The colored race multiplies like the locusts of Egypt. The grog-shop is its center of power. 'The safety of woman, of childhood, of the home, is menaced in a thousand localities at this moment, so that the men dare not go beyond the sight of their own roof-tree.' How little we know of all this, seated in comfort and affluence here at the North, descanting upon the rights of every man to cast one vote and have it fairly counted; that well-worn shibboleth invoked once more to dodge a living issue.

"The fact is that illiterate colored men will not vote at the South until the white population chooses to have them do so; and under similar conditions they would not at the North."

Here we have Miss Willard's words in full, condoning fraud, violence, murder, at the ballot box; rapine, shooting, hanging and burning; for all these things are done and being done now by the Southern white people. She does not stop there, but goes a step further to aid them in blackening the good name of an entire race, as shown by the sentences quoted in the paragraph above. These utterances, for which the colored people have never forgiven Miss Willard, and which Frederick Douglass has denounced as false, are to be found in full in the Voice of October 23, 1890, a temperance organ published at New York city.

This letter appeared in the May number of Fraternity, the organ of the first Anti-Lynching society of Great Britain. When Lady Henry Somerset learned through Miss Florence Balgarnie that this letter had been published she informed me that if the interview was published she would take steps to let the public know that my statements must be received with caution. As I had no money to pay the printer to suppress the edition which was already published and these ladies did not care to do so, the May number of Fraternity was sent to its subscribers as usual. Three days later there appeared in the daily Westminster Gazette an "interview" with Miss Willard, written by Lady Henry Somerset, which was so subtly unjust in its wording that I was forced to reply in my own defense. In that reply I made only statements which, like those concerning Miss Willard's Voice interview, have not been and cannot be denied. It was as follows:

LADY HENRY SOMERSET'S INTERVIEW
WITH MISS WILLARD

To the Editor of the Westminster Gazette: Sir—The interview published in your columns today hardly merits a reply, because of the indifference to suffering manifested. Two ladies are represented sitting under a tree at Reigate, and, after some preliminary remarks on the terrible subject of lynching, Miss Willard laughingly replies by cracking a joke. And the concluding sentence of the interview shows the object is not to determine how best they may help the Negro who is being hanged, shot and burned, but "to guard Miss Willard's reputation."

With me it is not myself nor my reputation, but the life of my people, which is at stake, and I affirm that this is the first time to my knowledge that Miss Willard has said a single word in denunciation of lynching or demand for law. The year 1890, the one in which the interview appears, had a larger lynching record than any previous year, and the number and territory have increased, to say nothing of the human beings burnt alive.

If so earnest as she would have the English public believe her to be, why was she silent when five minutes were given me to speak last June at Princes' Hall, and in Holborn Town Hall this May? I should say it was as President of the Women's Christian Temperance Union of America she is timid, because all these unions in the South emphasize the hatred of the Negro by excluding him. There is not a single colored woman admitted to the Southern W. C. T. U., but still Miss Willard blames the Negro for the defeat of Prohibition in the South. Miss Willard quotes from Fraternity, but forgets to add my immediate recognition of her presence on the platform at Holborn Town Hall, when, amidst many other resolutions on temperance and other subjects in which she is interested, time was granted to carry an anti-lynching resolution. I was so thankful for this crumb of her speechless presence that I hurried off to the editor of Fraternity and added a postscript to my article blazoning forth that fact.

Any statements I have made concerning Miss Willard are confirmed by the Hon. Frederick Douglass (late United States minister to Hayti) in a speech delivered by him in Washington in January of this year, which has since been published in a pamphlet. The fact is, Miss Willard is no better or worse than the great bulk of white Americans on the Negro questions. They are all afraid to speak out, and it is only British public opinion which will move them, as I am thankful to see it has already begun to move Miss Willard. I am, etc.,
May 21.   IDA B. WELLS.

Unable to deny the truth of these assertions, the charge has been made that I have attacked Miss Willard and misrepresented the W. C. T. U. If to state facts is misrepresentation, then I plead guilty to the charge.

I said then and repeat now, that in all the ten terrible years of shooting, hanging and burning of men, women and children in America, the Women's Christian Temperance Union never suggested one plan or made one move to prevent those awful crimes. If this statement is untrue the records of that organization would disprove it before the ink is dry. It is clearly an issue of fact and in all fairness this charge of misrepresentation should either be substantiated or withdrawn.

It is not necessary, however, to make any representation concerning the W. C. T. U. and the lynching question. The record of that organization speaks for itself. During all the years prior to the agitation begun against Lynch Law, in which years men, women and children were scourged, hanged, shot and burned, the W. C. T. U. had no word, either of pity or protest; its great heart, which concerns itself about humanity the world over, was, toward our cause, pulseless as a stone. Let those who deny this speak by the record. Not until after the first British campaign, in 1893, was even a resolution passed by the body which is the self constituted guardian for "God, home and native land."

Nor need we go back to other years. The annual session of that organization held in Cleveland in November, 1894, made a record which confirms and emphasizes the silence charged against it. At that session, earnest efforts were made to secure the adoption of a resolution of protest against lynching. At that very time two men were being tried for the murder of six colored men who were arrested on charge of barn burning, chained together, and on pretense of being taken to jail, were driven into the woods where they were ambushed and all six shot to death. The six widows of the butchered men had just finished the most pathetic recital ever heard in any court room, and the mute appeal of twenty-seven orphans for justice touched the stoutest hearts. Only two weeks prior to the session, Gov. Jones of Alabama, in his last message to the retiring state legislature, cited the fact that in the two years just past, nine colored men had been taken from the legal authorities by lynching mobs and butchered in cold blood—and not one of these victims was even charged with an assault upon womanhood.

It was thought that this great organization, in face of these facts, would not hesitate to place itself on record in a resolution of protest against this awful brutality towards colored people. Miss Willard gave assurance that such a resolution would be adopted, and that assurance was relied on. The record of the session shows in what good faith that assurance was kept. After recommending an expression against Lynch Law, the President attacked the anti-lynching movement, deliberately misrepresenting my position, and in her annual address, charging me with a statement I never made.

Further than that, when the committee on resolutions reported their work, not a word was said against lynching. In the interest of the cause I smothered the resentment. I felt because of the unwarranted and unjust attack of the President, and labored with members to secure an expression of some kind, tending to abate the awful slaughter of my race. A resolution against lynching was introduced by Mrs. Fessenden and read, and then that great Christian body, which in its resolutions had expressed itself in opposition to the social amusement of card playing, athletic sports and promiscuous dancing; had protested against the licensing of saloons, in-veighed against tobacco, pledged its allegiance to the Prohibition party, and thanked the Populist party in Kansas, the Republican party in California and the Democratic party in the South, wholly ignored the seven millions of colored people of this country whose plea was for a word of sympathy and support for the movement in their behalf. The resolution was not adopted, and the convention adjourned.

In the Union Signal Dec. 6, 1894, among the resolutions is found this one:

> Resolved, That the National W. C. T. U., which has for years counted among its departments that of peace and arbitration, is utterly opposed to all lawless acts in any and all parts of our common lands and it urges these principles upon the public, praying that the time may speedily come when no human being shall be condemned without due process of law; and when the unspeakable outrages which have so often provoked such lawlessness shall be banished from the world, and childhood, maidenhood and womanhood shall no more be the victims of atrocities worse than death.

This is not the resolution offered by Mrs. Fessenden. She offered the one passed last year by the W. C. T. U. which was a strong unequivocal denunciation of lynching. But she was told by the chairman of the committee on resolutions, Mrs. Rounds, that there was already a lynching resolution in the hands of the committee. Mrs. Fessenden yielded the floor on that assurance, and no resolution of any kind against lynching was submitted and none was voted upon, not even the one above, taken from the columns of the Union Signal, the organ of the national W. C. T. U.!

Even the wording of this resolution which was printed by the W. C. T. U., reiterates the false and unjust charge which has been so often made as an excuse for lynchers. Statistics show that less than one-third of the lynching victims are hanged, shot and burned alive for "unspeakable outrages against womanhood, maidenhood and childhood"; and that nearly a thousand, including women and children, have been lynched upon any pretext whatsoever; and that all have met death upon the unsupported word of white men and women. Despite these facts this resolution which was printed, cloaks an apology for lawlessness, in the same paragraph which affects to condemn it, where it speaks of "the unspeakable outrages which have so often provoked such lawlessness."

Miss Willard told me the day before the resolutions were offered that the Southern women present had held a caucus that day. This was after I, as fraternal delegate from the Woman's Mite Missionary Society of the A. M. E. Church at Cleveland, O., had been introduced to tender its greetings. In so doing I expressed the hope of the colored women that the W. C. T. U. would place itself on record as opposed to lynching which robbed them of husbands, fathers, brothers and sons and in many cases of women as well. No note was made either in the daily papers or the Union Signal of that introduction and greeting, although every other incident of that morning was published. The failure to submit a lynching resolution and the wording of the one above appears to have been the result of that Southern caucus.

On the same day I had a private talk with Miss Willard and told her she had been unjust to me and the cause in her annual address, and asked that she correct the statement that I had misrepresented the W. C. T. U., or that I had "put an imputation on one-half the white race in this country." She said that somebody in England told her it was a pity that I attacked the white women of America. "Oh," said I, "then you went out of your way to prejudice me and my cause in your annual address, not upon what you had heard me say, but what somebody had told you I said?" Her reply was that I must not blame her for her rhetorical expressions—that I had my way of expressing things and she had hers. I told her I most assuredly did blame her when those expressions were calculated to do such harm. I waited for an honest and unequivocal retraction of her statements based on "hearsay." Not a word of retraction or explanation was said in the convention and I remained misrepresented before that body through her connivance and consent.

The editorial notes in the Union Signal, Dec. 6, 1894, however, contains the following:

"In her repudiation of the charges brought by Miss Ida Wells against white women as having taken the initiative in nameless crimes between the races, Miss Willard said in her annual address that this statement 'put an unjust imputation upon half the white race.' But as this expression has been misunderstood she desires to declare that she did not intend a literal interpretation to be given to the language used, but employed it to express a tendency that might ensue in public thought as a result of utterances so sweeping as some that have been made by Miss Wells."

Because this explanation is as unjust as the original offense, I am forced in self-defense to submit this account of differences. I desire no quarrel with the W. C. T. U., but my love for the truth is greater than my regard for an alleged friend who, through ignorance or design misrepresents in the most harmful way the cause of a long suffering race, and then unable to maintain the truth of her attack excuses herself as it were by the wave of the hand, declaring that "she did not intend a literal interpretation to be given to the language used." When the lives of men, women and children are at stake, when the inhuman butchers of innocents attempt to justify their barbarism by fastening upon a whole race the obloquy of the most infamous of crimes, it is little less than criminal to apologize for the butchers today and tomorrow to repudiate the apology by declaring it a figure of speech.

CHAPTER IX
LYNCHING RECORD FOR 1894

The following tables are based on statistics taken from the columns of the Chicago Tribune, Jan. 1, 1895. They are a valuable appendix to the foregoing pages. They show, among other things, that in Louisiana, April 23–28, eight Negroes were lynched because one white man was killed by the Negro, the latter acting in self defense. Only seven of them are given in the list.

Near Memphis, Tenn., six Negroes were lynched—this time charged with burning barns. A trial of the indicted resulted in an acquittal, although it was shown on trial that the lynching was prearranged for them. Six widows and twenty-seven orphans are indebted to this mob for their condition, and this lynching swells the number to eleven Negroes lynched in and about Memphis since March 9, 1892.

In Brooks county, Ga., Dec. 23rd, while this Christian country was preparing for Christmas celebration, seven Negroes were lynched in twenty-four hours because they refused, or were unable to tell the whereabouts of a colored man named Pike, who killed a white man. The wives and daughters of these lynched men were horribly and brutally outraged by the murderers of their husbands and fathers. But the mob has not been punished and again women and children are robbed of their protectors whose blood cries unavenged to

Heaven and humanity. Georgia heads the list of lynching states.

Jan. 9, Samuel Smith, Greenville, Ala.; Jan. 11, Sherman Wagoner, Mitchell, Ind.; Jan. 12, Roscoe Parker, West Union, Ohio; Feb. 7, Henry Bruce, Gulch Co., Ark.; March 5, Sylvester Rhodes, Collins, Ga.; March 15, Richard Puryea, Stroudsburg, Pa.; March 29, Oliver Jackson, Montgomery, Ala.; March 30, —— Saybrick, Fisher's Ferry, Miss.; April 14, William Lewis, Lanison, Ala.; April 23, Jefferson Luggle, Cherokee, Kan.; April 23, Samuel Slaugate, Tallulah, La.; April 23, Thomas Claxton, Tallulah, La.; April 23, David Hawkins, Tallulah, La.; April 27, Thel Claxton, Tallulah, La.; April 27, Comp Claxton, Tallulah, La.; April 27, Scot Harvey, Tallulah, La.; April 27, Jerry McCly, Tallulah, La.; May 17, Henry Scott, Jefferson, Tex.; May 15, Coat Williams, Pine Grove, Fla.; June 2, Jefferson Crawford, Bethesda, S. C.; June 4, Thondo Underwood, Monroe, La.; June 8, Isaac Kemp, Cape Charles, Va.; June 13, Lon Hall, Sweethouse, Tex.; June 13, Bascom Cook, Sweethouse, Tex.; June 15, Luke Thomas, Biloxi, Miss.; June 29, John Williams, Sulphur, Tex.; June 29, Ulysses Hayden, Monett, Mo.; July 6, —— Hood, Amite, Miss.; July 7, James Bell, Charlotte, Tenn.; Sept. 2, Henderson Hollander, Elkhorn, W. Va.; Sept. 14, Robert Williams, Concordia Parish, La.; Sept. 22, Luke Washington, Meghee, Ark.; Sept. 22, Richard Washington, Meghee, Ark.; Sept. 22, Henry Crobyson, Meghee, Ark.; Nov. 10, Lawrence Younger, Lloyd, Va.; Dec. 17, unknown Negro, Williamston, S. C.; Dec. 23, Samuel Taylor, Brooks County, Ga.; Dec. 23, Charles Frazier, Brooks County, Ga.; Dec. 23, Samuel Pike, Brooks County, Ga.; Dec. 23, Harry,

Sherard, Brooks County, Ga.; Dec. 23, unknown Negro, Brooks County, Ga.; Dec. 23, unknown Negro, Brooks County, Ga.; Dec. 23, unknown Negro, Brooks County, Ga.; Dec. 26, Daniel McDonald, Winston County, Miss.; Dec. 26, William Carter, Winston County, Miss.

RAPE

Jan. 17, John Buckner, Valley Park, Mo.; Jan. 21, M. G. Campbell, Jellico Mines, Ky.; Jan. 27, unknown, Verona, Mo.; Feb. 11, Henry McCreeg, near Pioneer, Tenn.; April 6, Daniel Ahren, Greensboro, Ga.; April 15, Seymour Newland, Rushsylvania, Ohio; April 26, Robert Evarts, Jamaica, Ga.; April 27, James Robinson, Manassas, Va.; April 27, Benjamin White, Manassas, Va.; May 15, Nim Young, Ocala, Fla.; May 22, unknown, Miller County, Ga.; June 13, unknown, Blackshear, Ga.; June 18, Owen Opliltree, Forsyth, Ga.; June 22, Henry Capus, Magnolia, Ark.; June 26, Caleb Godly, Bowling Green, Ky.; June 28, Fayette Franklin, Mitchell, Ga.; July 2, Joseph Johnson, Hiller's Creek, Mo.; July 6, Lewis Bankhead, Cooper, Ala.; July 16, Marion Howard, Scottsville, Ky.; July 20, William Griffith, Woodville, Tex.; Aug. 12, William Nershbread, Rossville, Tenn.; Aug. 14, Marshall Boston, Frankfort, Ky.; Sept. 19, David Gooseby, Atlanta, Ga.; Oct. 15, Willis Griffey, Princeton, Ky.; Nov. 8, Lee Lawrence, Jasper County, Ga.; Nov. 10, Needham Smith, Tipton County, Tenn.; Nov. 14, Robert Mosely, Dolinite, Ala.; Dec. 4, William Jackson, Ocala, Fla.; Dec. 18, unknown, Marion County, Fla.

UNKNOWN OFFENSES

March 6, Lamsen Gregory, Bell's Depot, Tenn.; March 6, unknown woman, near Marche, Ark.; April 14, Alfred

Brenn, Calhoun, Ga.; June 8, Harry Gill, West Lancaster, S. C.; Nov. 23, unknown, Landrum, S. C.; Dec. 5, Mrs. Teddy Arthur, Lincoln County, W. Va.

DESPERADO

Jan. 14, Charles Willis, Ocala, Fla.

SUSPECTED INCENDIARISM

Jan. 18, unknown, Bayou Sarah, La.

SUSPECTED ARSON

June 14, J. H. Dave, Monroe, La.

ENTICING SERVANT AWAY

Feb. 10, —— Collins, Athens, Ga.

TRAIN WRECKING

Feb. 10, Jesse Dillingham, Smokeyville, Tex.

HIGHWAY ROBBERY

June 3, unknown, Dublin, Ga.

INCENDIARISM

Nov. 8, Gabe Nalls, Blackford, Ky.; Nov. 8, Ulysses Nalls, Blackford, Ky.

ARSON

Dec. 20, James Allen, Brownsville, Tex.

ASSAULT

Dec. 23, George King, New Orleans, La.

NO OFFENSE

Dec. 28, Scott Sherman, Morehouse Parish, La.

BURGLARY

May 29, Henry Smith, Clinton, Miss.; May 29, William James, Clinton, Miss.

ALLEGED RAPE

June 4, Ready Murdock, Yazoo, Miss.

ATTEMPTED RAPE

July 14, unknown Negro, Biloxi, Miss.; July 26, Vance McClure, New Iberia, La.; July 26, William Tyler, Carlisle, Ky.; Sept. 14, James Smith, Stark, Fla.; Oct. 8, Henry Gibson, Fairfield, Tex.; Oct. 20, —— Williams, Upper Marlboro, Md.; June 9, Lewis Williams, Hewett Springs, Miss.; June 28, George Linton, Brookhaven, Miss.; June 28, Edward White, Hudson, Ala.; July 6, George Pond, Fulton, Miss.; July 7, Augustus Pond, Tupelo, Miss.

RACE PREJUDICE

June 10, Mark Jacobs, Bienville, La.; July 24, unknown woman, Sampson County, Miss.

INTRODUCING SMALLPOX

June 10, James Perry, Knoxville, Ark.

KIDNAPPING

March 2, Lentige, Harland County, Ky.

CONSPIRACY

May 29, J. T. Burgis, Palatka, Fla.

HORSE STEALING

June 20, Archie Haynes, Mason County, Ky.; June 20, Burt Haynes, Mason County, Ky.; June 20, William Haynes, Mason County, Ky.

WRITING LETTER TO WHITE WOMAN

May 9, unknown Negro, West Texas.

GIVING INFORMATION

July 12, James Nelson, Abbeyville, S. C.

STEALING

Jan. 5, Alfred Davis, Live Oak County, Ark.

LARCENY

April 18, Henry Montgomery, Lewisburg, Tenn.

POLITICAL CAUSES

July 19, John Brownlee, Oxford, Ala.

CONJURING

July 20, Allen Myers, Rankin County, Miss.

ATTEMPTED MURDER

June 1, Frank Ballard, Jackson, Tenn.

ALLEGED MURDER

April 5, Negro, near Selma, Ala.; April 5, Negro, near Selma, Ala.

WITHOUT CAUSE

May 17, Samuel Wood, Gates City, Va.

BARN BURNING

April 22, Thomas Black, Tuscumbia, Ala.; April 22, John Williams, Tuscumbia, Ala.; April 22, Toney Johnson, Tuscumbia, Ala.; July 14, William Bell, Dixon, Tenn.; Sept. 1, Daniel Hawkins, Millington, Tenn.; Sept. 1, Robert Haynes, Millington, Tenn.; Sept. 1, Warner Williams, Millington, Tenn.; Sept. 1, Edward Hall, Millington, Tenn.; Sept. 1, John Haynes, Millington, Tenn.; Sept. 1, Graham White, Millington, Tenn.

ASKING WHITE WOMAN TO MARRY HIM

May 23, William Brooks, Galesline, Ark.

OFFENSES CHARGED FOR LYNCHING

Suspected arson, 2; stealing, 1; political causes, 1; murder, 45; rape, 29; desperado, 1; suspected incendiarism, 1; train wrecking, 1; enticing servant away, 1; kidnapping, 1; unknown offense, 6; larceny, 1; barn burning, 10; writing letters to a white woman, 1; without cause, 1; burglary, 1; asking white woman to marry, 1; conspiracy, 1; attempted murder, 1; horse stealing, 3; highway robbery, 1; alleged rape, 1; attempted rape, 11; race prejudice, 2; introducing smallpox, 1; giving information, 1; conjuring, 1; incendiarism, 2; arson, 1; assault, 1; no offense, 1; alleged murder, 2; total (colored), 134.

LYNCHING STATES

Mississippi, 15; Arkansas, 8; Virginia, 5; Tennessee, 15; Alabama, 12; Kentucky, 12; Texas, 9; Georgia, 19; South Carolina, 5; Florida, 7; Louisiana, 15; Missouri, 4; Ohio, 2; Maryland, 1; West Virginia, 2; Indiana, 1; Kansas, 1; Pennsylvania, 1.

LYNCHING BY THE MONTH

January, 11; February, 17; March, 8; April, 36; May, 16; June, 31; July, 21; August, 4; September, 17; October, 7; November, 9; December, 20; total colored and white, 197.

WOMEN LYNCHED

July 24, unknown woman, race prejudice, Sampson County, Miss.; March 6, unknown, woman, unknown offense, Marche, Ark.; Dec. 5. Mrs. Teddy Arthur, unknown cause, Lincoln County, W. Va.

CHAPTER X
THE REMEDY

It is a well established principle of law that every wrong has a remedy. Herein rests our respect for law. The Negro does not claim that all of the one thousand black men, women and children, who have been hanged, shot and burned alive during the past ten years, were innocent of the charges made against them. We have associated too long with the white man not to have copied his vices as well as his virtues. But we do insist that the punishment is not the same for both classes of criminals. In lynching, opportunity is not given the Negro to defend himself against the unsupported accusations of white men and women. The word of the accuser is held to be true and the excited blood-thirsty mob demands that the rule of law be reversed and instead of proving the accused to be guilty, the victim of their hate and revenge must prove himself innocent. No evidence he can offer will satisfy the mob; he is bound hand and foot and swung into eternity. Then to excuse its infamy, the mob almost invariably reports the monstrous falsehood that its victim made a full confession before he was hanged.

With all military, legal and political power in their hands, only two of the lynching States have attempted a check by exercising the power which is theirs. Mayor Trout, of Roanoke, Virginia, called out the militia in 1893, to protect a Negro prisoner, and in so doing nine men were killed and a number wounded. Then the mayor and militia withdrew, left the negro to his fate and he was promptly lynched. The business men realized the blow to the town's financial interests, called the mayor home, [and] the grand jury indicted and prosecuted the ringleaders of the mob. They were given light sentences, the highest being one of twelve months in State prison. The day he arrived at the penitentiary, he was pardoned by the governor of the State.

The only other real attempt made by the authorities to protect a prisoner of the law, and which was more successful, was that of Gov. McKinley, of Ohio, who sent the militia to Washington Courthouse, O., in October, 1894, and five men were killed and twenty wounded in maintaining the principle that the law must be upheld.

In South Carolina, in April, 1893, Gov. Tillman aided the mob by yielding up to be killed, a prisoner of the law, who had voluntarily placed himself under the Governor's protection. Public sentiment by its representatives has encouraged Lynch Law, and upon the revolution of this sentiment we must depend for its abolition.

Therefore, we demand a fair trial by law for those accused of crime, and punishment by law after honest conviction. No maudlin sympathy for criminals is solicited, but we do ask that the law shall punish all alike. We earnestly desire those that control the forces which make public sentiment to join with us in the demand. Surely the humanitarian spirit of this country which reaches out to denounce the treatment of the Russian Jews, the Armenian Christians, the laboring poor of Europe, the Siberian exiles and the native women of India— will no longer refuse to lift its voice on this subject. If it were known that the cannibals or the savage Indians had burned three human beings alive in the past two years, the whole of Christendom would be roused, to devise ways and means to put a stop to it. Can you remain silent and inactive when such things are done in our own community and country? Is your duty to humanity in the United States less binding?

What can you do, reader, to prevent lynching, to thwart anarchy and promote law and order throughout our land?

1st. You can help disseminate the facts contained in this book by bringing them to the knowledge of every one with whom you come in contact, to the end that public sentiment may be revolutionized. Let the facts speak for themselves, with you as a medium.

2d. You can be instrumental in having churches, missionary societies, Y.M.C.A.'s, W.C.T.U.'s and all Christian and moral forces in connection with your religious and social life, pass resolutions of condemnation and protest every time a lynching takes place; and see that they are sent to the place where these outrages occur.

3d. Bring to the intelligent consideration of Southern people the refusal of capital to invest where lawlessness and mob violence hold sway. Many labor organizations have declared the resolution that they would avoid lynch infested localities as they would the pestilence when seeking new homes. If the South wishes to build up its waste places quickly, there is no better way than to uphold the majesty of the law by enforcing obedience to the same, and meting out the same punishment to all classes of criminals, white as well as black. "Equality before the law," must become a fact as well as a theory before America is truly the "land of the free and the home of the brave."

4th. Think and act on independent lines in this behalf, remembering that after all, it is the white man's civilization and the white man's government which are on trial. This crusade will determine whether that civilization can maintain itself by itself, or whether anarchy shall prevail; whether this Nation shall write itself down a success at self government, or in deepest humiliation admit its failure complete; whether the precepts and theories of Christianity are professed and practiced by American white people as Golden Rules of thought and action, or adopted as a system of morals to be preached to heathen until they attain to the intelligence which needs the system of Lynch Law.

5th. Congressman Blair offered a resolution in the House of Representatives, August, 1894. The organized life of the country can speedily make this a law by sending resolutions to Congress indorsing Mr. Blair's bill and asking Congress to create the commission. In no better way can the question be settled, and the Negro does not fear the issue. The following is the resolution:

"Resolved, By the House of Representatives and Senate in congress assembled, That the committee on labor be instructed to investigate and report the number, location and date of all alleged assaults by males upon females throughout the country during the ten years last preceding the passing of this joint resolution, for or on account of which organized but unlawful violence has been inflicted or attempted to be inflicted. Also to ascertain and report all facts of organized but unlawful violence to the person, with the attendant facts and circumstances, which have been inflicted upon accused persons alleged to have been guilty of crimes punishable by due process of law which have taken place in any part of the country within the ten years last preceding the passage of this resolution. Such investigation shall be made by the usual methods and agencies of the Department of Labor, and report made to Congress as soon as the work can be satisfactorily done, and the sum of $25,000, or so much thereof as may be necessary, is hereby appropriated to pay the expenses out of any money in the treasury not otherwise appropriated."

The belief has been constantly expressed in England that in the United States, which has produced Wm. Lloyd Garrison, Henry Ward Beecher, James Russell Lowell, John G. Whittier and Abraham Lincoln there must be those of their descendants who would take hold of the work of inaugurating an era of law and order. The colored people of this country who have been loyal to the flag believe the same, and strong in that belief have begun this crusade. To those who still feel they have no obligation in the matter, we commend the following lines of Lowell on "Freedom."

> Men! whose boast it is that ye
> Come of fathers brave and free,
> If there breathe on earth a slave
> Are ye truly free and brave?
> If ye do not feel the chain,
> When it works a brother's pain,
> Are ye not base slaves indeed,
> Slaves unworthy to be freed?
>
> Women! who shall one day bear
> Sons to breathe New England air,
> If ye hear without a blush,
> Deeds to make the roused blood rush
> Like red lava through your veins,
> For your sisters now in chains,—

Answer! are ye fit to be
Mothers of the brave and free?

Is true freedom but to break
Fetters for our own dear sake,
And, with leathern hearts, forget
That we owe mankind a debt?
No! true freedom is to share
All the chains our brothers wear,
And, with heart and hand, to be
Earnest to make others free!

There are slaves who fear to speak
For the fallen and the weak;
They are slaves who will not choose
Hatred, scoffing, and abuse,
Rather than in silence shrink
From the truth they needs must think;
They are slaves who dare not be
In the right with two or three.

A FIELD FOR PRACTICAL WORK

The very frequent inquiry made after my lectures by interested friends is, "What can I do to help the cause?" The answer always is, "Tell the world the facts." When the Christian world knows the alarming growth and extent of outlawry in our land, some means will be found to stop it.

The object of this publication is to tell the facts, and friends of the cause can lend a helping hand by aiding in the distribution of these books. When I present our cause to a minister, editor, lecturer, or representative of any moral agency, the first demand is for facts and figures. Plainly, I can not then hand out a book with a twenty-five cent tariff on the information contained. This would be only a new method in the book agents' art. In all such cases it is a pleasure to submit this book for investigation, with the certain assurance of gaining a friend to the cause.

There are many agencies which may be enlisted in our cause by the general circulation of the facts herein contained. The preachers, teachers, editors and humanitarians of the white race, at home and abroad, must have facts laid before them, and it is our duty to supply these facts. The Central Anti-Lynching League, Room 9, 128 Clark st., Chicago, has established a Free Distribution Fund, the work of which can be promoted by all who are interested in this work.

Anti-lynching leagues, societies and individuals can order books from this fund at agents' rates. The books will be sent to their order, or, if desired, will be distributed by the League among those whose co-operative aid we so greatly need. The writer hereof assures prompt distribution of books according to order, and public acknowledgment of all orders through the public press.

MOB RULE
IN NEW ORLEANS

Robert Charles
and His Fight to the Death

The Story of His Life. Burning Human Beings Alive. Other
Lynching Statistics.

INTRODUCTION

Immediately after the awful barbarism which disgraced the State of Georgia in April of last year, during which time more than a dozen colored people were put to death with unspeakable barbarity, I published a full report showing that Sam Hose, who was burned to death during that time, never committed a criminal assault, and that he killed his employer in self-defense.

Since that time I have been engaged on a work not yet finished, which I interrupt now to tell the story of the mob in New Orleans, which, despising all law, roamed the streets day and night, searching for colored men and women, whom they beat, shot and killed at will.

In the account of the New Orleans mob I have used freely the graphic reports of the New Orleans Times-Democrat and the New Orleans Picayune. Both papers gave the most minute details of the week's disorder. In their editorial comment they were at all times most urgent in their defense of law and in the strongest terms they condemned the infamous work of the mob.

It is no doubt owing to the determined stand for law and order taken by these great dailies and the courageous action taken by the best citizens of New Orleans, who rallied to the support of the civic authorities, that prevented a massacre of colored people awful to contemplate.

For the accounts and illustrations taken from the above-named journals, sincere thanks are hereby expressed.

The publisher hereof does not attempt to moralize over the deplorable condition of affairs shown in this publication, but

Originally self-published in 1900 in Chicago.

SCENE OF THE
DOUBLE MURDER
THE NEARER BODY IS
THAT OF PATROLMAN
P. J. LAMB WHILE
CAPT DAY CAN BE PARTLY
SEEN FARTHER ON
BULLET HOLE IN DOOR

from New Orleans—Times-Democrat

simply presents the facts in a plain, unvarnished, connected way, so that he who runs may read. We do not believe that the American people who have encouraged such scenes by their indifference will read unmoved these accounts of brutality, injustice and oppression. We do not believe that the moral conscience of the nation—that which is highest and best among us—will always remain silent in face of such outrages, for God is not dead, and His Spirit is not entirely driven from men's hearts.

When this conscience wakes and speaks out in thunder tones, as it must, it will need facts to use as a weapon against injustice, barbarism and wrong. It is for this reason that I carefully compile, print and send forth these facts. If the reader can do no more, he can pass this pamphlet on to another, or send to the bureau addresses of those to whom he can order copies mailed.

Besides the New Orleans case, a history of burnings in this country is given, together with a table of lynchings for the past eighteen years. Those who would like to assist in the work of disseminating these facts, can do so by ordering copies, which are furnished at greatly reduced rates for gratuitous distribution. The bureau has no funds and is entirely dependent upon contributions from friends and members in carrying on the work.

Ida B. Wells-Barnett.
Chicago, Sept. 1, 1900.

SHOT AN OFFICER

The bloodiest week which New Orleans has known since the massacre of the Italians in 1892 was ushered in Monday, July 24th, by the inexcusable and unprovoked assault upon two colored men by police officers of New Orleans. Fortified by the assurance born of long experience in the New Orleans service, three policemen, Sergeant Aucoin, Officer Mora and Officer Cantrelle, observing two colored men sitting on doorsteps on Dryades street, between Washington avenue and 6th streets, determined, without a shadow of authority, to arrest them. One of the colored men was named Robert Charles, the other was a lad of nineteen named Leonard Pierce. The colored men had left their homes, a few blocks distant, about an hour prior, and had been sitting upon the doorsteps for a short time talking together. They had not broken the peace in any way whatever, no warrant was in the policemen's hands justifying their arrest, and no crime had been committed of which they were the suspects. The policemen, however, secure in the firm belief that they could do anything to a Negro that they wished, approached the two men, and in less than three minutes from the time they accosted them attempted to put both colored men under arrest. The younger of the two men, Pierce, submitted to arrest, for the officer, Cantrelle, who accosted him, put his gun in the young man's face ready to blow his brains out if he moved. The other colored man, Charles, was made a victim of a savage attack by Officer Mora, who used a billet and then drew a gun and tried to kill Charles. Charles drew his gun nearly as quickly as the policeman, and began a duel in the street, in which both participants were shot. The policeman got the worst of the duel, and fell helpless to the sidewalk. Charles made his escape. Cantrelle took Pierce, his captive, to the police station, to which place Mora, the wounded officer, was also taken, and a man hunt at once instituted for Charles, the wounded fugitive.

In any law-abiding community Charles would have been justified in delivering himself up immediately to the properly constituted authorities and asking a trial by a jury of his peers. He could have been certain that in resisting an unwarranted arrest he had a right to defend his life, even to the point of taking one in that defense, but Charles knew that his arrest in New Orleans, even for defending his life, meant nothing short of a long term in the penitentiary, and still more probable death by lynching at the hands of a cowardly mob. He very bravely determined to protect his life as long as he had breath in his body and strength to draw a hair trigger on his would-be murderers. How well he was justified in that belief is well shown by the newspaper accounts which were given of this transaction. Without a single line of evidence to justify the assertion, the New Orleans daily papers at once declared that both Pierce and Charles were desperadoes, that they were contemplating a burglary and that they began the assault upon the policemen. It is interesting to note how the two leading papers of New Orleans, the Picayune and the Times-Democrat, exert themselves to justify the policemen in the absolutely unprovoked attack upon the two colored men. As these two papers did all in their power to give an excuse for the action of the policemen, it is interesting to note their versions. The Times-Democrat of Tuesday morning, the 25th, says:

"Two blacks, who are desperate men, and no doubt will be proven burglars, made it interesting and dangerous for three bluecoats on Dryades street, between Washington avenue and Sixth street, the Negroes using pistols first and dropping Patrolman Mora. But the desperate darkies did not go free, for the taller of the two, Robinson, is badly wounded and under cover, while Leonard Pierce is in jail.

"For a long time that particular neighborhood has been troubled with bad Negroes, and the neighbors were complaining to the Sixth Precinct police about them. But of late Pierce and Robinson had been camping on a door step on the street, and the people regarded their actions as suspicious. It got to such a point that some of the residents were afraid to go to bed, and last night this was told Sergeant Aucoin, who was rounding up his men. He had just picked up Officers Mora and Cantrell, on Washington avenue and Dryades street, and catching a glimpse of the blacks on the steps, he said he would go over and warn the men to get away from the street. So the patrolmen followed, and Sergeant Aucoin asked the smaller fellow, Pierce, if he lived there. The answer was short and impertinent, the black saying he did not, and with that both Pierce and Robinson drew up to their full height.

"For the moment the sergeant did not think that the Negroes meant fight, and he was on the point of ordering them away when Robinson slipped his pistol from his pocket. Pierce had his revolver out, too, and he fired twice, point blank at the sergeant, and just then Robinson began shooting at the patrolmen. In a second or so the policemen and blacks were fighting with their revolvers, the sergeant having a duel with Pierce, while Cantrell and Mora drew their line of fire on Robinson, who was working his revolver for all he was worth. One of his shots took Mora in the right hip, another caught his index finger on the right hand, and a third struck the small finger of the left hand. Poor Mora was done for; he could not fight any more, but Cantrell kept up his fire, being answered by the big black. Pierce's revolver broke down, the cartridges snapping, and he threw up his hands, begging for quarter.

"The sergeant lowered his pistol and some citizens ran over to where the shooting was going on. One of the bullets that went at Robinson caught him in the breast and he began running, turning out Sixth street, with Cantrell behind him, shooting every few steps. He was loading his revolver again, but did not use it after the start he took, and in a little while Officer Cantrell lost the man in the darkness.

"Pierce was made a prisoner and hurried to the Sixth Precinct police station, where he was charged with shooting and wounding. The sergeant sent for an ambulance, and Mora was taken to the hospital, the wound in the hip being serious.

"A search was made for Robinson, but he could not be found, and even at 2 o'clock this morning Captain Day, with Sergeant Aucoin and Corporals Perrier and Trenchard, with a good squad of men, were beating the weeds for the black."

The New Orleans Picayune of the same date described the

occurrence, and from its account one would think it was an entirely different affair. Both of the two accounts cannot be true, and the unquestioned fact is that neither of them sets out the facts as they occurred. Both accounts attempt to fix the beginning of hostilities upon the colored men, but both were compelled to admit that the colored men were sitting on the doorsteps quietly conversing with one another when the three policemen went up and accosted them. The Times-Democrat unguardedly states that one of the two colored men tried to run away; that Mora seized him and then drew his billy and struck him on the head; that Charles broke away from him and started to run, after which the shooting began. The Picayune, however, declares that Pierce began the firing and that his two shots point blank at Aucoin were the first shots of the fight. As a matter of fact, Pierce never fired a single shot before he was covered by Aucoin's revolver. Charles and the officers did all the shooting. The Picayune's account is as follows:

"Patrolman Mora was shot in the right hip and dangerously wounded last night at 11:30 o'clock in Dryades street, between Washington and Sixth, by two Negroes, who were sitting on a door step in the neighborhood.

"The shooting of Patrolman Mora brings to memory the fact that he was one of the partners of Patrolman Trimp, who was shot by a Negro soldier of the United States government during the progress of the Spanish-American war. The shooting of Mora by the Negro last night is a very simple story. At the hour mentioned, three Negro women noticed two suspicious men sitting on a door step in the above locality. The women saw the two men making an apparent inspection of the building. As they told the story, they saw the men look over the fence and examine the window blinds, and they paid particular attention to the make-up of the building, which was a two-story affair. About that time Sergeant J. C. Aucoin and Officers Mora and J. D. Cantrell hove in sight. The women hailed them and described to them the suspicious actions of the two Negroes, who were still sitting on the step. The trio of bluecoats, on hearing the facts, at once crossed the street and accosted the men. The latter answered that they were waiting for a friend whom they were expecting. Not satisfied with this answer, the sergeant asked them where they lived, and the replied "down town," but could not designate the locality. To other questions put by the officers the larger of the two Negroes replied that they had been in town just three days.

"As this reply was made, the larger man sprang to his feet, and Patrolman Mora, seeing that he was about to run away, seized him. The Negro took a firm hold on the officer, and a scuffle ensued. Mora, noting that he was not being assisted by his brother officers, drew his billy and struck the Negro on the head. The blow had but little effect upon the man, for he broke away and started down the street. When about ten feet away, the Negro drew his revolver and opened fire on the officer, firing three or four shots. The third shot struck Mora in the right hip, and was subsequently found to have taken an upward course. Although badly wounded, Mora drew his pistol and returned the fire. At his third shot the Negro was noticed to stagger, but he did not fall. He continued his flight. At this moment Sergeant Aucoin seized the other Negro, who proved to be a youth, Leon Pierce. As soon as Officer Mora was shot he sank to the sidewalk, and the other officer ran to the nearest telephone, and sent in a call for the ambulance. Upon its arrival the wounded officer was placed in it and conveyed to the hospital. An examination by the house surgeon revealed the fact that the bullet had taken an upward course. In the opinion of the surgeon the wound was a dangerous one."

But the best proof of the fact that the officers accosted the two colored men and without any warrant or other justification attempted to arrest them, and did actually seize and begin to club one of them, is shown by Officer Mora's own statement. The officer was wounded and had every reason in the world to make his side of the story as good as possible. His statement was made to a Picayune reporter and the same was published on the 25th inst., and is as follows:

"I was in the neighborhood of Dryades and Washington streets, with Sergeant Aucoin and Officer Cantrell, when three Negro women came up and told us that there were two suspicious-looking Negroes sitting on a step on Dryades street, between Washington and Sixth. We went to the place indicated and found two Negroes. We interrogated them as to who they were, what they were doing and how long they had been here. They replied that they were working for some one and had been in town three days. At about this stage the larger of the two Negroes got up and I grabbed him. The Negro pulled, but I held fast, and he finally pulled me into the street. Here I began using my billet, and the Negro jerked from my grasp and ran. He then pulled a gun and fired. I pulled my gun and returned the fire, each of us firing about three shots. I saw the Negro stumble several times, and I thought I had shot him, but he ran away and I don't know whether any of my shots took effect. Sergeant Aucoin in the meantime held the other man fast. The man was about ten feet from me when he fired, and the three Negresses who told us about the men stood away about twenty-five feet from the shooting."

Thus far in the proceeding the Monday night episode

results in Officer Mora lying in the station wounded in the hip; Leonard Pierce, one of the colored men, locked up in the station, and Robert Charles, the other colored man, a fugitive, wounded in the leg and sought for by the entire police force of New Orleans. Not sought for, however, to be placed under arrest and given a fair trial and punished if found guilty according to the law of the land, but sought for by a host of enraged, vindictive and fearless officers, who were cooly ordered to kill him on sight. This order is shown by the Picayune of the 26th inst., in which the following statement appears:

"In talking to the sergeant about the case, the captain asked about the Negro's fighting ability, and the sergeant answered that Charles, though he called him Robinson then, was a desperate man, and it would be best to shoot him before he was given a chance to draw his pistol upon any of the officers."

This instruction was given before anybody had been killed, and the only evidence that Charles was a desperate man lay in the fact that he had refused to be beaten over the head by Officer Mora for sitting on a step quietly conversing with a friend. Charles resisted an absolutely unlawful attack, and a gun fight followed. Both Mora and Charles were shot, but because Mora was white and Charles was black, Charles was at once declared to be a desperado, made an outlaw, and subsequently a price put upon his head and the mob authorized to shoot him like a dog, on sight.

The New Orleans Picayune of Wednesday morning said:

"But he has gone, perhaps to the swamps, and the disappointment of the bluecoats in not getting the murderer is expressed in their curses, each man swearing that the signal to halt that will be offered Charles will be a shot."

In that same column of the Picayune it was said:

"Hundreds of policemen were about; each corner was

guarded by a squad, commanded either by a sergeant or a corporal, and every man had the word to shoot the Negro as soon as he was sighted. He was a desperate black and would be given no chance to take more life."

Legal sanction was given to the mob or any man of the mob to kill Charles at sight by the Mayor of New Orleans, who publicly proclaimed a reward of two hundred and fifty dollars, not for the arrest of Charles, not at all, but the reward was offered for Charles' body, "dead or alive." The advertisement was as follows:

"$250 REWARD.
"Under the authority vested in me by law, I hereby offer, in the name of the city of New Orleans, $250 reward for the capture and delivery, dead or alive, to the authorities of the city, the body of the Negro murderer,

"ROBERT CHARLES,
who, on Tuesday morning, July 24, shot and killed
"Police Captain John T. Day and Patrolman Peter J. Lamb, and wounded
"Patrolman August T. Mora.
"PAUL CAPDEVIELLE, Mayor."

This authority, given by the sergeant to kill Charles on sight, would have been no news to Charles, nor to any colored man in New Orleans, who, for any purpose whatever, even to save his life, raised his hand against a white man. It is now, even as it was in the days of slavery, an unpardonable sin for a Negro to resist a white man, no matter how unjust or unprovoked the white man's attack may be. Charles knew this, and knowing to be captured meant to be killed, he resolved to sell his life as dearly as possible.

The next step in the terrible tragedy occurred between 2:30 and 5 o'clock Tuesday morning, about four hours after the affair on Dryades street. The man hunt, which had been inaugurated soon after Officer Mora had been carried to the station, succeeded in running down Robert Charles, the wounded fugitive, and located him at 2023 4th street. It was nearly 2 o'clock in the morning when a large detail of police surrounded the block with the intent to kill Charles on sight. Capt. Day had charge of the squad of police. Charles, the wounded man, was in his house when the police arrived, fully prepared, as results afterward showed, to die in his own home. Capt. Day started for Charles' room. As soon as Charles got sight of him there was a flash, a report, and Day fell dead in his tracks. In another instant Charles was standing in the door, and seeing Patrolman Peter J. Lamb, he drew his gun, and Lamb fell dead. Two other officers, Sergeant Aucoin and Officer Trenchard, who were in the squad, seeing their comrades, Day and Lamb, fall dead, concluded to raise the siege, and both disappeared into an adjoining house, where they blew out their lights so that their cowardly carcasses could be safe from Charles' deadly aim. The calibre of their courage is well shown by the fact that they concluded to save themselves from any harm by remaining prisoners in that dark room until daybreak, out of reach of Charles' deadly rifle. Sergeant Aucoin, who had been so brave a few hours before when seeing the two colored men sitting on the steps talking together on Dryades street, and supposing that neither was armed, now showed his true calibre. Now he knew that Charles had a gun and was brave enough to use it, so he hid himself in a room two hours while Charles deliberately walked out of his room and into the street after killing both Lamb and Day. It is also shown, as further evidence of the bravery of some of New Orleans' "finest," that one of them, seeing Capt. Day fall, ran seven blocks before he stopped, afterwards giving the excuse that he was hunting for a patrol box.

At daybreak the officers felt safe to renew the attack upon Charles, so they broke into his room, only to find that—what they probably very well knew—he had gone. It appears that he made his escape by crawling through a hole in the ceiling to a little attic in his house. Here he found that he could not escape except by a window which led into an alley which had no opening on 4th street. He scaled the fence and was soon out of reach.

It was now 5 o'clock Tuesday morning, and a general alarm was given. Sergeant Aucoin and Corporal Trenchard, having received a new supply of courage by returning daylight, renewed their effort to capture the man that they had allowed to escape in the darkness. Citizens were called upon to participate in the man hunt and New Orleans was soon the scene of terrible excitement. Officers were present everywhere, and colored men were arrested on all sides upon the pretext that they were impertinent and "game niggers." An instance is mentioned in the Times-Democrat of the 25th and shows the treatment which unoffending colored men received at the hands of some of the officers. This instance shows Corporal Trenchard, who displayed such remarkable bravery on Monday night in dodging Charles' revolver, in his true light. It shows how brave a white man is when he has a gun attacking a Negro who is a helpless prisoner. The account is as follows:

"The police made some arrests in the neighborhood of the killing of the two officers. Mobs of young darkies gathered everywhere. These Negroes talked and joked about the affair, and many of them were for starting a race war on the spot. It was not until several of these little gangs amalgamated and started demonstrations that the police commenced to act. Nearly a dozen arrests were made within an hour, and everybody in the vicinity was in a tremor of excitement.

"It was about 1 o'clock that the Negroes on Fourth street became very noisy, and George Meyers, who lives on Sixth street, near Rampart, appeared to be one of the prime movers in a little riot that was rapidly developing. Policeman Exnicios and Sheridan placed him under arrest, and owing to the fact that the patrol wagon had just left with a number of prisoners, they walked him toward St. Charles avenue in order to get a conveyance to take him to the Sixth Precinct station.

"A huge crowd of Negroes followed the officers and their prisoners. Between Dryades and Baronne, on Sixth, Corporal Trenchard met the trio. He had his pistol in his hand and he came on them running. The Negroes in the wake of the officers and prisoner took to flight immediately. Some disappeared through gates and some over fences and into yards, for Trenchard, visibly excited, was waving his revolver in the air and was threatening to shoot. He joined the officers in their walk toward St. Charles street, and the way he acted led the white people who were witnessing the affair to believe that his prisoner was the wanted Negro. At every step he would punch him or hit him with the barrel of his pistol, and the onlookers cried, "Lynch him!" "Kill him!" and other expressions until the spectators were thoroughly wrought up. At St. Charles street Trenchard desisted, and, calling an empty ice wagon, threw the Negro into the body of the vehicle and ordered Officer Exnicios to take him to the Sixth Precinct station.

"The ride to the station was a wild one. Exnicios had all he could do to watch his prisoner. A gang climbed into the wagon and administered a terrible thrashing to the black en route. It took a half hour to reach the police station, for the mule that was drawing the wagon was not overly fast. When the station was reached a mob of nearly 200 howling white youths was awaiting it. The noise they made was something terrible. Meyers was howling for mercy before he reached the ground. The mob dragged him from the wagon, the officer with him. Then began a torrent of abuse for the unfortunate prisoner.

"The station door was but thirty feet away, but it took Exnicios nearly five minutes to fight his way through the mob to the door. There were no other officers present, and the station seemed to be deserted. Neither the doorman nor the clerk paid any attention to the noise on the outside. As the result, the maddened crowd wrought their vengeance on the Negro. He was punched, kicked, bruised and torn. The clothes were ripped from his back, while his face after that few minutes was unrecognizable."

This was the treatment accorded and permitted to a helpless prisoner because he was black. All day Wednesday the man hunt continued. The excitement caused by the deaths of Day and Lamb became intense. The officers of the law knew they were trailing a man whose aim was deadly and whose courage they had never seen surpassed. Commenting upon the marksmanship of the man which the paper styled a fiend, the Times-Democrat of Wednesday said:

"One of the extraordinary features of the tragedy was the marksmanship displayed by the Negro desperado. His aim was deadly and his coolness must have been something phenomenal. The two shots that killed Captain Day and patrolman Lamb struck their victims in the head, a circumstance remarkable enough in itself, considering the suddenness and fury of the onslaught and the darkness that reigned in the alley way.

"Later on Charles fired at Corporal Perrier, who was

standing at least seventy-five yards away. The murderer appeared at the gate, took lightning aim along the side of the house, and sent a bullet whizzing past the officer's ear. It was a close shave, and a few inches' deflection would no doubt have added a fourth victim to the list.

"At the time of the affray there is good reason to believe that Charles was seriously wounded, and at any event he had lost quantities of blood. His situation was as critical as it is possible to imagine, yet he shot like an expert in a target range. The circumstance shows the desperate character of the fiend, and his terrible dexterity with weapons makes him one of the most formidable monsters that has ever been loose upon the community."

Wednesday New Orleans was in the hands of a mob. Charles, still sought for and still defending himself, had killed four policemen, and everybody knew that he intended to die fighting. Unable to vent its vindictiveness and blood-thirsty vengeance upon Charles, the mob turned its attention to other colored men who happened to get in the path of its fury. Even colored women, as has happened many times before, were assaulted and beaten and killed by the brutal hoodlums who thronged the streets. The reign of absolute lawlessness began about 8 o'clock Wednesday night. The mob gathered near the Lee statue and was soon making its way to the place where the officers had been shot by Charles. Describing the mob, the Times-Democrat of Thursday morning says:

"The gathering in the square, which numbered about 700, eventually became in a measure quiet, and a large, lean individual, in poor attire and with unshaven face, leaped upon a box that had been brought for the purpose, and in a voice that under no circumstances could be heard at a very great distance, shouted: 'Gentlemen. I am the Mayor of

Kenner.' He did not get a chance for some minutes to further declare himself, for the voice of the rabble swung over his like a huge wave over a sinking craft. He stood there, however, wildly waving his arms and demanded a hearing, which was given him when the uneasiness of the mob was quieted for a moment or so.

  " 'I am from Kenner, gentlemen, and I have come down to New Orleans to-night to assist you in teaching the blacks a lesson. I have killed a Negro before, and in revenge of the wrong wrought upon you and yours, I am willing to kill again. The only way that you can teach these Niggers a lesson and put them in their place is to go out and lynch a few of them as an object lesson. String up a few of them, and the others will trouble you no more. That is the only thing to do—kill them, string them up, lynch them! I will lead you, if you will but follow. On to the Parish Prison and lynch Pierce!'

  "They bore down on the Parish Prison like an avalanche, but the avalanche split harmlessly on the blank walls of the jail, and Remy Klock sent out a brief message: 'You can't have Pierce, and you can't get in.' Up to that time the mob had had no opposition, but Klock's answer chilled them considerably. There was no deep-seated desperation in the crowd after all, only that wild lawlessness which leads to deeds of cruelty, but not to stubborn battle. Around the corner from the prison is a row of pawn and second-hand shops, and to these the mob took like the ducks to the proverbial mill-pond, and the devastation they wrought upon Mr. Fink's establishment was beautiful in its line.

  "Everything from breast pins to horse pistols went into the pockets of the crowd, and in the melee a man was shot down, while just around the corner somebody planted a long knife in the body of a little newsboy for no reason as yet shown.

Every now and then a Negro would be flushed somewhere in the outskirts of the crowd and left, beaten to a pulp. Just how many were roughly handled will never be known, but the unlucky thirteen had been severely beaten and maltreated up to a late hour, a number of those being in the Charity Hospital under the bandages and courtplaster of the doctors."

The first colored man to meet death at the hands of the mob was a passenger on a street car. The mob had broken itself into fragments after its disappointment at the jail, each fragment looking for a Negro to kill. The bloodthirsty cruelty of one crowd is thus described by the Times-Democrat:

" 'We will get a Nigger down here, you bet!' was the yelling boast that went up from a thousand throats, and for the first time the march of the mob was directed toward the downtown sections. The words of the rioters were prophetic, for just as Canal street was reached a car on the Villere line came along.

" 'Stop that car!' cried half a hundred men. The advance guard, heeding the injunction, rushed up to the slowly moving car, and several, seizing the trolley, jerked it down.

" 'Here's a Negro!' said half a dozen men who sprang upon the car.

"The car was full of passengers at the time, among them several women. When the trolley was pulled down and the car thrown in total darkness, the latter began to scream, and for a moment or so it looked as if the life of every person in the car was in peril, for some of the crowd with demoniacal yells of 'There he goes!' began to fire their weapons indiscriminately. The passengers in the car hastily jumped to the ground and joined the crowd, as it was evidently the safest place to be.

" 'Where's that Nigger?' was the query passed along the line, and with that the search began in earnest. The Negro, after jumping off the car, lost himself for a few moments in the crowd, but after a brief search he was again located. The slight delay seemed, if possible, only to whet the desire of the bloodthirsty crowd, for the reappearance of the Negro was the signal for a chorus of screams and pistol shots directed at the fugitive. With the speed of a deer, the man ran straight from the corner of Canal and Villere to Customhouse street. The pursuers, closely following, kept up a running fire, but notwithstanding the fact that they were right at the Negro's heels their aim was poor and their bullets went wide of the mark.

"The Negro, on reaching Customhouse street, darted from the sidewalk out into the middle of the street. This was the worst maneuver that he could have made, as it brought him directly under the light from an arc lamp, located on a nearby corner. When the Negro came plainly in view of the foremost of the closely following mob they directed a volley at him. Half a dozen pistols flashed simultaneously, and one of the bullets evidently found its mark, for the Negro stopped short, threw up his hands, wavered for a moment, and then started to run again. This stop, slight as it was, proved fatal to the Negro's chances, for he had not gotten twenty steps farther when several of the men in advance of the others reached his side. A burly fellow, grabbing him with one hand, dealt him a terrible blow on the head with the other. The wounded man sank to the ground. The crowd pressed around him and began to beat him and stamp him. The men in the rear pressed forward and those beating the man were shoved forward. The half-dead Negro, when he was freed from his assailants, crawled over to the gutter. The men behind, however, stopped pushing when those in front yelled, 'We've got him,' and then it was that the attack on the bleeding

Negro was resumed. A vicious kick directed at the Negro's head sent him into the gutter, and for a moment the body sank from view beneath the muddy, slimy water. 'Pull him out; don't let him drown,' was the cry, and instantly several of the men around the half-drowned Negro bent down and drew the body out. Twisting the body around they drew the head and shoulders up on the street, while from the waist down the Negro's body remained under the water. As soon as the crowd saw that the Negro was still alive they again began to beat and kick him. Every few moments they would stop and striking matches look into the man's face to see if he still lived. To better see if he was dead they would stick lighted matches to his eyes. Finally, believing he was dead, they left him and started out to look for other Negroes. Just about this time some one yelled, 'He ain't dead,' and the men came back and renewed the attack. While the men were beating and pounding the prostrate form with stones and sticks a man in the crowd ran up, and crying, 'I'll fix the d—— Negro,' poked the muzzle of a pistol almost against the body and fired. This shot must have ended the man's life, for he lay like a stone, and realizing that they were wasting energy in further attacks, the men left their victim lying in the street."

The same paper, on the same day, July 26th describes the brutal butchery of an aged colored man early in the morning:

"Baptiste Philo, a Negro, 75 years of age, was a victim of mob violence at Kerlerec and North Peters streets about 2:30 o'clock this morning. The old man is employed about the French Market, and was on his way there when he was met by a crowd and desperately shot. The old man found his way to the Third Precinct police station, where it was found that he had received a ghastly wound in the abdomen. The ambulance was summoned and he was conveyed to the Charity Hospital. The students pronounced the wound fatal after a superficial examination."

Mob rule continued Thursday, its violence increasing every hour, until 2 p.m., when the climax seemed to be reached. The fact that colored men and women had been made the victims of brutal mobs, chased through the streets, killed upon the highways and butchered in their homes, did not call the best element in New Orleans to active exertion in behalf of law and order. The killing of a few Negroes more or less by irresponsible mobs does not cut much figure in Louisiana. But when the reign of mob law exerts a depressing influence upon the stock market and city securities begin to show unsteady standing in money centers, then the strong arm of the good white people of the South asserts itself and order is quickly brought out of chaos.

It was so with New Orleans on that Thursday. The better element of the white citizens began to realize that New Orleans in the hands of a mob would not prove a promising investment for Eastern capital, so the better element began to stir itself, not for the purpose of punishing the brutality against the Negroes who had been beaten, or bringing to justice the murderers of those who had been killed, but for the purpose of saving the city's credit. The Times-Democrat, upon this phase of the situation, on Friday morning says:

"When it became known later in the day that State bonds had depreciated from a point to a point and a half on the New York market a new phase of seriousness was manifest to the business community. Thinking men realized that a continuance of unchecked disorder would strike a body blow to the credit of the city and in all probability would complicate the negotiation of the forthcoming improvement bonds. The bare thought that such a disaster might be brought about by a few irresponsible boys, tramps and ruffians, inflamed popular indignation to fever pitch. It was all that was needed to bring to the aid of the authorities the active personal cooperation of the entire better element."

With the financial credit of the city at stake, the good citizens rushed to the rescue, and soon the Mayor was able to mobilize a posse of 1,000 willing men to assist the police in maintaining order, but rioting still continued in different sections of the city. Colored men and women were beaten, chased and shot whenever they made their appearance upon the street. Late in the night a most despicable piece of villainy occurred on Rousseau street, where an aged colored woman was killed by the mob. The Times-Democrat thus describes the murder:

"Hannah Mabry, an old Negress, was shot and desperately wounded shortly after midnight this morning while sleeping in her home at No. 1929 Rousseau street. It was the work of a mob, and was evidently well planned so far as escape was concerned, for the place was reached by police officers and a squad of the volunteer police within a very short time after the reports of the shots, but not a prisoner was secured. The square was surrounded, but the mob had scattered in several directions, and, the darkness of the neighborhood aiding them, not one was taken.

"At the time the mob made the attack on the little house there were also in it David Mabry, the 62-year-old husband of the wounded woman; her son, Harry Mabry; his wife, Fannie, and an infant child. The young couple with their babe could not be found after the whole affair was over, and they either escaped or were hustled off by the mob. A careful search of the whole neighborhood was made, but no trace of them could be found.

"The little place occupied by the Mabry family is an old

cottage on the swamp side of Rousseau street. It is furnished
with slat shutters to both doors and windows. These shutters
had been pulled off by the mob and the volleys fired through
the glass doors. The younger Mabrys, father, mother and
child, were asleep in the first room at the time. Hannah
Mabry and her old husband were sleeping in the next room.
The old couple occupied the same bed, and it is miraculous
that the old man did not share the fate of his spouse.

"Officer Bitterwolf, who was one of the first on the scene,
said that he was about a block and a half away with Officers
Fordyce and Sweeney. There were about twenty shots fired,
and the trio raced to the cottage. They saw twenty or thirty
men running down Rousseau street. Chase was given and the
crowd turned toward the river and scattered into several
vacant lots in the neighborhood.

"The volunteer police stationed at the Sixth Precinct had
about five blocks to run before they arrived. They also moved
on the reports of the firing, and in a remarkably short time
the square was surrounded, but no one could be taken. As
they ran to the scene they were assailed on every hand with
vile epithets and the accusation of 'Nigger lovers.'

"Rousseau street, where the cottage is situated, is a particularly dark spot, and no doubt the members of the mob were
well acquainted with the neighborhood, for the officers said
that they seemed to sink into the earth, so completely and
quickly did they disappear after they had completed their
work, which was complete with the firing of the volley.

"Hannah Mabry was taken to the Charity Hospital in the
ambulance, where it was found on examination that she had
been shot through the right lung, and that the wound was a
particularly serious one.

"Her old husband was found in the little wrecked home
well nigh distracted with fear and grief. It was he who

informed the police that at the time of the assault the younger Mabrys occupied the front room. As he ran about the little home as well as his feeble condition would permit he severely lacerated his feet on the glass broken from the windows and door. He was escorted to the Sixth Precinct station, where he was properly cared for. He could not realize why his little family had been so murderously attacked, and was inconsolable when his wife was driven off in the ambulance piteously moaning in her pain.

"The search for the perpetrators of the outrage was thorough, but both police and armed force of citizens had only their own efforts to rely on. The residents of the neighborhood were aroused by the firing, but they would give no help in the search and did not appear in the least concerned over the affair. Groups were on almost every doorstep, and some of them even jeered in a quiet way at the men who were voluntarily attempting to capture the members of the mob. Absolutely no information could be had from any of them, and the whole affair had the appearance of being the work of roughs who either lived in the vicinity, or their friends."

DEATH OF CHARLES

Friday witnessed the final act in the bloody drama begun by the three police officers, Aucoin, Mora and Cantrelle. Betrayed into the hands of the police, Charles, who had already sent two of his would-be murderers to their death, made a last stand in a small building, 1210 Saratoga street, and, still defying his pursuers, fought a mob of twenty thousand people, single-handed and alone, killing three more men, mortally wounding two more and seriously wounding nine others. Unable to get to him in his stronghold, the besiegers set fire to his house of refuge. While the building was burning Charles was shooting, and every crack of his death-dealing rifle added another victim to the price which he had placed upon his own life. Finally, when fire and smoke became too much for flesh and blood to stand, the long sought for fugitive appeared in the door, rifle in hand, to charge the countless guns that were drawn upon him. With a courage which was indescribable, he raised his gun to fire again, but this time it failed, for a hundred shots riddled his body, and he fell dead face fronting to the mob. This last scene in the terrible drama is thus described in the Times-Democrat of July 26th:

"Early yesterday afternoon, at 3 o'clock or thereabouts, Police Sergeant Gabriel Porteus was instructed by Chief Gaster to go to a house at No. 1210 Saratoga street, and search it for the fugitive murderer, Robert Charles. A private 'tip' had been received at the headquarters that the fiend was hiding somewhere on the premises.

"Sergeant Porteus took with him Corporal John R. Lally and Officers Zeigel and Essey. The house to which they were directed is a small, double frame cottage, standing flush with Saratoga street, near the corner of Clio. It has two street entrances and two rooms on each side, one in front and one in the rear. It belongs to the type of cheap little dwellings commonly tenanted by Negroes.

"Sergeant Porteus left Ziegel and Essey to guard the outside and went with Corporal Lally to the rear house, where he found Jackson and his wife in the large room on the left. What immediately ensued is only known by the Negroes. They say the sergeant began to question them about their lodgers and finally asked them whether they knew anything about Robert Charles. They strenuously denied all knowledge of his whereabouts.

"The Negroes lied. At that very moment the hunted and

desperate murderer lay concealed not a dozen feet away. Near the rear, left-hand corner of the room is a closet or pantry, about three feet deep, and perhaps eight feet long. The door was open and Charles was crouching, Winchester in hand, in the dark further end.

"Near the closet was a bucket of water, and Jackson says that Sergeant Porteous walked toward it to get a drink. At the next moment a shot rang out and the brave officer fell dead. Lally was shot directly afterward. Exactly how and where will never be known, but the probabilities are that the black fiend sent a bullet into him before he recovered from his surprise at the sudden onslaught. Then the murderer dashed out of the back door and disappeared.

"The neighborhood was already agog with the tragic events of the two preceding days, and the sound of the shots was a signal for wild and instant excitement. In a few moments a crowd had gathered and people were pouring in by the hundred from every point of the compass. Jackson and his wife had fled and at first nobody knew what had happened, but the surmise that Charles had recommenced his bloody work was on every tongue and soon some of the bolder found their way to the house in the rear. There the bleeding forms of the two policemen told the story.

"Lally was still breathing, and a priest was sent for to administer the last rites. Father Fitzgerald responded, and while he was bending over the dying man the outside throng was rushing wildly through the surrounding yards and passageways searching for the murderer. 'Where is he?' 'What has become of him?' were the questions on every lip.

"Suddenly the answer came in a shot from the room directly overhead. It was fired through a window facing Saratoga street, and the bullet struck down a young man named Alfred J. Bloomfield, who was standing in the narrow passage-way between the two houses. He fell on his knees and a second bullet stretched him dead.

"When he fled from the closet Charles took refuge in the upper story of the house. There are four windows on that floor, two facing toward Saratoga street and two toward Rampart. The murderer kicked several breaches in the frail central partition, so he could rush from side to side, and like a trapped beast, prepared to make his last stand.

"Nobody had dreamed that he was still in the house, and when Bloomfield was shot there was a headlong stampede. It was some minutes before the exact situation was understood. Then rifles and pistols began to speak, and a hail of bullets poured against the blind frontage of the old house. Every one hunted some coign of vantage, and many climbed to adjacent roofs. Soon the glass of the four upper windows was shattered by flying lead. The fusillade sounded like a battle, and the excitement upon the streets was indescribable.

"Throughout all this hideous uproar Charles seems to have retained a certain diabolical coolness. He kept himself mostly out of sight, but now and then he thrust the gleaming barrel of his rifle through one of the shattered window panes and fired at his besiegers. He worked the weapon with incredible rapidity, discharging from three to five cartridges each time before leaping back to a place of safety. These replies came from all four windows indiscriminately, and showed that he was keeping a close watch in every direction. His wonderful marksmanship never failed him for a moment, and when he missed it was always by the narrowest margin only.

"On the Rampart street side of the house there are several sheds, commanding an excellent range of the upper story. Detective Littleton, Andrew Van Kuren of the Workhouse force and several others climbed upon one of these and opened fire on the upper windows, shooting whenever they could catch a glimpse of the assassin. Charles responded with his rifle, and presently Van Kuren climbed down to find a better position. He was crossing the end of the shed when he was killed.

"Another of Charles' bullets found its billet in the body of Frank Evans, an ex-member of the police force. He was on the Rampart street side firing whenever he had an opportunity. Officer J. W. Bofill and A. S. Leclerc were also wounded in the fusillade.

"While the events thus briefly outlined were transpiring time was a-wing, and the cooler headed in the crowd began to realize that some quick and desperate expedient must be adopted to insure the capture of the fiend and to avert what might be a still greater tragedy than any yet enacted. For nearly two hours the desperate monster had held his besiegers at bay, darkness would soon be at hand and no one could predict what might occur if he made a dash for liberty in the dark.

"At this critical juncture it was suggested that the house be fired. The plan came as an inspiration, and was adopted as the only solution of the situation. The wretched old rookery counted for nothing against the possible continued sacrifice of human life, and steps were immediately taken to apply the torch. The fire department had been summoned to the scene soon after the shooting began; its officers were warned to be ready to prevent a spread of the conflagration, and several men rushed into the lower right-hand room and started a blaze in one corner.

"They first fired an old mattress, and soon smoke was pouring out in dense volumes. It filled the interior of the ramshackle structure, and it was evident that the upper story would soon become untenable. An interval of tense excitement followed, and all eyes were strained for a glimpse of the murderer when he emerged.

"Then came the thrilling climax. Smoked out of his den, the desperate fiend descended the stairs and entered the lower room. Some say he dashed into the yard, glaring around vainly for some avenue of escape; but, however that may be, he was soon a few moments later moving about behind the lower windows. A dozen shots were sent through the wall in the hope of reaching him, but he escaped unscathed. Then suddenly the door on the right was flung open and he dashed out. With head lowered and rifle raised ready to fire on the instant, Charles dashed straight for the rear door of the front cottage. To reach it he had to traverse a little walk shaded by a vineclad arbor. In the back room, with a cocked revolver in his hand, was Dr. C. A. Noiret, a young medical student, who was aiding the citizens' posse. As he sprang through the door Charles fired a shot, and the bullet whizzed past the doctor's head. Before it could be repeated Noiret's pistol cracked and the murderer reeled, turned half around and fell on his back. The doctor sent another ball into his body as he struck the floor, and half a dozen men, swarming into the room from the front, riddled the corpse with bullets.

"Private Adolph Anderson of the Connell Rifles was the first man to announce the death of the wretch. He rushed to the street door, shouted the news to the crowd, and a moment later the bleeding body was dragged to the pavement and made the target of a score of pistols. It was shot, kicked and beaten almost out of semblance to humanity.

*   *   *

"The limp dead body was dropped at the edge of the sidewalk and from there dragged to the muddy roadway by half a hundred hands. There in the road more shots were fired into the body. Corporal Trenchard, a brother-in-law of Porteus, led the shooting into the inanimate clay. With each shot there was a cheer for the work that had been done and curses and imprecations on the inanimate mass of riddled flesh that was once Robert Charles.

"Cries of 'Burn him! Burn him' were heard from Clio street all the way to Erato street, and it was with difficulty that the crowd was restrained from totally destroying the wretched dead body. Some of those who agitated burning even secured a large vessel of kerosene, which had previously been brought to the scene for the purpose of firing Charles' refuge, and for a time it looked as though this vengeance might be wreaked on the body. The officers, however, restrained this move, although they were powerless to prevent the stamping and kicking of the body by the enraged crowd.

"After the infuriated citizens had vented their spleen on the body of the dead Negro it was loaded into the patrol wagon. The police raised the body of the heavy black from the ground and literally chucked it into the space on the floor of the wagon between the seats. They threw it with a curse hissed more than uttered and born of the bitterness which was rankling in their breasts at the thought of Charles having taken so wantonly the lives of four of the best of their fellow-officers.

"When the murderer's body landed in the wagon it fell in such a position that the hideously mutilated head, kicked, stamped and crushed, hung over the end.

"As the wagon moved off, the followers, who were protesting against its being carried off, declaring that it should be burned, poked and struck it with sticks, beating it into such a condition that it was utterly impossible to tell what the man ever looked like.

"As the patrol wagon rushed through the rough street,

jerking and swaying from one side of the thoroughfare to the other, the gory, mud-smeared head swayed and swung and jerked about in a sickening manner, the dark blood dripping on the step and spattering the body of the wagon and the trousers of the policemen standing on the step."

MOB BRUTALITY

The brutality of the mob was further shown by the unspeakable cruelty with which it beat, shot and stabbed to death an unoffending colored man, name unknown, who happened to be walking on the street with no thought that he would be set upon and killed because he was a colored man. The Times-Democrat's description of the outrage is as follows:

"While the fight between the Negro desperado and the citizens was in progress yesterday afternoon at Clio and Saratoga streets another tragedy was being enacted downtown in the French quarter, but it was a very one-sided affair. The object of the white man's wrath was, of course, a Negro, but, unlike Charles, he showed no fight, but tried to escape from the furious mob which was pursuing him, and which finally put an end to his existence in a most cruel manner.

"The Negro, whom no one seemed to know—at any rate no one could be found in the vicinity of the killing who could tell who he was—was walking along the levee, as near as could be learned, when he was attacked by a number of white longshoremen or screwmen. For what reason, if there was any reason other than the fact that he was a Negro, could not be learned, and immediately they pounced upon him he broke ground and started on a desperate run for his life.

"The hunted Negro started off the levee toward the French Vegetable Market, changed his course out the sidewalk toward

Gallatin street. The angry, yelling mob was close at his heels, and increasing steadily as each block was traversed. At Gallatin street he turned up that thoroughfare, doubled back into North Peters street and ran into the rear of No. 1216 of that street, which is occupied by Chris Reuter as a commission store and residence.

"He rushed frantically through the place and out on to the gallery on the Gallatin street side. From this gallery he jumped to the street and fell flat on his back on the sidewalk. Springing to his feet as soon as possible, with a leaden hail fired by the angry mob whistling about him, he turned to his merciless pursuers in an appealing way, and, throwing up one hand, told them not to shoot any more, that they could take him as he was.

"But the hail of lead continued, and the unfortunate Negro finally dropped to the sidewalk, mortally wounded. The mob then rushed upon him, still continuing the fusillade, and upon reaching his body a number of Italians, who had joined the howling mob, reached down and stabbed him in the back and buttock with big knives. Others fired shots into his head until his teeth were shot out, three shots having been fired into his mouth. There were bullet wounds all over his body.

"Others who witnessed the affair declared that the man was fired at as he was running up the stairs leading to the living apartments above the store, and that after jumping to the sidewalk and being knocked down by a bullet he jumped up and ran across the street, then ran back and tried to get back into the commission store. The Italians, it is said, were all drunk, and had been shooting firecrackers. Tiring of this, they began shooting at Negroes, and when the unfortunate man who was killed ran by they joined in the chase.

"No one was arrested for the shooting, the neighborhood having been deserted by the police, who were sent up to the place where Charles was fighting so desperately. No one could or would give the names of any of those who had participated in the chase and the killing, nor could any one be found who knew who the Negro was. The patrol wagon was called and the terribly mutilated body sent to the morgue and the coroner notified.

"The murdered Negro was copper colored, about 5 feet 11 inches in height, about 35 years of age, and was dressed in blue overalls and a brown slouch hat. At 10:30 o'clock the vicinity of the French Market was very quiet. Squads of special officers were patrolling the neighborhood, and there did not seem to be any prospects of disorder."

During the entire time the mob held the city in its hands and went about holding up street cars and searching them, taking from them colored men to assault, shoot and kill, chasing colored men upon the public square, through alleys and into houses of anybody who would take them in, breaking into the homes of defenseless colored men and women and beating aged and decrepit men and women to death, the police and the legally-constituted authorities showed plainly where their sympathies were, for in no case reported through the daily papers does there appear the arrest, trial and conviction of one of the mob for any of the brutalities which occurred. The ring-leaders of the mob were at no time disguised. Men were chased, beaten and killed by white brutes, who boasted of their crimes, and the murderers still walk the streets of New Orleans, well known and absolutely exempt from prosecution. Not only were they exempt from prosecution by the police while the town was in the hands of the mob, but even now that law and order is supposed to resume control, these men, well known, are not now, nor ever will be, called to account for the unspeakable brutalities of that terrible week.

On the other hand, the colored men who were beaten by the police and dragged into the station for purposes of intimidation, were quickly called up before the courts and fined or sent to jail upon the statement of the police. Instances of Louisiana justice as it is dispensed in New Orleans are here quoted from the Times-Democrat of July 26th:

"JUSTICE DEALT OUT TO FOLKS WHO TALKED TOO MUCH

"All the Negroes and whites who were arrested in the vicinity of Tuesday's tragedy had a hard time before Recorder Hughes yesterday. Lee Jackson was the first prisoner, and the evidence established that he made his way to the vicinity of the crime and told his Negro friends that he thought a good many more policemen ought to be killed. Jackson said he was drunk when he made the remark. He was fined $25 or thirty days.

"John Kennedy was found wandering about the street Tuesday night with an open razor in his hand, and he was given $25 or thirty days.

"Edward McCarthy, a white man, who arrived only four days since from New York, went to the scene of the excitement at the corner of Third and Rampart streets, and told the Negroes that they were as good as any white man. This remark was made by McCarthy, as another white man said the Negroes should be lynched. McCarthy told the recorder that he considered a Negro as good as a white in body and soul. He was fined $25 or thirty days.

"James Martin, Simon Montegut, Eddie McCall, Alex Washington and Henry Turner were up for failing to move on. Martin proved that he was at the scene to assist the police and was discharged. Montegut, being a cripple, was also released, but the others were fined $25 or thirty days each.

"Eddie Williams for refusing to move on was given $25 or thirty days.

"Matilda Gamble was arrested by the police for saying that two officers were killed and it was a pity more were not shot. She was given $25 or thirty days. ["]

INSOLENT BLACKS

"Recorder Hughes received Negroes in the first recorder's office yesterday morning in a way that they will remember for a long time, and all of them were before the magistrate for having caused trouble through incendiary remarks concerning the death of Captain Day and Patrolman Lamb."

"Lee Jackson was before the recorder and was fined $25 or thirty days. He was lippy around where the trouble happened Tuesday morning, and some white men punched him good and hard and the police took him. Then the recorder gave him a dose, and now he is in the parish prison."

"John Kennedy was another black who got into trouble. He said that the shooting of the police by Charles was a good thing, and for this he was pounded. Patrolman Lorenzo got him and saved him from being lynched, for the black had an open razor. He was fined $25 or thirty days."

"Edward McCarthy, a white man, mixed up with the crowd, and an expression of sympathy nearly cost him his head, for some whites about started for him, administering licks and blows with fists and umbrellas. The recorder fined him $25 or thirty days. He is from New York."

"Then James Martin, a white man, and Simon Montegut, Eddie Call, Henry Turner and Alex. Washington were before the magistrate for having failed to move on when the police ordered them from the square where the bluecoats were

Tuesday, waiting in the hope of catching Charles. All save Martin and Montegut were fined."

"Eddie Williams, a little Negro who was extremely fresh with the police, was fined $10 or ten days."

SHOCKING BRUTALITY

The whole city was at the mercy of the mob and the display of brutality was a disgrace to civilization. One instance is described in the Picayune as follows:

"A smaller party detached itself from the mob at Washington and Rampart streets, and started down the latter thoroughfare. One of the foremost spied a Negro, and immediately there was a rush for the unfortunate black man. With the sticks they had torn from fences on the line of march the young outlaws attacked the black and clubbed him unmercifully, acting more like demons than human beings. After being severely beaten over the head, the Negro started to run with the whole gang at his heels. Several revolvers were brought into play and pumped their lead at the refugee. The Negro made rapid progress and took refuge behind the blinds of a little cottage in Rampart street, but he had been seen, and the mob hauled him from his hiding place and again commenced beating him. There were more this time, some twenty or thirty, all armed with sticks and heavy clubs, and under their incessant blows the Negro could not last long. He begged for mercy, and his cries were most pitiful, but a mob has no heart, and his cries were only answered with more blows.

" 'For God's sake, boss, I ain't done nothin'. Don't kill me. I swear I ain't done nothin'.'

"The white brutes turned

"A DEAF EAR TO THE PITYING CRIES

of the black wretch and the drubbing continued. The cries subsided into moans, and soon the black swooned away into unconsciousness. Still not content with their heartless work, they pulled the Negro out and kicked him into the gutter. For the time those who had beaten the black seemed satisfied and left him groaning in the gutter, but others came up, and, regretting that they had not had a hand in the affair, they determined to evidence their bravery to their fellows and beat the man while he was in the gutter, hurling rocks and stones at his black form. One thoughtless white brute, worse even than the black slayer of the police officers, thought to make himself a hero in the eyes of his fellows and fired his revolver repeatedly into the helpless wretch. It was dark and the fellow probably aimed carelessly. After firing three or four shots he also left without knowing what extent of injury he inflicted on the black wretch who was left lying in the gutter."

MURDER ON THE LEVEE

One part of the crowd made a raid on the tenderloin district, hoping to find there some belated Negro for a sacrifice. They were urged on by the white prostitutes, who applauded their murderous mission. Says an account:

"The red light district was all excitement. Women—that is, the white women—were out on their stoops and peeping over their galleries and through their windows and doors, shouting to the crowd to go on with their work, and kill Negroes for them.

" 'Our best wishes, boys,' they encouraged; and the mob answered with shouts, and whenever a Negro house was sighted a bombardment was started on the doors and windows."

No colored men were found on the streets until the mob reached Custom House place and Villiers streets. Here a victim was found and brutally put to death. The Picayune description is as follows:

"Some stragglers had run a Negro into a car at the corner of Bienville and Villere streets. He was seeking refuge in the conveyance, and he believed that the car would not be stopped and could speed along. But the mob determined to stop the car, and ordered the motorman to halt. He put on his brake. Some white men were in the car.

" 'Get out, fellows,' shouted several of the mob.

" 'All whites fall out,' was the second cry, and the poor Negro understood that it was meant that he should stay in the car.

"He wanted to save his life. The poor fellow crawled under the seats. But some one in the crowd saw him and yelled that he was hiding. Two or three men climbed through the windows with their pistols; others jumped over the motorman's board, and dozens tumbled into the rear of the car. Big, strong hands got the Negro by the shirt. He was dragged out of the conveyance, and was pushed to the street. Some fellow ran up and struck him with a club. The blow was heavy, but it did not fell him, and the Negro ran toward Canal street, stealing along the wall of the Tulane Medical Building. Fifty men ran after him, caught the poor fellow and hurried him back into the crowd. Fists were aimed at him, then clubs went upon his shoulders, and finally the black plunged into the gutter.

"A gun was fired, and the Negro, who had just gotten to his feet, dropped again. He tried to get up, but a volley was sent after him, and in a little while he was dead.

"The crowd looked on at the terrible work. Then the lights in the houses of ill-fame began to light up again, and women peeped out of the blinds. The motorman was given the order to go on. The gong clanged and the conveyance sped out of the way. For half an hour the crowd held their place at the corner, then the patrol wagon came and the body was picked up and hurried to the morgue.

"Coroner Richard held an autopsy on the body of the Negro who was forced out of car 98 of the Villere line and shot down. It was found that he was wounded four times, the most serious wound being that which struck him in the right side, passing through the lungs, and causing hemorrhages, which brought about death.

"Nobody tried to identify the poor fellow and his name is unknown."

A VICTIM IN THE MARKET

Soon after the murder of the man on the street car many of the same mob marched down to the market place. There they found a colored market man named Louis Taylor, who had gone to begin his early morning's work. He was at once set upon by the mob and killed. The Picayune account says:

"Between 1 and 2 o'clock this morning a mob of several hundred men and boys, made up of participants in many of the earlier affairs, marched on the French Market. Louis Taylor, a Negro vegetable carrier, who is about 30 years of age, was sitting at the soda water stand. As soon as the mob saw him fire was opened and the Negro took to his heels. He ran directly into another section of the mob and any number of shots were fired at him. He fell, face down, on the floor of the market.

"The police in the neighborhood rallied hurriedly and found the victim of mob violence seemingly lifeless. Before they arrived the Negro had been beaten severely about the head and body. The ambulance was summoned and Taylor was carried to the charity hospital, where it was found that he had been shot through the abdomen and arm. The examination was a hurried one, but it sufficed to show that Taylor was mortally wounded.

"After shooting Taylor the members of the mob were pluming themselves on their exploit. 'The Nigger was at the soda water stand and we commenced shooting him,' said one of the rioters. 'He put his hands up and ran, and we shot until he fell. I understand that he is sill alive. If he is, he is a wonder. He was certainly shot enough to be killed.'

"The members of the mob readily admitted that they had taken part in the assaults which marked the earlier part of the evening.

" 'We were up on Jackson avenue and killed a Nigger on Villere street. We came down here, saw a nigger and killed him, too.' This was the way they told the story.

" 'Boys, we are out of ammunition,' said some one.

" 'Well, we will keep on like we are, and if we can't get some before morning, we will take it. We have got to keep this thing up, now we have started.'

"This declaration was greeted by a chorus of applauding yells, and the crowd started up the levee. Half of the men in the crowd, and they were all of them young, were drunk.

"Taylor, when seen at the charity hospital, was suffering greatly, and presented a pitiable spectacle. His clothing was covered with blood, and his face was beaten almost into a pulp. He said that he had gone to the market to work and was quietly sitting down when the mob came and began to fire on him. He was not aware at first that the crowd was after him. When he saw its purpose he tried to run, but fell. He didn't know any of the men in the crowd. There is hardly a chance that Taylor will recover.

"The police told the crowd to move on, but no attempt was made to arrest any one."

A GRAY-HAIRED VICTIM

The bloodthirsty barbarians, having tasted blood, continued their hunt and soon ran across an old man of 75 years. His life had been spent in hard work about the French market, and he was well known as an unoffending, peaceable and industrious old man.

But that made no difference to the mob. He was a Negro, and with a fiendishness that was worse than that of cannibals they beat his life out. The report says:

"There was another gang of men parading the streets in the lower part of the city, looking for any stray Negro who might be on the streets. As they neared the corner of Dauphine and Kerleree, a square below Esplanade avenue, they came upon Baptiste Thilo, an aged Negro, who works in the French Market.

"Thilo for years has been employed by the butchers and fish merchants to carry baskets from the stalls to the wagons, and unload the wagons as they arrive in the morning. He was on his way to the market, when the mob came upon him. One of the gang struck the old Negro, and as he fell, another in the crowd, supposed to be a young fellow, fired a shot. The bullet entered the body just below the right nipple.

"As the Negro fell the crowd looked into his face and they discovered then that the victim was very old. The young man who did the shooting said: 'Oh, he is an old Negro. I'm sorry that I shot him.'

"This is all the old Negro received in the way of consolation.

"He was left where he fell, but later staggered to his feet and made his way to the third precinct station. There the police summoned the ambulance and the students pronounced the wound very dangerous. He was carried to the hospital as rapidly as possible.

"There was no arrest."

Just before daybreak the mob found another victim. He too, was on his way to market, driving a meat wagon. But little is told of his treatment, nothing more than the following brief statement:

"At nearly 3 o'clock this morning a report was sent to the Third Precinct station that a negro was lying on the sidewalk at the corner of Decatur and St. Philip. The man had been pulled off of a meat wagon and riddled with bullets.

"When the police arrived he was insensible and apparently dying. The ambulance students attended the Negro and pronounced the wounds fatal.

"There was nothing found which would lead to the discovery of his identity."

FUN IN GRETNA

If there are any persons so deluded as to think that human life in the South is valued any more than the life of a brute, he will be speedily undeceived by reading the accounts of unspeakable barbarism committed by the mob in and around New Orleans. In no other civilized country in the world, nay, more, in no land of barbarians would it be possible to duplicate the scenes of brutality that are reported from New Orleans. In the heat of blind fury one might conceive how a mad mob might beat and kill a man taken red-handed in a brutal murder. But it is almost past belief to read that civilized white people, men who boast of their chivalry and blue blood, actually had fun in beating, chasing and shooting men who had no possible connection with any crime.

But this actually happened in Gretna, a few miles from New Orleans. In its description of the scenes of Tuesday night, the Picayune mentions the brutal chase of several colored men whom the mob sought to kill. In the instances mentioned, the paper said:

"Gretna had its full share of excitement between 8 and 11 o'clock last night, in connection with a report that spread through the town that a Negro resembling the slayer of Police Captain Day, of New Orleans, had been seen on the outskirts of the place.

"It is true that a suspicious-looking Negro was observed by the residents of Madison and Amelia streets lurking about the fences of that neighborhood just after dark, and shortly before 8 o'clock John Fist, a young white man, saw the Negro on Fourth street. He followed the darkey a short distance, and, coming upon Robert Moore, who is known about town as the 'black detective.' Fist pointed the Negro out and Moore at once made a move toward the stranger. The latter observed Moore making in his direction, and, without a word, he sped in the direction of the Brooklyn pasture, Moore following and firing several shots at him. In a few minutes a half hundred white men, including Chief of Police Miller, Constable Dannenhauer, Patrolman Keegan and several special officers, all well-armed, joined in the chase, but in the darkness the negro escaped.

"Just as the pursuing party reached town again, two of the residents of Layfayette avenue, Peter Leson and Robert Henning, reported that they had just chased and shot at a Negro, who had been seen in the yard of the former's house. They were positive the Negro had not escaped from the square. Their report was enough to set the appetite of the crowd on edge, and the square was quickly surrounded, while several dozens of men, armed with lanterns and revolvers, made a search of every yard and under every house in the square. No Negro was found.

"The crowd of armed men was constantly swelling, and at 10 o'clock it had reached the proportions of a small army. At 10:30 o'clock an outbound freight train is due to pass through Gretna on the Texas and Pacific Road, and the crowd, believing that Captain Day's slayer might be aboard one of the cars attempting to leave the scene of his crime, resolved to inspect the train. As the train stopped at the Madison street crossing the engineer was requested to pull very slowly through the town, in order that the trucks of the cars might be examined. There was a string of armed men on each side of the railroad track and in a few moments a Negro was espied riding between two cars. A half dozen weapons were pointed at him and he was ordered to come out. He sprang out with alacrity and was pounced upon almost before he reached the ground. Robert Moore grabbed him and pushed an ugly looking Derringer under his nose and the Negro threw up both hands. Constable Dannenhauer and Patrolman Keegan took charge of him and hustled him off to jail, where he was locked up. The Negro does not at all resemble Robert Charles, but it was best for his sake that he was placed under lock and key. The crowd was not in a humor to let any Negro pass muster last night. The prisoner gave his name as Luke Wallace.

"But now came the real excitement. The train had slowed down almost to a standstill, in the very heart of town. Somebody shouted: 'There he goes, on top of the train!' And sure enough, somebody was going. It was a Negro, too, and he was making a bee-line for the front end of the train. A veritable shower of bullets, shot and rifle balls greeted the flying form, but on it sped. The locomotive had stopped in the middle of the square between Lavoisier and Newton streets, and the Negro, flying with the speed of the wind along the top of the cars, reached the first car of the train and jumped to the tender and then into the cab. As he did several white men standing at the locomotive made a rush into the cab. The Negro sprang swiftly out of the other side, on to the sidewalk. But there were several more men, and as he realized that he was rushing right into their arms he made a spring to leap over the fence of Mrs. Linden's home, on the wood side of the track. Before the Negro got to the top one white man had hold of his legs, while another rushed up, pistol in hand. The man who was holding the darkey's legs was jostled out of the way and the man with the pistol, standing directly beneath the Negro, sent two bullets at him.

"There was a wild scramble, and the vision of a fleeing form in the Linden yard, but that was the last seen of the black man. The yard was entered and searched, and neighboring yards were also searched, but not even the trace of blood was found. It is almost impossible to believe that the Negro was not wounded, for the man who fired at him held the pistol almost against the Negro's body.

"The shots brought out almost everybody—white—in town, and though there was nothing to show for the exciting work, except the arrest of the Negro, who doesn't answer the description of the man wanted, Gretna's male population had its little fun and felt amply repaid for all the trouble it was put to, and all the ammunition it wasted."

BRUTALITY IN NEW ORLEANS

Mob rule reigned supreme Wednesday, and the scenes that were enacted challenge belief. How many colored men and women were abused and injured is not known, for those who escaped were glad to make a place of refuge and took no time to publish their troubles. The mob made no attempt to find Charles; its only purpose was to pursue, beat and kill any colored man or woman who happened to come in sight. Speaking editorially, the Picayune of Thursday, the 26th of July, said:

[Text appears to be missing in original.]

ESCAPED WITH THEIR LIVES

At the Charity Hospital Wednesday night more than a score of people were treated for wounds received at the hands of the mob. Some were able to tell of their mistreatment, and their recitals are briefly given in the Picayune as follows:

"Alex. Ruflin, who is quite seriously injured, is a Pullman car porter, a native of Chicago. He reached New Orleans at 9:20 o'clock last night, and after finishing his work, boarded a Henry Clay avenue car to go to Delachaise street, where he has a sick son.

" 'I hadn't ridden any way," said he, 'when I saw a lot of white folks. They were shouting to 'Get the Niggers.' I didn't know they were after every colored man they saw, and sat still. Two or three men jumped on the car and started at me. One of them hit me over the head with a slungshot, and they started to shooting at me. I jumped out of the car and ran, although I had done nothing. They shot me in the arm and in the leg. I would certainly have been killed had not some gentleman taken my part. If I known New Orleans was so excited I would never have left my car.'

"George Morris is the name of a Negro who was badly injured by a mob which went through the Poydras Market. Morris is employed as watchman there. He heard the noise of the passing crowd and looked out to see what the matter was. As soon as the mob saw him its members started after him.

" 'One man hit me over the head with a club,' said George, after his wounds had been dressed, 'and somebody cut me in the back. I didn't hardly think what was the matter at first, but when I saw they were after me I ran for my life. I ran to the coffee stand, where I work, for protection, but they were right after me, and somebody shot me in the back. At last the police got me away from the crowd. Just before I was hit a friend of mine, who was in the crowd, said, 'You had better go home, Nigger; they're after your kind.' I didn't know then what he meant. I found out pretty quick.'

"Morris is at the hospital. He is a perfect wreck, and while he will probably get well, he will have had a close call.

"Esther Fields is a Negro washerwoman who lives at South Claiborne and Toledano streets. She was at home when she heard a big noise and went out to investigate. She ran into the arms of the mob, and was beaten into insensibility in less time than it takes to tell it. Esther is being treated at the charity hospital, and should be able to get about in a few days. The majority of her bruises are about the head.

"T. P. Sanders fell at the hands of the Jackson avenue

mob. He lives at 1927 Jackson avenue, and was sitting in front of his home when he saw the crowd marching out the street. He stayed to see what the excitement was all about, and was shot in the knee and thorax and horribly beaten about the head before the mob came to the conclusion that he had been done for, and passed on. The ambulance was called and he was picked up and carried to the charity hospital, where his wounds were dressed and pronounced serious.

"Oswald McMahon is nothing more than a boy. He was shot in the leg and afterward carried to the hospital. His injuries are very slight.

"Dan White is another charity hospital patient. He is a Negro roustabout and was sitting in the bar room at Poydras and Franklin streets when a mob passed along and espied him. He was shot in the hand, and would have been roughly dealt with had some policeman not been luckily near and rescued him.

"In addition to the Negroes who suffered from the violence of the mob there were several patients treated at the hospital during the night who had been with the rioters and had been struck by stray bullets or injured in scuffles. None of this class were hurt to any extent. They got their wounds dressed and went out again."

WAS CHARLES A DESPERADO?

The press of the country has united in declaring that Robert Charles was a desperado. As usual, when dealing with a negro, he is assumed to be guilty because he is charged. Even the most conservative of journals refuse to ask evidence to prove that the dead man was a criminal, and that his life had been given over to law-breaking. The minute that the news was flashed across the country that he had shot a white man it was at once declared that he was a fiend incarnate, and that when he was killed the community would be ridden of a black-hearted desperado.

The reporters of the New Orleans papers, who were in the best position to trace the record of this man's life, made every possible effort to find evidence to prove that he was a villain unhung. With all the resources at their command, and inspired by intense interest to paint him as black a villain as possible, these reporters signally failed to disclose a single indictment which charged Robert Charles with a crime. Because they failed to find any legal evidence that Charles was a lawbreaker and desperado his accusers gave full license to their imagination and distorted the facts that they had obtained, in every way possible, to prove a course of criminality, which the records absolutely refuse to show.

Charles had his first encounter with the police Monday night, in which he was shot in the street duel which was begun by the police after Officer Mora had beaten Charles three or four times over the head with his billy in an attempt to make an illegal arrest. In defending himself against the combined attack of two officers with a billy and their guns upon him, Charles shot Officer Mora and escaped.

Early Tuesday morning Charles was traced to Dryades street by officers who were instructed to kill him on sight. There, again defending himself, he shot and killed two officers. This, of course, in the eyes of the American press, made him a desperado. The New Orleans press, in substantiating the charges that he was a desperado, make statements which will be interesting to examine.

In the first place the New Orleans Times-Democrat, of July 25th, calls Charles a "ravisher and a daredevil." It says that from all sources that could be searched "the testimony was cumulative that the character of the murderer, Robert Charles, is that of a daredevil and a fiend in human form." Then in the same article it says:

"The belongings of Robert Charles which were found in his room were a complete index to the character of the man. Although the room and its contents were in a state of chaos on account of the frenzied search for clews by officers and citizens, an examination of his personal effects revealed the mental state of the murderer and the rancor in his heart toward the Caucasian race. Never was the adage; 'A little learning is a dangerous thing,' better exemplified than in the case of the negro who shot to death the two officers."

His room was searched, and the evidence upon which the charge that he was a desperado consisted of pamphlets in support of Negro emigration to Liberia. On his mantel-piece there was found a bullet mold and an outfit for reloading cartridges. There were also pistol scabbards and a bottle of cocaine. The other evidences that Charles was a desperado the writer described as follows:

"In his room were found negro periodicals and other 'race' propaganda, most of which was in the interest of the negro's emigration to Liberia. There were Police Gazettes strewn about his room and other papers of a similar character. Well-worn text-books, bearing his name written in his own scrawling handwriting, and well-filled copybooks found in his trunk showed that he had burnt the midnight oil, and was desirous of improving himself intellectually in order that he might conquer the hated white race. Much of the literature found among his chattels was of a superlatively vituperative character, and attacked the white race in unstinted language and asserted the equal rights of the Negro.

"Charles was evidently the local agent of the 'Voice of Missions,' a 'religious' paper, published at Atlanta, as great bundles of that sheet were found. It is edited by one Bishop Turner, and seems to be the official organ of all haters of the white race. Its editorials are anarchistic in the extreme, and urge upon the negro that the sooner he realizes that he is as good as the white man the better it will be for him. The following verses were clipped from the journal; they were marked 'till forbidden,' and appeared in several successive numbers:

"OUR SENTIMENTS
"H.M.T.

"My country, 'tis of thee,
Dear land of Africa,
    Of thee we sing.
Land where our fathers died,
Land of the Negro's pride,
    God's truth shall ring.

"My native country, thee,
Land of the black and free,
    Thy name I love;
To see thy rocks and rills,
Thy woods and matchless hills,
    Like that above.

"When all thy slanderous ghouls,
In the bosom of sheol,
    Forgotten lie,
Thy monumental name shall live,
And suns thy royal brow shall gild,
Upheaved to heaven high,
    O'ertopping thrones."

"There were no valuables in his room, and if he was a professional thief he had his headquarters for storing his plunder at some other place than his room on Fourth street.

Nothing was found in his room that could lead to the belief that he was a thief, except fifty or more small bits of soap. The inference was that every place he visited he took all of the soap lying around, as all of the bits were well worn and had seen long service on the washstand.

"His wearing apparel was little more than rags, and financially he was evidently not in a flourishing condition. He was in no sense a skilled workman, and his room showed, in fact, that he was nothing more than a laborer.

"The 'philosopher in the garret' was a dirty wretch, and his room, his bedding and his clothing were nasty and filthy beyond belief. His object in life seemed to have been the discomfiture of the white race, and to this purpose he devoted himself with zeal. He declared himself to be a 'patriot,' and wished to be the Moses of his race."

Under the title of "The Making of a Monster," the reporter attempts to give "something of the personality of the arch-fiend, Charles." Giving his imagination full vent, the writer says:

"It is only natural that the deepest interest should attach to the personality of Robert Charles. What manner of man was this fiend incarnate? What conditions developed him? Who were his preceptors? From what ancestral strain, if any, did he derive his ferocious hatred of the whites, his cunning, his brute courage, the apostolic zeal which he displayed in spreading the propaganda of African equality? These are questions involving one of the most remarkable psychological problems of modern times."

In answer to the questions which he propounds, the reporter proceeds to admit that he did not learn anything of a very desperate nature connected with Charles. He says:

"Although Charles was a familiar figure to scores of Negroes in New Orleans, and they had been more or less intimately acquainted with him for over two years, curiously little can be learned of his habits or mode of life. Since the perpetration of his terrible series of crimes it goes without saying that his former friends are inclined to be reticent, but it is reasonably certain that they have very little to tell. In regard to himself, Charles was singularly reticent for a Negro. He did not even indulge in the usual lying about his prowess and his adventures. This was possibly due to the knowledge that he was wanted for a couple of murders. The man had sense enough to know that it would be highly unwise to excite any curiosity about his past.

"When Charles first came to New Orleans he worked here and there as a day laborer. He was employed at different times in a sawmill, on the street gangs, as a roustabout on the levee, as a helper at the sugar works and as a coal shoveler in the engine room of the St. Charles Hotel. At each of the places where he worked he was known as a quiet, rather surly fellow, who had little to say to anybody, and generally performed his tasks in morose silence. He managed to convey the impression, however, of being a man of more than ordinary intelligence.

"A Negro named William Butts, who drives a team on the levee and lives on Washington street, near Baronne, told a Times-Democrat reporter yesterday that Charles got a job about a year ago as agent for a Liberian Immigration Society, which has headquarters at Birmingham, and was much elated at the prospect of making a living without hard labor."

According to the further investigations of this reporter, Charles was also agent for Bishop Turner's "Voice of Missions," the colored missionary organ of the African Methodist Church, edited by H. M. Turner, of Atlanta, Georgia. Concerning his service as agent for the "Voice of Missions," the reporter says:

"He secured a number of subscribers and visited them once a month to collect the installments. In order to insure regular payments it was necessary to keep up enthusiasm, which was prone to wane, and Charles consequently became an active and continual preacher of the propaganda of hatred. Whatever may have been his private sentiments at the outset, this constant harping on one string must eventually have had a powerful effect upon his own mind.

"Exactly how he received his remuneration is uncertain, but he told several of his friends that he got a 'big commission.' Incidentally he solicited subscribers for a Negro paper called the Voice of the Missions, and when he struck a negro who did not want to go to Africa himself, he begged contributions for the 'good of the cause.'

"In the course of time Charles developed into a fanatic on the subject of the Negro oppression and neglected business to indulge in wild tirades whenever he could find a listener. He became more anxious to make converts than to obtain subscribers, and the more conservative darkies began to get afraid of him. Meanwhile he got into touch with certain agitators in the North and made himself a distributing agent for their literature, a great deal of which he gave away. Making money was a secondary consideration to 'the cause.'

"One of the most enthusiastic advocates of the Liberian scheme is the colored Bishop H. M. Turner, of Atlanta. Turner is a man of unusual ability, has been over to Africa personally several times, and has made himself conspicuous by denouncing laws which he claimed discriminated against the blacks. Charles was one of the bishop's disciples and evidence has been found that seems to indicate they were in correspondence."

This was all that the Times-Democrat's reporters could find after the most diligent search to prove that Charles was the fiend incarnate which the press of New Orleans and elsewhere declared him to be.

The reporters of the New Orleans Picayune were no more successful than their brethren of the Times-Democrat. They, too, were compelled to substitute fiction for facts in their attempt to prove Charles a desperado. In the issue of the 26th of July it was said that Charles was well-known in Vicksburg, and was there a consort of thieves. They mentioned that a man named Benson Blake was killed in 1894 or 1895, and that four Negroes were captured, and two escaped. Of the two escaped they claim that Charles was one. The four negroes who were captured were put in jail, and as usual, in the high state of civilization which characterizes Mississippi, the right of the person accused of crime to an indictment by legal process and a legal trial by jury was considered an useless formality if the accused happened to be black. A mob went to the jail that night, the four colored men were delivered to the mob, and all four were hanged in the court-house yard. The reporters evidently assumed that Charles was guilty, if, in fact, he was ever there, because the other four men were lynched. They did not consider it was a fact of any importance that Charles was never indicted. They called him a murderer on general principles.

DIED IN SELF-DEFENSE

The life, character and death of Robert Charles challenges the thoughtful consideration of all fair-minded people. In the frenzy of the moment, when nearly a dozen men lay dead, the victims of his unerring and death-dealing aim, it was natural for a prejudiced press and for citizens in private life to denounce him as a desperado and a murderer. But sea depths are not measured when the ocean rages, nor can absolute justice be determined while public opinion is lashed into fury. There must be calmness to insure correctness of judgment. The fury of the hour must abate before we can deal justly with any man or any cause.

That Charles was not a desperado is amply shown by the discussion in the preceding chapter. The darkest pictures which the reporters could paint of Charles were quoted freely, so that the public might find upon what grounds the press declared him to be a lawbreaker. Unquestionably the grounds are wholly insufficient. Not a line of evidence has been presented to prove that Charles was the fiend which the first reports of the New Orleans charge him to be.

Nothing more should be required to establish his good reputation, for the rule is universal that a reputation must be assumed to be good until it is proved bad. But that rule does not apply to the Negro, for as soon as he is suspected the public judgment immediately determines that he is guilty of whatever crime he stands charged. For this reason, as a matter of duty to the race, and the simple justice to the memory of Charles, an investigation has been made of the life and character of Charles before the fatal affray which led to his death.

Robert Charles was not an educated man. He was a student who faithfully investigated all the phases of oppression from which his race has suffered. That he was a student is amply shown by the Times-Democrat report of the 25th, which says:

"Well-worn text-books, bearing his name written in his own scrawling handwriting, and well-filled copy-books found in his trunk, showed that he had burned the midnight oil, and desired to improve himself intellectually in order that he might conquer the hated white race." From this quotation it

will be seen that he spent the hours after days of hard toil in
trying to improve himself, both in the study of text-books
and in writing.

He knew that he was a student of a problem which required
all the intelligence that a man could command, and he was
burning his midnight oil gathering knowledge that he might
better be able to come to an intelligent solution. To his aid
and the study of this problem he sought the aid of a Christian
newspaper,The Voice of Missions, the organ of the African
Methodist Episcopal Church. He was in communication with
its editor, who is a bishop, and is known all over this country
as a man of learning, a lover of justice and the defender of
law and order. Charles could receive from Bishop Turner
not a word of encouragement to be other than an earnest,
tireless and God-fearing student of the complex problems
which affected the race.

For further help and assistance in his studies, Charles
turned to an organization which has existed and flourished
for many years, at all times managed by men of high Christian
standing and absolute integrity. These men believe and preach
a doctrine that the best interests of the Negro will be subserved
by an emigration from America back to the Fatherland, and
they do all they can to spread the doctrine of emigration and
to give material assistance to those who desire to leave America
and make their future homes in Africa. This organization is
known as "The International Migration Society." It has its
headquarters in Birmingham, Alabama. From this place it
issues pamphlets, some of which were found in the home of
Robert Charles, and which pamphlets the reporters of the
New Orleans papers declare to be incendiary and dangerous
in their doctrine and teaching.

Nothing could be further from the truth. Copies of any
and all of them may be secured by writing to D. J. Flummer

who is President and in charge of the home office in Birmingham, Alabama. Three of the pamphlets found in Charles' room are named respectively:

First, "Prospectus of the Liberian Colonization Society:" which pamphlet in a few brief pages tells of the work of the society, plans, prices and terms of transportation of colored people who choose to go to Africa. These pages are followed by a short, conservative discussion of the Negro question, and close with an argument that Africa furnishes the best asylum for the oppressed Negroes in this country.

The second pamphlet is entitled "Christian Civilization of Africa." This is a brief statement of the advantages of the Republic of Liberia, and an argument in support of the superior conditions which colored people may attain to by leaving the South and settling in Liberia.

The third pamphlet is entitled "The Negro and Liberia." This is a larger document than the other two, and treats more exhaustively the question of emigration, but from the first page to the last there is not an incendiary line or sentence. There is not even a suggestion of violence in all of its thirty-two pages, and not a word which could not be preached from every pulpit in the land.

If it is true that the workman is known by his tools, certainly no harm could ever come from the doctrines which were preached by Charles or the papers and pamphlets distributed by him. Nothing ever written in the "Voice of Missions," and nothing ever published in the pamphlets above alluded to in the remotest way suggest that a peacable man should turn lawbreaker, or that any man should dye his hands in his brother's blood.

In order to secure as far as possible positive information about the life and character of Robert Charles, it was plain that the best course to pursue was to communicate with those with whom he had sustained business relations. Accordingly a letter was forwarded to Mr. D. J. Flummer, who is president of the colonization society, in which letter he was asked to state in reply what information he had of the life and character of Robert Charles. The result was a very prompt letter in response, the text of which is as follows:

Birmingham, Ala., Aug. 21, 1900

Mrs. Ida B. Wells Barnett, Chicago, Ill.:

Dear Madam—Replying to your favor of a recent date requesting me to write you giving such information as I may have concerning the life, habits and character of Robert Charles, who recently shot and killed police officers in New Orleans, I wish to say that my knowledge of him is only such as I have gained form his business connection with the International Migration Society during the past five or six years, during which time I was president of the society.

He having learned that the purpose of this society was to colonize the colored people in Liberia, West Africa, and thereby lessen or destroy the friction and prejudice existing in this country between the two races, set about earnestly and faithfully distributing the literature that we issued from time to time. He always appeared to be mild but earnest in his advocacy of emigration, and never to my knowledge used any method or means that would in the least appear unreasonable, and had always kept within the bounds of law and order in advocating emigration.

The work he performed for this society was all gratuitous, and apparently prompted from his love of humanity, and desires to be instrumental in building up a Negro Nationality in Africa.

If he ever violated a law before the killing of the policemen, I do not know of it. Yours very truly,

D. J. Flummer

Besides this statement, Mr. Flummer enclosed a letter received by the Society two days before the tragedy at New

Orleans. This letter was written by Robert Charles, and it attests his devotion to the cause of emigration which he had espoused. Memoranda on the margin of the letter show that the order was filled by mailing the pamphlets. It is very probable that these were the identical pamphlets which were found by the mob which broke into the room of Robert Charles and seized upon these harmless documents and declared they were sufficient evidence to prove Charles a desperado. In the light of subsequent events the letter of Charles, which follows, sounds like a voice from the tomb:

New Orleans, July 30, 1900.

Mr. D. J. Fummer:

Dear Sir—I received your last pamphlets and they are all given out. I want you to send me some more, and I enclose you the stamps. I think I will go over in Greenville, Miss., and give my people some pamphlets over there. Yours truly,
Robert Charles.

The latest word of information comes from New Orleans from a man who knew Charles intimately for six years. For obvious reasons, his name is withheld. In answer to a letter sent him he answers as follows:

New Orleans, Aug. 23, 1900.

Mrs. Ida B. Wells Barnett:

Dear Madam—It affords me great pleasure to inform you as far as I know of Robert Charles. I have been acquainted with him about six years in this city. He never has, as I know, given any trouble to anyone. He was quiet and a peaceful man and was very frank in speaking. He was too much of a hero to die; few can be found to equal him. I am very sorry to say that I do not know anything of his birthplace, nor his parents, but enclosed find letter from his uncle, from which you may find more information. You will also find one of the circulars in which Charles was in possession of which was styled as a crazy document. Let me say, until our

preachers preach this document we will always be slaves. If
you can help circulate this "crazy" doctrine I would be glad
to have you do so, for I shall never rest until I get to that
heaven on earth: that is,the west coast of Africa, in Liberia.

   With best wishes to you I still remain, as always, for the
good of the race,   ————

By only those whose anger and vindictiveness warp their
judgment is Robert Charles a desperado. Their word is not
supported by the statement of a single fact which justifies
their judgment, and no criminal record shows that he was
ever indicted for any offense, much less convicted of crime.
On the contrary, his work for many years had been with
Christian people, circulating emigration pamphlets and active
as agent for a mission publication. Men who knew him say
that he was a law-abiding, quiet, industrious, peaceable man.
So he lived.

So he lived and so he would have died had not he raised
his hand to resent unprovoked assault and unlawful arrest
that fateful Monday night. That made him an outlaw, and
being a man of courage he decided to die with his face to the
foe. The white people of this country may charge that he was
a desperado, but to the people of his own race Robert Charles
will always be regarded as the hero of New Orleans.

BURNING HUMAN BEINGS ALIVE

Not only has life been taken by mobs in the past twenty years,
but the ordinary procedure of hanging and shooting have
been improved upon during the past ten years. Fifteen human
beings have been burned to death in the different parts of the
country by mobs. Men, women and children have gone to
see the sight, and all have approved the barbarous deeds done

in the high light of the civilization and Christianity of this country.

In 1891 Ed Coy was burned to death in Texarkana, Ark. He was charged with assaulting a white woman, and after the mob had securely tied him to a tree, the men and boys amused themselves for some time sticking knives into Coy's body and slicing off pieces of flesh. When they had amused themselves sufficiently, they poured coal oil over him and the women in the case set fire to him. It is said that fifteen thousand people stood by and saw him burned. This was on a Sunday night, and press reports told how the people looked on while the Negro burned to death.

Feb. 1st, 1893, Henry Smith was burned to death in Paris, Texas. The entire county joined in that exhibition. The district attorney himself went for the prisoner and turned him over to the mob. He was placed upon a float and drawn by four white horses through the principal streets of the city. Men, women and children stood at their doors and waved their handkerchiefs and cheered the echoes. They knew that the man was to be burned to death because the newspaper had declared for three days previous that this would be so. Excursions were run by all the railroads, and the mayor of the town gave the children a holiday so that they might see the sight.

Henry Smith was charged with having assaulted and murdered a little white girl. He was an imbecile, and while he had killed the child, there was no proof that he had criminally assaulted her. He was tied to a stake on a platform which had been built ten feet high, so that everybody might see the sight. The father and brother and uncle of the little white girl that had been murdered was upon that platform about fifty minutes entertaining the crowd of ten thousand persons by burning the victim's flesh with red-hot irons. Their own newspapers told how they burned his eyes out and ran the red-hot iron down his throat, cooking his tongue, and how the crowd cheered with delight. At last, having declared themselves satisfied, coal oil was poured over him and he was burned to death, and the mob fought over the ashes for bones and pieces of his clothes.

July 7th, 1893, in Bardwell, Ky., C. J. Miller was burned to ashes. Since his death this man has been found to be absolutely innocent of the murder of the two white girls with which he was charged. But the mob would wait for no justification. They insisted that, as they were not sure he was the right man, they would compromise the matter by hanging him instead of burning. Not to be outdone, they took the body down and made a huge bonfire out of it.

July 22d, 1893, at Memphis Tenn., the body of Lee Walker was dragged through the street and burned before the court house. Walker had frightened some girls in a wagon along a country road by asking them to let him ride in their wagon. They cried out; some men working in a field near by said it was at attempt of assault, and of course began to look for their prey. There was never any charge of rape; the women only declared that he attempted an assault. After he was apprehended and put in jail and perfectly helpless, the mob dragged him out, shot him, cut him, beat him with sticks, built a fire and burned the legs off, then took the trunk of the body down and dragged further up the street, and at last burned it before the court house.

Sept. 20th, 1893, at Roanoke, Va., the body of a Negro who had quarreled with a white woman was burned in the presence of several thousand persons. These people also wreaked their vengeance upon this helpless victim of the mob's wrath by sticking knives into him, kicking him and beating him with stones and otherwise mutilating him before life was extinct.

June 10th, 1898, at Knoxvill, Ark., James Perry was shut up in a cabin because he had smallpox and burned to death. He had been quarantined in this cabin when it was declared that he had this disease and the doctor sent for. When the physician arrived he found only a few smoldering embers. Upon inquiry some railroad hands who were working near by revealed the fact that they had fastened the door of the cabin and set fire to the cabin and burned man and hut together.

Feb. 22d, 1898, at Lake City, S. C., Postmaster Baker and his infant child were burned to death by a mob that had set fire to his house. Mr. Baker's crime was that he had refused to give up the postoffice, to which he had been appointed by the National Government. The mob had tried to drive him away by persecution and intimidation. Finding that all else had failed, they went to his home in the dead of night and set fire to his house, and as the family rushed forth they were greeted by a volley of bullets. The father and his baby were shot through the open door and wounded so badly that they fell back in the fire and were burned to death. The remainder of the family, consisting of the wife and five children, escaped with their lives from the burning house, but all of them were shot, one of the number made a cripple for life.

Jan. 7th, 1898, two Indians were tied to a tree at Maud Postoffice, Indian Territory, and burned to death by a white mob. They were charged with murdering a white woman. There was no proof of their guilt except the unsupported word of the mob. Yet they were tied to a tree and slowly roasted to death. Their names were Lewis McGeesy and

Hond Martin. Since that time these boys have been found to be absolutely innocent of the charge. Of course that discovery is too late to be of any benefit to them, but because they were Indians the Indian Commissioner demanded and received from the United States Government an indemnity of $13,000.

April 23d, 1899, at Palmetto, Ga., Sam Hose was burned alive in the presence of a throng, on Sunday afternoon. He was charged with killing a man named Cranford, his employer, which he admitted he did because his employer was about to shoot him. To the fact of killing the employer was added the absolutely false charge that Hose assaulted the wife. Hose was arrested and no trial was given him. According to the code of reasoning of the mob, none was needed. A white man had been killed and a white woman was said to have been assaulted. That was enough. When Hose was found he had to die.

The Atlanta Constitution, in speaking of the murder of Cranford, said that the Negro who was suspected would be burned alive. Not only this, but it offered $500 reward for his capture. After he had been apprehended, it was publicly announced that he would be burned alive. Excursion trains were run and bulletins were put up in the small towns. The Governor of Georgia was in Atlanta while excursion trains were being made up to take visitors to the burning. Many fair ladies drove out in their carriages on Sunday afternoon to witness the torture and burning of a human being. Hose's ears were cut off, then his toes and fingers, and passed round to the crowd. His eyes were put out, his tongue torn out and flesh cut in strips by knives. Finally they poured coal oil on him and burned him to death. They dragged his half-consumed trunk out of the flames, cut it open, extracted his heart and liver, and sold slices for ten cents each for souvenirs, all of which was published most promptly in the daily papers of Georgia and boasted over by the people of that section.

Oct. 19th, 1889, at Canton, Miss., Joseph Leflore was burned to death. A house had been entered and its occupants murdered during the absence of the husband and father. When the discovery was made, it was immediately supposed that the crime was the work of a Negro, and the motive that of assaulting white women.

Bloodhounds were procured and they made a round of the village and discovered only one colored man absent from his home. This was taken to be proof sufficient that he was the perpetrator of the deed. When he returned home he was apprehended, taken into the yard of the house that had been burned down, tied to a stake, and was slowly roasted to death.

Dec. 6th, 1899, at Maysville, Ky., Wm. Coleman also was burned to death. He was slowly roasted, first one foot and then the other, and dragged out of the fire so that the torture might be prolonged. All of this without a shadow of proof or scintilla of evidence that the man had committed the crime.

Thus have the mobs of this country taken the lives of their victims within the past ten years. In every single instance except one these burnings were witnessed by from two thousand to fifteen thousand people, and no one person in all these crowds throughout the country had the courage to raise his voice and speak out against the awful barbarism of burning human beings to death.

Men and women of America, are you proud of this record which the Anglo-Saxon race has made for itself? Your silence seems to say that you are. Your silence encourages a continuance of this sort of horror. Only by earnest, active, united endeavor to arouse public sentiment can we hope to put a stop to these demonstrations of American barbarism.

_____

LYNCHING RECORD

The following table of lynchings has been kept year by year by the Chicago Tribune, beginning with 1882, and shows the list of Negroes that have been lynched during that time.

1882, Negroes murdered by mobs 52
1883, Negroes murdered by mobs 39
1884, Negroes murdered by mobs 53
1885, Negroes murdered by mobs 164
1886, Negroes murdered by mobs 136
1887, Negroes murdered by mobs 128
1888, Negroes murdered by mobs 143
1889, Negroes murdered by mobs 127
1890, Negroes murdered by mobs 176
1891, Negroes murdered by mobs 192
1892, Negroes murdered by mobs 241
1893, Negroes murdered by mobs 200
1894, Negroes murdered by mobs 190
1895, Negroes murdered by mobs 171
1896, Negroes murdered by mobs 131
1897, Negroes murdered by mobs 156
1898, Negroes murdered by mobs 127
1899, Negroes murdered by mobs 107

Of these thousands of men and women who have been put to death without judge or jury, less than one-third of them have been even accused of criminal assault. The world at large has accepted unquestionably the statement that Negroes are lynched only for assaults upon white women. Of those who were lynched from 1882 to 1891, the first ten years of the tabulated lynching record, the charges are as follows:

Two hundred and sixty-nine were charged with rape; 253 with murder; 44 with robbery; 37 with incendiarism; 4 with burglary; 27 with race prejudice; 13 quarreled with white men; 10 with making threats; 7 with rioting; 5 with miscegenation; in 32 cases no reasons were given, the victims were lynched on general principles.

During the past five years the record is as follows:

Of the 171 persons lynched in 1895 only 34 were charged with this crime. In 1896, out of 131 persons who were lynched, only 34 were said to have assaulted women. Of the 156 in 1897, only 32 . In 1898, out of 127 persons lynched, 24 were charged with the alleged "usual crime." In 1899, of the 107 lynchings, 16 were said to be for crimes against women. These figures, of course, speak for themselves, and to the unprejudiced, fair-minded person it is only necessary to read and study them in order to show that the charge that the Negro is a moral outlaw is a false one, made for the purpose of injuring the Negro's good name and to create public sentiment against him.

If public sentiment were alive, as it should be upon the subject, it would refuse to be longer hoodwinked, and the voice of conscience would refuse to be stilled by these false statements. If the laws of the country were obeyed and respected by the white men of the country who charge that the Negro has no respect for law, these things could not be, for every individual, no matter what the charge, would have a fair trial and an opportunity to prove his guilt or innocence before a tribunal of law.

That is all the Negro asks—that is all the friends of law and order need to ask, for once the law of the land is supreme, no individual who commits crime will escape punishment.

Individual Negroes commit crimes the same as do white men, but that the Negro race is peculiarly given to assault upon women, is a falsehood of the deepest dye. The tables given above show that the Negro who is saucy to white men is lynched as well as the Negro who is charged with assault upon women. Less than one-sixth of the lynchings last year, 1899, were charged with rape.

The Negro points to his record during the war in rebuttal of this false slander. When the white women and children of the South had no protector save only these Negroes, not one instance is known where the trust was betrayed. It is remarkably strange that the Negro had more respect for womanhood with the white men of the South hundreds of miles away, than they have to-day, when surrounded by those who take their lives with impunity and burn and torture, even worse than the "unspeakable Turk."

Again, the white women of the North came South years ago, threaded the forests, visited the cabins, taught the schools and associated only with the Negroes whom they came to teach, and had no protectors near at hand. They had no charge or complaint to make of the danger to themselves after association with this class of human beings. Not once has the country been shocked by such recitals form them as come from the women who are surrounded by their husbands, brothers, lovers, and friends. If the Negro's nature is bestial, it certainly should have proved itself in one of these two instances. The Negro asks only justice and an impartial consideration of these facts.